James Harmon Hoose

On the Province of Methods of Teaching

A Professional Study

James Harmon Hoose

On the Province of Methods of Teaching
A Professional Study

ISBN/EAN: 9783337004910

Printed in Europe, USA, Canada, Australia, Japan

Cover: Foto ©Thomas Meinert / pixelio.de

More available books at **www.hansebooks.com**

ON THE PROVINCE

OF

METHODS OF TEACHING.

A PROFESSIONAL STUDY.

BY

JAMES H. HOOSE, A.M., Ph.D.,

PRINCIPAL OF THE STATE NORMAL AND TRAINING
SCHOOL, CORTLAND, N. Y.,

*Author of "Studies in Articulation," "Notes on the Public School
System of England and Scotland," "Vindication of the Free
School System," "Practical Suggestions to Americans
Visiting Europe," etc., etc.*

WITH AN INTRODUCTION
BY
CHARLES W. BENNETT, D.D.,

PROFESSOR OF HISTORY AND LOGIC IN SYRACUSE UNIVERSITY.

SYRACUSE, N. Y.:
C. W. BARDEEN, PUBLISHER.
1886.

TO EDUCATORS

THIS STUDY IS RESPECTFULLY

𝔇𝔢𝔡𝔦𝔠𝔞𝔱𝔢𝔡,

AS A CONTRIBUTION

TO THE

PROFESSION OF TEACHING.

PROFESSIONAL MAXIMS AND DEFINITIONS.

"In whatever line of study distinction is sought the advantage of good teaching is great."—I. TODHUNTER.

"A point which I have incidentally brought forward deserves some consideration; I mean the gradual decay in the educational value of a subject as it falls into feebler hands to administer."—IBID.

"I am afraid it must be allowed that no art of equal importance to mankind, has been so little investigated scientifically as the art of teaching."—SIR HENRY SUMNER MAINE.

"A good *principle* not rightly understood may prove as hurtful as a bad."—MILTON.

The Investigation of the Principles of Adjusting Subject-matter to the Faculties and capabilities of the learning Mind—the Process of discovering Methods of Teaching—constitutes the conception of the Science of Teaching. (See § 214.)

The Investigation of Ways of applying Methods of Teaching in practice—The Invention of Modes of Teaching—is the conception of the Art of Teaching. (See § 215.)

The Investigation of the Science and the Art of Teaching constitutes the Profession of Teaching. (See § 216.)

TO THE PROFESSIONAL STUDENT.

"The *Thoughtful* person considers carefully, and acts with reflection in regard to the circumstances of a case."—C. J. SMITH.

"When I have a case before me, I can't help thinking of it beforehand, and perhaps feeling grieved too, afterward, if in any respect I might have conducted it better. If I am at dinner, the merriment or the philosophy of the *table-talk* suggests something, which I put away into a pigeon-hole in my mind for the case; and when I read, be it poetry or prose, the case hangs over the page like a magnet, and attracts to itself whatever seems to be pertinent or applicable. Success or failure leaves a bright or a dark hue on my mind, often for days."—HORACE MANN, *Life*, p. 74.

"There is a certain reaction against the conservatism of scientific men at the present time, and the uneducated man believes that chance and genius outweigh years of the careful accumulation and sifting of facts. . . It is, to say the least, improbable at this stage of the world's progress that an ignorant or a merely practical man should discover a new force in Nature. That dame certainly does not put a premium on ignorance."—*The Nation*, p. 396, No. 704, Dec. 26, 1878.

"Another error is the over-early and peremptory reduction of knowledge into arts and methods; from which time commonly sciences receive small or no augmentation. But as young men, when they knit and shape perfectly, do seldom grow to a further stature ; so knowledge, while it is in aphorisms and observations, it is in growth : but when it once is comprehended in exact methods, it may perchance be further polished and illustrated and accommodated for use and practice ; but it increaseth no more in bulk and substance.

"Another error which doth succeed that which we last mentioned, is, that after the distribution of particular arts and sciences, men have abandoned universality, or *philosophia prima:* which cannot but cease and stop all progression. For no perfect discovery can be made upon a flat or level : neither is it possible to discover the more remote and deeper parts of any science, if you stand but upon the level of the same science, and ascend not to a higher science."— BACON, *Advancement of Learning*, pp. 39, 40, Ed. 1866, Oxford.

A LIST OF AUTHORS AND WORKS QUOTED IN THIS VOLUME.

John W. Armstrong, D.D.—"On Method" (An Article).
Thomas Arnold, D.D.—"Life and Correspondence," by Arthur P. Stanley, M.A.
"The Art Journal."—Monthly, New York.
Charles W. Bennett, D.D.—"History of the Philosophy of Pedagogics."
Alexander Bain, M.A.—Article in "Mind."
——— "A Brief English Grammar on a Logical Method."
——— "Senses and Intellect."
Francis Bacon.—"Advancement of Learning."
Joseph Bosworth, D.D., F.R.S., F.S.A.—"A Compendious Anglo-Saxon and English Dictionary."
Wilhelm Adolf Becker.—"Charicles," translated by Frederick Metcalfe, M.A.
Francis Bowen, LL.D.—"A Treatise on Logic; or, The Laws of Pure Thought."
M. Bautain, Professor at the Sorbonne.—"The Art of Extempore Speaking."
Joseph Butler, D.C.L.—"The Analogy of Religion."
Henry Calderwood, LL.D., F.R.S.E.—"On Teaching: Its Ends and Means."
——— "Hand-Book of Moral Philosophy."
Chambers' Encyclopædia.
Henry Coppée, A.M.—"Elements of Logic."
George Crabb, M.A.—"English Synonyms."
B. F. Cocker, D.D., LL.D.—"The Theistic Conception of the World."
Henry N. Day, LL.D.—"Elements of Logic."
——— "Outlines of Ontological Science."

LIST OF AUTHORS AND WORKS.

Davies and Peck—" Dictionary of Mathematics."
Epictetus—" Discourses translated by George Long."
English Cyclopædia—Ed. 1867.
William Fleming, D.D.—" The Vocabulary of Philosophy."
Leo H. Grindon—" Life."
Thomas Henry Huxley, LL.D., F.R.S.—" Lay Sermons, Addresses, and Reviews."
Thomas Hill, LL.D.—" The True Order of Studies."
Levi Hedge, LL.D.—" Elements of Logick."
Sir William Hamilton—" Metaphysics."
W. Stanley Jevons, LL.D., M.A., F.R.S.—Article in "Mind."
———— " The Principles of Science."
———— " Elementary Lessons in Logic."
William James—Article in "Mind."
Dionysius Longinus—" On the Sublime," translated by William Smith.
S. S. Laurie, A.M.—" Inaugural Address—Chair of Education in University of Edinburgh."
———— " Synopsis of Lectures."
Horace Mann—" Life," by his Wife.
"Mind"—A Quarterly—London.
J. D. M. Meiklejohn, M.A.—" Inaugural Address, Bell Chair of Education, University of St. Andrews."
J. Clark Murray—" Outlines of Sir William Hamilton's Philosophy."
John Stuart Mill—" A System of Logic, Ratiocinative and Inductive; being a Connected View of the Principles of Evidence and the Method of Scientific Investigation."
Michael Seigneur De Montaigne—" Essays."
Sir Henry Sumner Maine, R.C.S.Q., LL.D., F.R.S.— " Village Communities and Miscellanies."
L. Mariotti—" Conferences De Pedagogie."
Henry Longueville Mansel, B.D.—" Metaphysics."
———— " Prolegomena Logica."
James McCosh, LL.D.—" Intuitions of the Mind."

LIST OF AUTHORS AND WORKS.

John Ferguson McLennan. M.A., LL.D."—"Primitive Marriage."
J. H. Newman, M.A.—"The Idea of A University."
"The Nation"—A Weekly—New York.
David P. Page, M.A.—"Theory and Practice of Teaching."
Noah Porter, D.D.—"The Human Intellect."
Jean Paul Frederick Richter—"Levana."
Karl Rosenkranz—"The Philosophy of Education, or Pedagogics as a System," translated by Anna C. Brackett.
Jean Jacques Rousseau—"Emilius and Sophia," 4 vols. Ed. 1783. London.
James E. Thorold Rogers, M.A.—"Education in Oxford."
Laurence Sterne—"Life and Opinions of Tristram Shandy."
Karl Schmidt—Quoted by Dr. Bennett.
Henry Sidgwick, M.A.—"The Methods of Ethics."
C. J. Smith—"Synonyms Discriminated."
Herbert Spencer—"Education."
J. A. Stewart—Article in "Mind."
Sydney Smith—"Essays."
Louis Soldan—"Method and Manner," in Transactions of Nat. Ed. Association for 1874.
James Fitzjames Stephen, Q.C.—"Liberty, Equality, Fraternity."
I. Todhunter, M.A., F.R.S.—"The Conflict of Studies, and other Essays."
Edward B. Tylor, LL.D., F.R.S.—"Primitive Culture," 2 volumes.
William Thompson, D.D.—"An Outline of the Necessary Laws of Thought."
Frederick Ueberweg—"System of Logic, and History of Logical Doctrines," translated by Thomas M. Lindsay, M.A., F.R.S.E.
Varro—Quoted by Rousseau.
William Whewell, D.D.—"Novum Organon Renovatum."
Richard Whately—"Elements of Logic."

PREFACE.

The following STUDY has grown out of one branch of the investigations which have occupied my time more or less during an extended period of years of public labors in teaching. This volume has gradually assumed form for my own classes in professional researches. I have been impressed long with the thought that, as teachers and educators of the United States, we are too impatient and superficial in our professional inquiries. The consequences are, that our theories of teaching rest too heavily upon notions of present expediency and brief experience. As a body we are in full sympathy with the general spirit of the nation—we are satisfied with only immediate results. Parents urge us to hasten their children into the mysteries of learning, for soon they must be placed at work, or must enter the advanced schools. The legitimate consequences are at our doors: the cry of the upper schools is, that candidates for admission are too poorly prepared for the work in store for them; the experienced men of business complain that the youth are not properly grounded in the principles underlying their daily routine of labors; the educated unite in proclaiming the masses uneducated. Thus have we been between these upper and nether millstones, crushed and thrown out if immediate scholarship was not forthcoming, while we are censured in after-years for not having secured more valuable products for the study expended by the children in their early school-days.

In this dilemma we have recollected the wisdom of the Dutch proverb, "Economy is a great revenue," and the German, "Necessity teaches even the lame to dance," and the Italian, "Even the dog gets bread by wagging his tail," and have endeavored to insure to the pupils a scholarship that is frequently too insufficient to be valuable, but which has secured for us an ephemeral reputation and a jeopardized support. Under all the circumstances, perhaps we have done as well as we could in our schools.

Because we have yielded so far to the popular demands, we are to-day without a sharply defined and outlined philosophy in our theories of education and of teaching. In our experimentation for sudden fruitage we have apparently forgotten that the most practical thing in existence is a thoroughly matured philosophical theory. Experiments without this theory are at random; they may be successful—probably they will not be. Under a correct theory, experiments can be tested philosophically, and failures reduced to a minimum in number and in degree of disaster. In this respect we can learn much from those nations that have passed their eager and experimental age, and are now in their enlightened maturity. In our ambition to "make scholars," irrespective of the elements of necessary time and application, we have overlooked the fact that scholars can never be "made;" they must grow: the faculties become powers only as time and application enucleate them. The active energies of the Profession have been too much absorbed in inventing artificial aids, helps, short-cuts, and "royal roads" to learning, to enter into patient and continued study to discover the philosophical nature of the Profession as an Art and as a Science. It is time for us to turn our attention to find a firmer basis for our practice. This is found only in Philosophy.

"The beginning of philosophy to him at least who only enters on it in the right way and by the door, is a consciousness of his own weakness and inability about necessary things."—EPICTETUS.

The work now submitted is an attempt to outline one subject which is included within the conception of a complete Philosophy of Education—that of the Province of Methods of Teaching. Although the subject is not first in the order of classification in the general investigation of Education, yet because of its practical nature it has been directly approached.

The treatment is somewhat out of the ordinary mode of authorship. While I have steadily kept to the line of the investigation, yet I have permitted a wide range of related matter to incorporate itself into the body of the text, even at the risk of seeming to be pedantic. The disadvantages of this apparent heterogeneity are more than compensated by the greater suggestiveness of the materials admitted. Besides, he who would erect a "liberty-pole" that shall remain permanently standing as a beacon must imbed it deeply into the firmest of soil which the past and present have deposited from the attrition of the Ages.

"The reader will please to take it patiently if he find what has been already printed again printed here. What has been printed is necessary as the bond and bast-matting of what has not been printed; but the bast-matting must not cover the whole garden, instead of merely tying up the trees. But there are two still better excuses. Known rules in education gain new force if new experience verifies them. The author has three times been in the position of trying them upon different children of all ages and talents; and he now enjoys with his own the pedagogic *jus trium liberorum* (law of three children); and every other person's experience related in this book has been made his own. Secondly, printing-ink now is like sympathetic ink, it becomes as quickly invisible as visible; wherefore it is good to repeat old thoughts in the newest books, because the old works in which they stand are not read. New translations of many truths, as of foreign standard works, must be given forth every half century. And, indeed, I wish that even old German standard books were turned into new German from time to time, and so could find their way into the circulating libraries.

"Why are there flower and weed gleanings of every thing, but no wine or corn gleanings of the innumerable works on education? Why should one single good observation or rule be lost because it is imprisoned in some monstrous folio, or blown away in some single sheet? For dwarfs and giants, even in books, do not live long. Our age, this balloon, or air-ship, which, by simultaneous lighting of new lamps, and throwing out of old ballast, has constantly mounted higher and higher, might now, I should think, cease to throw out, and rather lovingly endeavor to collect than to disperse the old.

"However little so disjointed a collection of thoughts could teach rules, it would yet arouse and sharpen the educational sense, from which they originally sprung. . . . .

"Something very different from such a progressive cabinet of noble thoughts, or even from my weak *Levana*, with her fragments in her arms, is the usual kind of complete system of education which one person after another has written, and will write. It is difficult,—I mean the end, not the means. For it is very easy to proceed with book-binder's and bookmaker's paste, and fasten together a thousand selected thoughts with five of your own, especially if you conscientiously remark in the Preface that you have availed yourself of the labors of your predecessors, yet make no mention of one in the work itself, but sell such a miniature library in one volume to the reader as a mental *fac-simile* of yourself. How much better in this case were a hole-maker than a hole-hider! How much better were it if associated authors (I mean those friendly hundreds who move along one path, uttering precisely the same sound) entirely died out—as Humboldt tells us that in the tropical regions there are none of those sociable plants which make our forests monotonous, but next each tree a perfectly different one grows. A diary about an ordinary child would be much better than a book upon children by an ordinary writer. Yes, every man's opinion about education would be valuable if he only wrote what he did not copy. The author, unlike a partner, should always only say 'I,' and no other word."—JEAN PAUL RICHTER, *Levana*, Author's Preface, pp. xii–xv, ed. 1863.

Although Methods of Teaching occupied the attention of some of the Greek philosophers, and have continued before the minds of educators in portions of Europe down to the present date, and have of late engaged thought in the United States, yet they have been confounded generally with Methods of Education, Modes and Manners of Teaching, rather than apprehended as constituting a province by themselves. The subject of the inquiry being intricate in its character, it has been no easy task to elaborate it. I have diligently sought nothing but Truth. Should subsequent researches, observations, or experience, from whatever source, reveal aught of error in the positions advanced, no one shall outdo the author in haste to accept the facts as they shall appear. If this investigation, with all of its imperfections of style, matter, and treatment, shall prove as interesting to the Fraternity as it has to the writer, it will serve its purpose. "Indeed, its largeness, its infinity, embarrass me. It is like an attempt to lift the earth : the arms are too short to get hold of it. However, I hope to get hold of a few handfuls." HORACE MANN, *Life*, p. 87, Boston, 1865.

"I have long known that no man can apply himself to any worthy subject, either of thought or action, but he will forthwith find it develop into dimensions and qualities of which before he had no conception. If this be true of all subjects worthy of rational attention, how extensively true is it of the all-comprehending subject of education ! This expansion of any object to which our attention is systematically directed may be compared to the opening of a continent upon the eye of an approaching mariner. At first he descries some minute point, just emerging in the distance,—the lofty summit of some mountain. As he approaches, other elevated points seem to rise out of nothing, and stand upon the horizon; then they are perceived to be connected together; then hills, cities, towns, plains, rivers, which the eye cannot count for their numbers, nor embrace for their distance, fill up the admiring vision. So it is in approaching any of the intellectual or moral systems which Nature has established."—*Ibid.*, pp. 84, 85.

J. H. H.

ANALYTICAL TABLE OF CONTENTS.

	PAGE
DEDICATION.................................	iii
PROFESSIONAL MAXIMS...........................	v
TO THE PROFESSIONAL STUDENT....................	vi-vii
A LIST OF AUTHORS AND WORKS QUOTED.........	viii-x
PREFACE.......................................	xi-xvi
TABLE OF CONTENTS.............................	xvii-xxx
INTRODUCTION—By Dr. Charles W. Bennett.........	xxxi-xxxvii

ANALYTICAL TABLE OF CONTENTS.

PART FIRST.

INTRODUCTORY DISCUSSION — On Pedagogics, Education, Teaching, Authorities..............................

I. ON PEDAGOGICS.

SECTION		PAGE
1. Pedagogics—definition of...................	From Soldan	3
2. Pedagogics—definition of............	From Rosenkranz	4
3. Pedagogics—definition of.....	From Schmidt, quoted by Bennett	4

II. ON EDUCATION.

4. Education—province of...		5
5. Education—province of.................	From Rousseau	5
6. Education—province of..............	From Rosenkranz	6
7. Education—province of...................	From Rogers	9
8. Education—province of.....................	From Bain	9
9. Education—province of.....................	From Jevons	20
10. Education—province of	From Varro	22
11. Education and Training.	From Smith	22
12. Education—province of.....	From Hill	23
13. Education—province of.............	From Page	24
14. Education—province of.....	From Huxley	26
15. Education—province of...................	From Laurie	30
16. Education—province of............. ..	From Richter	34
17. Education vs. Instruction...	From Richter	42
18. Education vs. Teaching.................................		43
19. Education vs. Teaching..	From Calderwood	43

ANALYTICAL TABLE OF CONTENTS. xix

III. On Teaching.

SECTION	PAGE
20. Language—represents......................................	44
21. Teaching—meaning of..................From the Greek	45
22. Teaching—meaning of....... ....From the Latin	47
23. Teaching—meaning of..........From the Anglo-Saxon	49
24. Methods of Teaching—expression determined...........	50
25. Authority in Anglo-Saxon Conception of Teaching— illustrated........................From Todhunter	51
26. Same idea—illustrated......................From Jevons	51
27. Same idea—illustrated................From Calderwood	52
28. Conception of Teacher limited to Persons...............	54
29. Teach, Instruct, Inform—defined...........From Crabb	55
30. Teach, Instruct, Inform—defined...........From Smith	57

IV. On Authorities.

31. Authority—defined... ....From Crabb	60
32. Authority—defined........................From Smith	60
33. Authority, Consent, Assent, Belief—defined. From Fleming	61
34. Authority—general discussion..............From Bacon	69

35....................V. Recapitulation................... 77

PART SECOND.

On Method in General.

36. Method—defined...	79
37. Method—refers to subject-matter........................	80
38. Methods of Business—customary use of Expression....	80
39. Methods of Business—illustrated..From "The Nation"	81
40. Three distinct Elements in an Investigation—(1) Object-matter, the end ; (2) Way in which faculties proceed ; (3) State of Investigator......................	82
41. I. Object-matter of Study—considered—ends in *System*.	83
42. II. Ways of Procedure of Mind—considered—Are modes of method...	85
43. (a) *Analysis*—defined............................	85

xx ANALYTICAL TABLE OF CONTENTS.

SECTION		PAGE
44.	*Analysis vs. Separation*............................	86
45.	(*b*) *Synthesis*—defined...............................	87
46.	*Synthesis* and *Definition*..........................	87
47.	*Abstraction*—defined................................	87
48.	Analysis and Synthesis are parts of same Method. From Hamilton	87
49.	Synthesis *vs. Reconstruction*........................	88
50.	(*c*) *Generalization*—defined.........................	89
51.	(*d*) *Classification*—defined.........................	89
52.	(*e*) *Induction*—defined.............................	90
53.	*Induction vs. Interpretation*........................	90
54.	*Induction vs. Repetition*............................	92
55.	(*f*) *Deduction*—defined.............................	93
56.	III. State, or Ways of Investigator—give rise to *Manner*.	93
57.	Manner Systematized is *Mode*........................	94

PART THIRD.

I. ON THE THEORY OF METHODS OF TEACHING.

58. Introduction—Need of Better Methods.....From Maine 96
59. Theory of Methods of Teaching—based upon Psychology and nature of subject-matter....................... 98
60. Nature of Faculty—defined.............................. 98
61. Character of Faculty—defined........................... 98
62. Psychology—defined..................................... 98
63. Psychology—province of.............. ....From Stewart 98
64. Objects and Limitations of Present Investigation....... 101
65. Knowing—forms of knowledge........From Ueberweg 102
66. Form and Matter.....................From Thompson 103
67. Form and Matter....................... From Jevons 105
68. Form and Matter.....................From McCosh 105
69. Form and Matter.....................From Newman 107
70. Form of Matter—(*a*) Illustrated...From "The Nation"
    (*b*) Illustrated....................From Rousseau 107
71. Knowledge, Learning, Erudition—defined..From Crabb 108

ANALYTICAL TABLE OF CONTENTS. xxi

SECTION	PAGE
72. Knowledge—defined.. .. ..From Day	110
73. Knowledge—defined.........................From Day	111
74. Knowledge—aim of, is truth............From Ueberweg	112
75. Knowledge—stages of, in acquiring : (1) Source of—resides in mind ; (2) Rational way of procedure is under Will ; (3) End of activity is Knowledge......	113
76. Teaching—defined...	114
77. Self-Informed is Self-educated—defined and amplified...	114
78. Teachers are a Necessity to Learners—Teacher, what is —Adjust, defined......................From Smith	115
79. Teaching—defined..	116
80. Teacher—duties of, to analyze and separate subject-matter.................................	117
81. Teacher—duty to note both form and matter of knowledge in mind of learner............................	117
82. How to Teach ?—is great question................	118
83. Teaching—Conception of, requires examination of : (1) Mind of learner—learner ; (2) Mind of teacher—teacher ; (3) Things to be learned—subject-matter..	118
84. Teaching—Conception of, resolves itself into: (1) Teacher must know subject-matter ; (2) Teacher must know mind ; (3) Teacher must know Way in which mind proceeds when learning—Constitute Profession of Teaching...	119
85. Recapitulation of §§ 82, 83............................	120
86. PROVINCE OF METHODS OF TEACHING—that of Principles of Adaptation of Subject-matter to Faculties of Mind...	121
87. Principle—defined.....................From Fleming	122
88. Principle—defined.. ....From Smith	122
89. Methods of Teaching—require system of subject-matter.	123
90. Systems and Methods—compared......................	123
91. Province of Methods of Teaching, not that of Pedagogics or Ethology..	125
92. Ethics—defined....:....................From Sidgwick	125
93. Teaching is Handmaid of Education...................	126
94. Methods of Pedagogics, Scope of—equivalent to Methods of Education........................·.............	127

xxii ANALYTICAL TABLE OF CONTENTS.

SECTION　　　　　　　　　　　　　　　　　　　　　　　PAGE
95. Methodick of Education—defined. (1) Educator must be a Guide—Processes: Analytic, Synthetic, Inductive. (2) Educator must guide Morals—Methodick of Education is Methodology, Way, Procedure—Methodick—rests on the Will. Departments of—particular methods........................... From Laurie 129
96. Methods of Education regard Growth of Mind as an End—They consider: (1) What Subjects to be Taught—purpose of. (2) How to Instruct for Right Judgments. Answers: To (1) Doctrine of the Real—To (2) Formal Discipline .... From Laurie 131
97. Growth and Development—contrasted... From Spencer 132
Growth—defined......................... From Smith 132
98. Methods of Teaching regard Growth of Mind as a Means 135
99. Methods of Teaching Examined in their Relation to "How to Study".................................... 136
100. Methods of Teaching do not distinguish between Truth and Error of Subject-matter taught.................. 138
101. Methods of Teaching assume innate Activity of Mind—Examined in relation to "Waking up Mind"—Conception of "Variety" examined..................... 139
102. Attention—defined and examined........From Richter 139
103. Excite, Awaken, Rouse, Incite, Stimulate—defined.
From Smith 141
104. Methods of Teaching—not responsible for Form of Knowledge in Mind of Learner..................... 142
105. "Development of Ideas"—analyzed.................... 144
106. Thorough Teaching—defined............ 144
107. Develop, Unfold, Unravel—defined....... From Smith 145
108. Methods of Teaching must regard Procedure of Faculties when learning.................................. 148
109. Methods of Discovery and of Instruction. From Jevons 149
110. Methods of Teaching must respect Inherited "Cast of Mind"... 160
111. Methods of Teaching—difficult to suit, because of evanescence of psychological phenomena............... 162
112. Methods of Teaching—in present state of Psychology, not absolutely invariable.. 163

ANALYTICAL TABLE OF CONTENTS. xxiii

| SECTION | PAGE |

113. Methods of Teaching examined in relation to "Class-Drill"... 164
114. Methods of Teaching do not regard Individuality of Teacher.. 165
115. Manner—Examined and defined............................. 165
116. Teacher can have "His Manner," not "His Method". 166
117. Methods of Teaching—are not method in general..... 166
118. Method and Manner—contrasted........From Soldau 167
119. Mode of Teaching—defined................................ 168
120. Methods, Modes, Manners—compared.................. 168
121. In Perfect Knowledge, all Teachers would Teach alike in their Modes.. 169
122. Methods of Teaching—Misconception of occasions Misuse of the Expression..................................... 170
123. Mode, Manner—defined.................From Smith
     Mode, Manner—used............From "The Nation" 171
124. System, Method—defined...............From Smith
     System—defined........................From Jevons 172
125. Method, Procedure—defined............From Mariotti 172
126. Method, Mode—defined...............From Armstrong 173
127. Principle, Law, Rule—defined........From Armstrong 173
128. Method, Mode, Manner—difference. (*a*) Illustrated by Figure of a Bridge; (*b*) Illustrated by Water as buoying-up power; (*c*) Illustrated by Gravity, Animal Power, Steam; (*d*) Illustrated by Horse Power, Carriage, Landau................................. 174
129. Mode—properly used........................From Page 175
130. Mode of Teaching—illustrated...........From Page 175
131. Method—improperly used..............From Rousseau 176
132. Method—Socratic Mode—illustrated...From Epictetus 178
133. Methods of Teaching—for Modes and Manners—Critique upon.............................From Meiklejohn 184
134. "Methods of Nature"—Conception of, Examined—Illustration............................From Rousseau
     Illustration...........................From McLennan 188
135. Artificial—Conception of, examined..................... 190
136. Natural, in general, is not Natural in the Individual.... 192
137. Natural—defined........................From Butler 193

xxiv ANALYTICAL TABLE OF CONTENTS.

SECTION   PAGE

138. Nature—defined............ ....From Cocker 193
139. Nature—Law of—defined................From Cocker 194
140. Nature—Universality of Order of—defined—not Invariable................................From Cocker 194
141. Nature—defined........................From Fleming 196
142. Natural—Instance of...................From Epictetus 200
143. Natural and Artificial Education—discriminated.
                                                  From Huxley 202

      II. ON THE PRACTICE OF METHODS OF TEACHING.
      (A) *On the Knowing Faculties of the Mind.*

144. Purpose of this Division is to submit a Basis for Methods of Teaching....... 203
145. Psychological Phenomena—classified. (1) Phenomena of Cognitions ; (2) Phenomena of Feelings ; (3) Phenomena of Conations...............From Hamilton 204
146. Consciousness—defined. Involves : (1) A Knowing Subject, the Ego ; (2) A Recognized Modification of Ego ; (3) A Recognition by the Subject of the Modification........................(a) From Hamilton
                                                  (b) From James 204
147. I. Presentative Faculties............From Hamilton 205
148. II. Memory—Faculty of......... ......From Hamilton 207
149. III. Reproductive Faculty............ From Hamilton 207
150. IV. Imagination........... ....From Hamilton 208
151. V. Elaborative Faculty..............From Hamilton 208
152. VI. Regulative Faculty....:...........From Hamilton 209
153. Recapitulation of Cognitive Faculties..From Hamilton 210
154. Will, the Principal Faculty in acquiring Knowledge.
                                                  From Richter 211
155. Will—same idea..........................From Laurie 213
156. Will—same idea.........................From Cocker 213
157. Imagination—(a) The Poetic........ .....From Porter 214
158. Imagination—(b) The Philosophic.........From Porter 214
159. Imagination—(c) The Ethical Uses of.....From Porter 216
160. Imagination—(d) Relation to Religious Faith.
                                                  From Porter 217
161. Imagination is Over-developed in the Youth of India.
                                                  From Maine 218

ANALYTICAL TABLE OF CONTENTS.

SECTION	PAGE

162. Memory—Modification—defined...................... 219
163. Memory—Active—Childhood need not Understand all it Learns..............................From Arnold 219
164. Memory, Imagination, and Hope are the same Faculty.
   From Mansel 220
165. Memory—Permanence of................From Grindon 221
166. Memory—Limited in its Growth.........From Richter 224
167. Memory—Retains best from Contrasts...From Richter 226
168. Memory—a Goddess..................From Montaigne 227
169. Memory—a Personal Reminiscence....From Montaigne 227
170. Memory and "Cram"...... ....From Maine 235
171. Memory and "Cram".... ....From Todhunter 240
172. Memory and "Cram," and Thinking Faculties—A Question-Begging Epithet; Analysis of "Cram;" "Good Cram" and "Bad Cram" defined; Dulness and "Cram;" Book-work and "Cram;" Examinations are Tests; Repetition in Teaching Necessary; Purpose of "Good Cramming;" Intense "Cramming" is Real Education; Remarks of Home-Secretary Cross; Mr. Cross Answered; Slow and Deliberate Teaching compared with Rapid; Object of School; Purpose of Liberal Education; Not Desirable to Remember things Taught in School; Source of Error not in Memory, but in Distinguishing between Form and Matter; Retention; Barristers must Forget; Work of Teachers not to make Philosophers, and Scholars, and Geniuses—these are Born; Business of Educator is "to Cram"........................ .....From Jevons 241
173. Knowing, Act of—defined.............From Ueberweg 257
174. Knowledge—defined...................From Ueberweg 258
175. Human Thought—determined.........From Ueberweg 258
176. Knowledge—Activity necessary to.....From Ueberweg 258
177. Knowledge—defined.................From Calderwood 259
178. Thought—Difference between, and other Phenomena of Mind—Intuition, Conception, Concept, Consciousness, Representation, Perception, Imagination...................... ....From Mansel 259

SECTION	PAGE

179. Thought—defined.....................From Mansel 265

180. Thought—Faculty of—defined—Judgment; Apprehension; Conception is a Psychological Judgment; Conceiving; Language is a sign of Intuitions; Abstraction; Concept; Common Language and Common Thought; Identity; Reasoning defined; Syllogism; Recapitulation...............From Mansel 266

181. Powers—Mental, employed in acquiring Knowledge—Discrimination; Power of Detecting Identity; Power of Retention...........................From Jevons 274

182. Identity and Difference—Laws of. (1) Law of Identity; (2) Law of Contradiction; (3) Law of Duality.
From Jevons 277

183. Thought—First Gradation of, is the Formation of *Judgment*—Proposition; Sentence; Concept; Conceiving; Reasoning; Perception; Regulative Faculty, or Faculty of Intuition; Being; Existence; Matter of Thought; Analysis; Abstraction; Attention; Comparison; Synthesis; Subject; Predicate; Terms of a Proposition; Copula...............From Day 279

184. Thought—Second Gradation of, is the Formation of *Concept*—Judgments; Forming Concepts; Terms; Concept in Comprehension; Conception; Faculty; Act; Product; Law of Identity; Base; Relative Cognition; Concepts differ from Judgments; Concept not Expressed; Concept implies Judgments; Base of Concept; Concepts are Products of Thought; Thought aggregated by single Words....From Day 288

185. Thought—Third Gradation of, is *Reasoning*—Reasoning derived from Judgment; Reasoning not a Conclusion; Reasoning defined; Ratiocination; Discourse; Discursive; Argumentation; Inference or Illation; Conclusion; Syllogism; Parts of Reasoning; Antecedent; Consequent; Immediate Reasoning; Mediate Reasoning............From Day 296

186. Reason—has no Relation to Body.......From Grindon 301

187. Thinking is Conversation of Soul with itself.
From Mansel 301

ANALYTICAL TABLE OF CONTENTS. xxvii

(B) *On the Nature of Subject-Matter.*

SECTION   PAGE
188. Methods of Teaching—Teacher to discover, must know Mind and Nature of Subject-matter........ 302
189. Subject-matter—defined................................ 302
190. Subject-matter—Material—Exists outside of Mind..... 302
191. Subject-matter—Immaterial—Created wholly by Mind. 302
192. Object Teaching—Conception of, Analyzed............ 303
193. Object Teaching—when Valuable..................... .. 304
194. Object Teaching—when Possible........ 304
195. Illustrative Teaching—defined... 304
196. Ideas—Succeed each other according to Laws of Association..... 305
197. Illustrations—defined, by Illustrations—defined........................... ....From Smith
Analogy—defined.........................From Smith
Analogy and Induction—Difference.....From Fleming 305
198. Illustrations—Example of................From Sterne 306
199. Illustrative Teaching—Analogous Extension of Meaning of Words........................From Jevons 309
200. Illustration—differs from Example.................... 309
201. Illustrative Teaching is Objective Teaching............ 309
202. Illustrative Teaching—Conception of, misunderstood for Object Teaching, has occasioned abuse of the Expression.. 310
203. Mathematics—cannot be taught by Object Teaching—only Illustratively.................................. 310
204. Mathematics—Nature of Arithmetical Numbers.
From Jevons
Number—defined...............From Davies and Peck 312
205. Mathematical Judgments—on Nature of..From Mansel 314
206. Mathematical Judgments—on Arithmetic, Geometry.
From Eng. Cycl. 324
207. Mathematical Judgments—on Numeration.
From Whewell 326
208. Object Teaching—Branches that can be Taught in this way...................................... 327
209. Objects—when their Value ceases in Teaching and Learning.................................... 328
210. Object Teaching—must be succeeded by Thought...... 329

(C) *On Discovering Methods of Teaching Special Subjects.*

SECTION PAGE

211. System of Subject-matter must be constructed by Teacher—Principle of Adaptation must be Discovered for Method of Teaching...... 330
212. Addition—on Discovering the Method of Teaching it... 331
    (1) On the Nature of the Subject-matter............... 331
    (2) On the Faculties primarily active in Learning Addition............ 332
    (3) On Inventing the Mode of Teaching Addition...... 333
213. Mode and Manner of Teaching Addition—Recapitulated................ 333
214. SCIENCE OF TEACHING—defined.................. 334
215. ART OF TEACHING—defined..................... 334
216. PROFESSION OF TEACHING—defined............... 334

III. CONCLUDING REFLECTIONS.

217. To Teach—Qualifications Requisite................ 335
218. Growth—Evil effects of missing Opportunities for.
     From Meiklejohn 335
219. Teacher—Should be a Learner........ ...From Arnold 336
220. Teacher—Value of Common-Sense..... From Sidgwick 338
221. Teacher—Value of Common-Sense for..From Whately 339
222. Teacher—Best Talent for, is Judging Right upon Imperfect Materials....................From Stephen 344
223. Difference between Theory and Practice—of Degree only, not of Kind................. ..From Mansel 344
224. Science of Human Nature—Possible........From Mill 344

APPENDIX OF QUOTATIONS.

SECTION	PAGE
225. A.—On METHOD.	
1. From Hedge	346
2. From Coppée	347
3. From Day	348
4. From Fleming	350
5. From Bain	356
6. From Whewell	357
7. From Bowen	361
8. From Day	368
9. From Comte	373
226. B.—On SYSTEM.	
1. From Fleming	376
227. C.—On ANALYSIS.	
1. From Fleming	380
228. D.—On SYNTHESIS.	
1. From Fleming	383
229. E.—On DEFINITION.	
1. From Fleming	385
2. From Mill	389
230. F.—On ABSTRACTION.	
1. From Fleming	390
231. G.—On GENERALIZATION.	
1. From Fleming	392
2. From Jevons	395
232. H.—On CLASSIFICATION.	
1. From Fleming	398
2. From Jevons	401
233. I.—On INDUCTION.	
1. From Smith	413
2. From Day	415

xxx   APPENDIX OF QUOTATIONS.

SECTION   PAGE
          3. From Fleming............................. 416
          4. From Whewell............................. 422
          5. From Eng. Cyclop. 423
          6. From Jevons.............................. 434
          7. From Mill................................ 451
234. J.—On INTERPRETATION.
          1. From Davies and Peck..................... 473
          2. From Smith............................... 477
235. K.—On DEDUCTION,
          1. From Fleming............................. 478
          2. From Day................................. 480
          3. From Bowen............................... 482
          4. From Hedge............................... 484

INTRODUCTION.

BY
CHARLES W. BENNETT, D.D.

INTRODUCTION.

The subject of education is each year assuming growing prominence. It cannot be justly charged that the Eastern, Middle, and Western States of the American Union have been indifferent to the claims of their citizens to enjoy opportunities of instruction and enlightenment. Nearly all of them have made generous provisions for primary and intermediate instruction, and in some have been elaborated complete systems of education from lowest to highest.

Nor has the question of Training Schools for teachers been neglected. Good general education presupposes good schools, and good schools presupposes good teachers; hence that State which fails to provide for good teachers exhibits a plain lack of practical wisdom. These Normal or Training Schools have been subjected to severe criticism, both as to the scope and character of their work, as well as the products which they have yielded to the State. Many able thinkers have believed that the nature and province of the instruction in these State schools was not sufficiently definitive to warrant their independent existence and exceptional support;

that the Common Schools, Academies, and Seminaries of the State were doing essentially all which was accomplished by the expensive machinery of Normal Schools ; that the conception of the use and design of Teachers' Training Schools, as entertained by those who had inaugurated and managed them, was essentially erroneous ; that they had failed to elevate teaching to the dignity, honor, and emoluments of a profession ; that a large fraction of those who had been thus educated chiefly at the public expense had not rendered to the State adequate remuneration in superior service and skilled labor. Doubtless some of the writing and speaking on this subject has been hypercritical ; since the difficulties of the educational problem have not been sufficiently appreciated, and the amount and quality of the hard work done by those who have had charge of these Training Schools have not been properly recognized. Nevertheless, that the expectations of the best friends of education have not been fully satisfied must be frankly acknowledged. Too much time and energy have been consumed in the mere preliminaries to strictly Training Schools. The requirements for admission have been too low. The three great departments of Psychology, History of Pedagogics, and Methodology and Training, which should occupy by far the largest portion of the course of study, have been in too many instances but meagrely examined, and in most of these schools the historical examination has scarcely been touched upon at all.

We, therefore, welcome the present work of Dr. Hoose as a promise that a better day for Normal School Training is dawning. It shows that at least one Chief in these Schools is fully awake to the necessity of careful and exact thinking on one of the few subjects of study which legitimately belong to Training Schools. The importance of the branch of education here treated can hardly be over-emphasized. Lack of clearness here brings obscurity and partial failure into the whole career of the teacher. He may, by long experimentation with mind, correct some mistakes ; but unless the principle which underlies Method is fully understood in the outset, it is difficult to compute the mischief which may ensue.

The work which is here presented professes to reveal and discuss this principle. As stated in his preface, during the ten years of his supervision of one of the largest Training Schools of New York, the author has been continually studying, and yearly developing this subject before the classes which have been under his tuition. Like most valuable products it has, therefore, been a growth from the experience and close observation of an eminently practical teacher. This should greatly enhance its value. In the directness, brevity, and pertinence of statement and illustration, the author seems to have the wants of his classes ever distinctly before him. Evidently he is no recluse thinker, but a busy man among busy men and women who need his help, and whom he wants to help.

The extended quotations from so many eminent thinkers and educators may, in the opinion of some, smack a little of pedantry. But since one great object of such a work is to stimulate to further research, as well as to instruct the uninitiated, these references to and quotations from the works of philosophic thinkers must be regarded not only pertinent, but invaluable. Moreover, the assumption of originality may be cheap with those of slender information, but the real student becomes quite content at times to sit at the feet of those giants who have wrestled with the hard problems of education, and endeavor to reduce their thoughts to practical and efficient uses. He usually does most for his pupils and readers who opens up to them the literature of his subject, and directs them to the sources of his own inspiration and quickening. The teacher in Training Schools especially must ever consider that he is dealing with minds of greater or less maturity, who are, with himself, desirous to go to the fountain-heads of knowledge and truth, and there drink for themselves. While this course of procedure may prove terribly iconoclastic to those who may be worshipping the false idol of originality, it will always be most helpful to the real lover of truth, and become most beneficent to our fellow-workers.

It is highly probable that some positions of the author will not pass unchallenged. Some readers may be inclined to believe that his boldness sometimes verges on rashness, and that in some points he has not fully established what he claims : but in all the work there breathes the spirit of honest conviction ; and honest thinking cannot long remain wrong thinking after the wrong has been pointed out. If by frank and generous criticism it shall be shown that the author has inadvertently been led to make any misstatements of fact or principle, these corrections will probably be thankfully received, and can be easily incorporated into the text of some future edition.

The subject here presented by Dr. Hoose is specially worthy of investigation and attention on the part of the directors of Training Schools ; indeed, none are of greater value. Hence we must believe that this work will be cordially welcomed by the teachers of Normal Schools, by the graduating classes of these schools, and by all thorough teachers, as supplying a long-felt need.

CHAS. W. BENNETT.
SYRACUSE UNIVERSITY, January 1, 1879.

PART FIRST.

§§ 1-35.

INTRODUCTORY DISCUSSION.

I. ON PEDAGOGICS, ... §§ 1-3.
II. ON EDUCATION, ... §§ 4-19.
III. ON TEACHING, . . . §§ 20-30.
IV. ON AUTHORITIES, . . . §§ 31-34.
V. RECAPITULATION, ... § 35.

I.

ON PEDAGOGICS.

1. " By Pedagogics we mean the science of the realization of the human rational potentiality into actuality. In the human mind lie certain capabilities which do not manifest themselves unless drawn out by external influence or an inherent principle of development. Although there be no development of these faculties, they may still exist, but are not manifest. They remain in a dormant or latent state, they exist as possibilities, or *in* **potentia.** By an educating or developing influence these latent capabilities become manifest, and from the state of potentiality pass over to the state of actuality. To use an illustration, we may say that the seed makes the growth of the plant possible : it contains the possibility of the plant. Hence, to express the same thought in a different way : The seed is the potentiality of the plant ; sun and soil will transform this potentiality into actuality, the plant itself. All actual, finite existence must have passed through the stage of potential existence. Pedagogics is the science of the transition of man from his natural potentiality to actuality." (*Proceedings of the National Educational Asso-*

ciation, 1874, p. 246. Paper by Prof. Louis Soldan.)

2. "Pedagogics as a science must (1) unfold the general idea of Education ; (2) must exhibit the particular phases into which the general work of Education divides itself, and (3) must describe the particular standpoint upon which the general idea realizes itself, or should become real in its special processes at any particular time. . . . It busies itself with developing **a priori** the idea of Education in the universality and necessity of that idea. . . . Pedagogics as an art is the concrete individualizing of this abstract idea in any given case. . . . The idea of Pedagogics in general must distinguish, (1) The nature of Education in general ; (2) Its form ; (3) Its limits." (Rosenkranz, *Pedagogics as a System*, pp. 7–9, ed. 1873. Translated by Anna C. Brackett.)

3. "**Pedagogics** is the science and art of so developing, by means of **conscious influence** on the physical, intellectual, and moral powers of man, the ideas of truth, freedom, and love, that lie at the foundation of his God-derived nature, that he can meet spontaneously, and independently, his human responsibilities." (Schmidt, *Geschichte der Erziehung*, p. 1, quoted by Dr. C. W. Bennett in *History of the Philosophy of Pedagogics*, p. 2, a paper published by E. Steiger, New York, 1877.)

II.

ON EDUCATION.

4. Man lives upon the earth as a member of a family, as a member of society, as a member of the state, and as an individual. These ethical relations and the natural surroundings constitute the environment which encircle and mould him. Whatever influence this environment has upon his native capacities and faculties to occasion them to grow into powers, or habits, is called Education.

5. " We are born weak, we have need of help; we are born destitute of every thing, we stand in need of assistance; we are born stupid, we have need of understanding. All that we are not possessed of at our birth, and which we require when grown up, is bestowed on us by education. This education we receive from nature, from men, or from circumstances. The constitutional exertion of our organs and faculties is the education of nature; the uses we are taught to make of that exertion constitute the education given us by men; and in the acquisitions made by our own experience, on the objects that surround us, consists our education from circumstances. We are formed, therefore, by three kinds of masters.

The pupil, in whom the effects of their different lessons are contradictory, is badly educated, and can never be consistent with himself. He, in whom they are perfectly consonant, and always tend to the same point, hath only attained the end of a complete education. His life and actions demonstrate this, and that he alone is well brought up. Of these three different kinds of education, that of nature depends not on ourselves ; and but in a certain degree that of circumstances : the third, which belongs to men, is that only we have in our power : and even of this we are masters only in imagination ; for who can flatter himself he will be able entirely to govern the discourse and actions of those who are about a child ?" (Rousseau, *Emilius and Sophia*, vol. 1, pp. 4, 5. London, 4 vols., 1783.)

6. "Education is the influencing of man by man, and it has for its end to lead him to actualize himself through his own efforts. . . . It is the nature of education only to assist in the producing of that which the subject would strive most earnestly to develop for himself if he had a clear idea of himself. . . . Man, therefore, is the only fit subject for education. We often speak, it is true, of the education of plants and animals ; but even when we do so, we apply, unconsciously perhaps, other expressions, as ' raising ' and ' training,' in order to distinguish these. The general form of Education is determined by the nature of the mind, that it really is nothing but what it makes itself to be. The mind is (1) immediate (or potential), but (2) it must estrange itself from itself as it were, so that it may place itself over against itself as a special object of attention ; (3) this estrangement is finally removed through a further acquaintance with the object. . . . Education cannot create : it can only help to develop to reality the previously existent possibility ; it can only help to bring forth to light the hidden life. . . . Education seeks to transform every particular condition so that it shall no longer seem strange to the mind or in any wise foreign to its own nature. This identity of consciousness, and the special character of any thing done or endured by it, we call Habit (habitual conduct or behavior). It conditions formally all progress ; for that which is not yet become habit, but which we perform with design and an exercise of our will, is not yet a part of ourselves. . . . The limits of Education are found in the idea of its nature, which is to fashion the individual into theoretical and practical rationality." (Rosenkranz, *Pedagogics as a System*, pp. 7–23, ed. 1872, St. Louis. Translated by Anna C. Brackett.)

7. " Education differs from information or knowledge. The latter is of a special character, the purport of which is to fit a man for bringing about certain definite results by the immediate operation of that knowledge which he possesses. We talk, indeed, of the education of a lawyer, a doctor, and a clergyman—of an engineer, a soldier, or a sailor ; generally meaning by it the information or knowledge which he has acquired

for the immediate exercise of his vocation. But law, medicine, divinity, mechanics, strategics, and navigation, are not education. A man may possess any one of them and be well-nigh illiterate, though of course some can more possibly co-exist with want of education than others. One can conceive that a man may have a profound practical acquaintance with law, and be an uneducated person. Again, to quote an instance, the first Duke of Marlborough was one of the most skilful generals ever known, but he could not spell, and hardly write. Some men who have had the most marvellous aptitude and quickness in mechanical science, have been unable, from sheer ignorance, to sustain a common conversation. Education, on the other hand, deals with formalities. It does not so much aim at setting the mind right on particular points, as on getting the mind into the way of being right. It does not deal with matter, but with method. It purposes to train the thinking powers of man, not to fill the mind with facts. Hence, were it perfect, it would cultivate the intelligence so largely as to render easy the acquisition of any knowledge. It deals, in short, either directly or indirectly, with logical order and the reasoning powers. That it falls short of effecting what it purposes, is due to defects in its system, to defects in man's mind, to defects in this or that man's mind. As, however, its operation is not immediate, but only indirect, its best methods are frequently cavilled at as useless. It may teach logical method of thinking and reasoning. This, however, is generally too abstract for most minds, except they be more or less matured, and more or less informed on some one or two subjects. In place of this, then, it teaches ordinarily something, which is as exact an illustration of logical method as can be, and which, being unfailing in its inferences, trains the mind in method, and often stores it with facts. In a greater or less degree, but in some degree at least, this inculcation of an abstract method is necessary for any kind of education, and even, except it be a mere knack, for information." (Rogers, *Education in Oxford*, pp. 1–3. London, 1861.)

8. In the following quotation the extension of the term education is limited substantially to the work of the teacher. This limitation is unusual, and the advantages gained by it are hardly evident: " First, let me quote the definition (of Education) embodied in the ideal of the founders of the Prussian National System. It is given shortly as ' the harmonious and equable evolution of the human powers ;' at more length, in the words of Stein, ' by a method based on the nature of the mind, every power of the soul to be unfolded, every crude principle of life stirred up and nourished, all one-sided culture avoided, and the impulses on which the strength and worth of men rest, carefully attended to.' (Donaldson's *Lectures on Education*, p. 38.) This definition, which is pointed against narrowness generally, may have had special reference to the many omissions in the schooling of the foregone times : the leaving out of such things as bodily or muscular training ; training in the senses or observation ; training in art or refinement. It farther insinuates that hitherto the professed teacher may not have done much even for the intellect, for the higher moral training, nor for the training with a view to happiness or enjoyment. . . .

"In the very remarkable article on education contributed by James Mill to the *Encyclopædia Britannica*, the end of education is stated to be 'to render the individual, as much as possible, an instrument of happiness, first to himself, and next to other beings.' This, however, should be given as an amended answer to the first question of the Westminster Catechism—'What is the chief end of man?' The utmost that we could expect of the educator, who is not everybody, is to contribute his part to the promotion of human happiness in the order stated. No doubt the definition goes more completely to the root of the matter than the German formula. It does not trouble itself with the harmony, the many-sidedness, the wholeness, of the individual development ; it would admit these just as might be requisite for securing the final end.

"James Mill is not singular in his over-grasping view of the subject. The most usual subdivision of Education is into Physical, Intellectual, Moral, Religious, Technical. Now when we inquire into the meaning of Physical Education, we find it to mean the rearing of a healthy human being, by all the arts and devices of nursing feeding, clothing, and general regimen. Mill includes this subject in his article, and Mr. Herbert Spencer devotes a very interesting chapter to it in his work on Education. It seems to me, however, that this department may be kept quite separate, important though it be. It does not at all depend upon the principles and considerations that the educator, properly so called, has in view in the carrying on of his work. The discussion of the subject does not in any way help us in educational matters, as most commonly understood; nor does it derive any illumination from being placed side by side with the arts of the recognized teacher. The fact of bodily health or vigor is a leading postulate in bodily or mental training, but the trainer does not take upon himself to lay down the rules of hygiene.

"The inadvertence, for so I regard it, of coupling the Art of Health with Education is easily disposed of, and does not land us in any arduous controversies. Very different is another aspect of these definitions: that wherein the end of Education is propounded as the promotion of human happiness, human virtue, human perfection. Probably the qualification will at once be conceded, that Education is but one of the means, a single contributing agency to the all-including end. Nevertheless, the openings for difference of opinion as to what constitutes happiness, virtue or perfection, are very wide. Moreover, the discussion has its proper place in Ethics and in Theology, and if brought into the field of Education, should be received under protest.

"Before entering upon the consideration of this difficulty, the greatest of all, I will advert to some of the other views of education that seem to err on the side of taking in too much. Here, I may quote from the younger Mill, who, like his father, and unlike the generality of theorists, starts **more scientifico** with a definition. Education, according to him, ' includes whatever we do for ourselves, and whatever is done for us by others, for the express purpose of bringing us nearer to the perfection of our nature ; in its largest acceptation, it comprehends even the indirect effects produced on character and on the human faculties by things of which the direct purposes are different ; by laws, by forms of government, by the industrial arts, by modes of social life ; nay even by physical facts not dependent on the human will ; by climate, soil, and local position.' He admits, however, that this is a very wide view of the subject, and for his own immediate purpose advances a narrower view, namely, ' the culture which each generation purposely gives to those who are to be its successors, in order to qualify them for at least keeping up, and if possible for raising, the improvement which has been attained.' (*Inaugural Address at St. Andrew's*, p. 4.)

"Besides involving the dispute as to what constitutes ' perfection,' the first and larger statement is, I think, too wide for the most comprehensive Philosophy of Education. The influences exerted on the human character by climate and geographical position, by arts, laws, government and modes of social life, constitute a very interesting department of Sociology, and have their place there and nowhere else. What we do for ourselves, and what others do for us, to bring us nearer to the perfection of our nature, may be education in a precise sense of the word, and it may not. I do not see the propriety of including under the subject the direct operation of rewards and punishments. No doubt we do something to educate ourselves, and society does something to educate us, in a sufficiently proper acceptation of the word ; but the ordinary influence of society, in the dispensing of punishment and reward, is not the essential fact of Education, as I propose to regard it, although an adjunct to some of its legitimate functions.

"Mill's narrow expression of the scope of the subject is not exactly erroneous ; the moulding of each generation by the one preceding is not improperly described as an Education. It is, however, grandiose rather than scientific. Nothing is to be got out of it. It does not give the lead to the subsequent exposition.

"I find in the article ' Education,' in *Chambers's Encyclopædia*, a definition to the following effect : ' In the widest sense of the word a man is **educated**, either for good or for evil, by every thing that he experiences from the cradle to the grave [say, rather, " formed," " made," " influenced "]. But in the more limited and usual sense, the term Education is confined to the efforts made, of set purpose, to train men in a particular way—the efforts of the grown-up part of the community to inform the intellect and mould the character of the young [rather too much stress on the fact of influence from without] ; and more especially to the labours of professional educators or schoolmasters.' The concluding clause is the nearest to the point—the arts and methods employed by the schoolmasters ; for, although he is not alone in the work that he is expressly devoted to, yet he it is that typifies the process in its greatest singleness and purity. If by any investigations, inventions or discussions, we can improve his art to the ideal pitch, we shall have done nearly all that can be required of a science and art of Education." (Bain, *Education as a Science*, Art. I., in *Mind*, pp. 1-4, No. 5, January, 1877.)

9. " The true view of education is to regard it as a course of training. The youth in a gymnasium practises upon the horizontal bar, in order to develop his muscular powers generally ; he does not intend to go on posturing upon horizontal bars all through life. School is a place where the mental fibres are to be exercised, trained, expanded, developed, and strengthened. . . . It is the very purpose of a **liberal education**, as it is correctly called, to develop and train the plastic fibres of the youthful brain, so as to prevent them taking too early a definite ' set,' which will afterwards narrow and restrict the range of acquisition and judgment. I will even go so far as to say that it is hardly desirable for the actual things taught at school to stay in the mind for life. The source of error is the failure to distinguish between the **form** and the **matter** of knowledge, between the facts themselves and the manner in which the mental powers deal with facts. . . . It is the purpose of education so to exercise the faculties of mind that the infinitely various experience of after-life may be observed and reasoned upon to the best effect." (Jevons, in *Mind*, pp. 197-207, No. VI., April, 1877.) (Reinserted under " Memory and Cram," § 172.)

10. " Educit obstetrix, educat nutrix, instituit pedagogus, docet magister." (Varro. See also *An. and St'd Lat. Lex.*, unabridged.)

11. " Training (Fr. *trainer*) is development by instruction, exercise, and discipline, and is applicable to the whole nature of a man, or, specifically, to the faculties which he possesses. It denotes no more than a process of purposed habituation, and is equally applicable to the physical and mental powers, so that it may include both at the same time." (Smith, *Syn. Discriminated*, Art. *Education*, ed. 1878.) This sense of training is the ordinary meaning now attached to education.

12. " A thorough and complete education ought to preserve and increase the pupil's bodily health and strength ; give him command of his own muscular and mental powers ; increase his quickness in perceiving through his five senses, and quicken his mental perception ; form in him the habit of prompt and accurate judgment ; lead to delicacy and depth in every right feeling ; and make him inflexible in his conscientious and steadfast devotion to all his duties. In other words, an integral education must include at least these four branches :—gymnastics, or care of the body ; noetics, or training of the mind ; æsthetics, or cultivation of the tastes ; and ethics, which shall include religion as well as duty. And in every part of each branch of education, there will be a double end in view, namely, the increase of knowledge, and the increase of skill. Each study may be made the object of thought, or the object of action ; in the one case it is pursued as a science ; in the other case as an art." (Thomas Hill, *The True Order of Studies*, pp. 7, 8, ed. 1876.)

13. " The conclusions of the honest and intelligent inquirer after the truth in this matter, will be something like the following :—That education (from *e* and *duco*, to lead forth) is development ; that it is not instruction merely—knowledge, facts, rules—communicated by the teacher, but it is discipline, it is a waking up of the mind, a growth of the mind,—growth by a healthy assimilation of wholesome aliment. It is an inspiring of the mind with a thirst for knowledge, growth, enlargement,—and then a disciplining of its powers so far that it can go on to educate itself. It is the arousing of the child's mind to think, without thinking for it ; it is the awakening of its powers to observe, to remember, to reflect, to combine. It is not a cultivation of the memory to the neglect of every thing else ; but it is a calling forth of all the faculties into harmonious action. If to possess facts simply is education, then an encyclopædia is better educated than a man." (Page, *Theory and Practice of Teaching*, p. 70, ed. 1853.)

14. "Suppose it were perfectly certain that the life and fortune of every one of us would, one day or other, depend upon his winning or losing a game at chess. Don't you think that we should all consider it to be a primary duty to learn at least the names and the moves of the pieces ; to have a notion of a gambit, and a keen eye for all the means of giving and getting out of check ? Do you not think that we should look with disapprobation amounting to scorn, upon the father who allowed his son, or the state which allowed its members, to grow up without knowing a pawn from a knight ?

"Yet it is a very plain and elementary truth, that the life, the fortune, and the happiness of every one of us, and, more or less, of those who are connected with us, do depend upon our knowing something of the rules of a game infinitely more difficult and complicated than chess. It is a game which has been played for untold ages, every man and woman of us being one of the two players in a game of his or her own. The chess-board is the world, the pieces are the phenomena of the universe, the rules of the game are what we call the laws of Nature. The player on the other side is hidden from us. We know that his play is always fair, just, and patient. But also we know, to our cost, that he never overlooks a mistake, or makes the smallest allowance for ignorance. To the man who plays well the highest stakes are paid, with that sort of overflowing generosity with which the strong shows delight in strength. And one who plays ill is checkmated—without haste, but without remorse.

"My metaphor will remind some of you of the famous picture in which Retzsch has depicted Satan playing at chess with man for his soul. Substitute for the mocking fiend in that picture, a calm, strong angel who is playing for love, as we say, and would rather lose than win —and I should accept it as an image of human life.

"Well, what I mean by Education is learning the rules of this mighty game. In other words, education is the instruction of the intellect in the laws of Nature, under which name I include not merely things and their forces, but men and their ways; and the fashioning of the affections and of the will into an earnest and loving desire to move in harmony with those laws. For me, education means neither more nor less than this. Any thing which professes to call itself education must be tried by this standard, and if it fails to stand the test, I will not call it education, whatever may be the force of authority, or of numbers, upon the other side.

"It is important to remember that, in strictness, there is no such thing as an uneducated man. Take an extreme case. Suppose that an adult man, in the full vigour of his faculties, could be suddenly placed in the world, as Adam is said to have been, and then left to do as he

best might. How long would he be left uneducated? Not five minutes. Nature would begin to teach him, through the eye, the ear, the touch, the properties of objects. Pain and pleasure would be at his elbow telling him to do this and avoid that; and by slow degrees the man would receive an education, which, if narrow, would be thorough, real, and adequate to his circumstances, though there would be no extras and very few accomplishments. . . .
The great mass of mankind are the ' Poll,' who pick up just enough to get through without much discredit. Those who won't learn at all are plucked; and then you can't come up again. Nature's pluck means extermination. . . .
Nature's discipline is not even a word and a blow, and the blow first; but the blow without the word. It is left to you to find out why your ears are boxed." (Huxley, *Lay Sermons*, pp. 31–34, ed. 1870. London.)

15. " As theory, Education allies itself to Psychology, Physiology, and Sociology. The materials of its teaching it draws from these philosophies, from the practice of the schoolroom, and from the rich domain of History. . . .
I have some sympathy with the cynical Love Peacock, who, in describing certain social bores in the shape of men of one idea who hold forth in season and out of season, says :—' The worst of all bores was the third. His subject had no beginning, middle, nor end. It was Education. Never was such a journey through the desert of mind, the great Sahara of intellect. The

very recollection makes me thirsty.' Such men are not educationists in any sense in which that term is applicable within these walls. They are men of leisure who have restless minds, and if they have not one fixed idea or crotchet, will find another. An educationist has no crotchets. That man has crotchets who, having seized on that particular corner of a large and many-sided subject which has some secret affinity with his own mind, or affords the quickest passage to notoriety, pursues it to the death. Now, an educationist is, by virtue of his very name and vocation, inaccessible to all petty fanaticisms. He has to deal with a subject of infinite variety, and so variously related to life, that he is more apt to be lost in hesitations and scepticisms than to be the victim of a fixed idea. If you wish to meet with educational crotchets, you must go to the specialist in this or that department of knowledge, who is unfortunate enough to take up the question of Education, as you see he often in moments of aberration takes up other subjects which are outside his own range of intellectual experience. It is only in such cases that you will find the confidence and self-assurance which is born of limited knowledge, and the pertinacious insistence which flows from these habits of mind. To him whose subject is Education crotchets are prohibited, because his opinions on this or that point are related on the one side to rational and comprehensive theory, and on the other to the daily practice of the schoolroom and the needs of life. . . .

The more abstract treatment of the theory of Education is doubtless, if true in its philosophy, of universal application. It sweeps the whole field. But this will engage our attention only within carefully prescribed limits, and when we leave this portion of our subject, we have to restrict ourselves on all sides. The education of every human being is determined by potent influences which do not properly fall within the range of our consideration here. The breed of men to which the child belongs, the character of his parents, the human society into which he is born, the physical circumstances by which he is surrounded, are silently but irresistibly forming him. The traditions of his country, its popular literature, its very idioms of speech, its laws and customs, its religious life, its family life, constitute an aggregate of influence which chiefly make him what he is. . . . By their constant presence they mould the future man, himself unconscious. They are the atmosphere of the humanity of his particular time and place, and in breathing it he is essentially a **passive** agent. . . . The passive activity of our nature is not to be ignored in our educational methods; it is to be turned to use as one of our most potent instruments, but it is mainly the self-conscious forces that we have to educe and direct. Even in doing this we are bound by external conditions, and must take note not only of the almost irresistible forces around us, but of minor conditions of time, place, and circumstance. Each successive century, and the traditions and circumstances of each country, nay, the genius of each people, present to us the educational problem in ever-changing aspects. Educational systems cannot be manufactured in the study. Our theory of the end of all education and the means by which that end has to be attained may be, or rather ought to be, always the same; but the application of that theory must vary with varying external conditions. What present defects have we **here** and **now**, and to what dangers are we exposed? is the form which the practical question must take with us." (Laurie, *Inaugural Address, Chair of Education*, pp. 21-24. Edinburgh, 1876.)

16. "To write upon education, means to write upon almost every thing at once; for it has to care for, and watch over, the development of an entire, though miniature, world in little, —a microcosm of the microcosm. All the energies with which nations have labored and signalized themselves once existed as germs in the hand of the educator. If we carried the subject still further, every century, every nation, and even every boy and every girl, would require a distinct system of education, a different primer, and domestic French governess, &c. . . . But although the spirit of education, always watching over the whole, is nothing more than an endeavor to liberate, by means of a freeman, the ideal human being which lies concealed in every child; and though, in the application of the divine to the child's nature, it must scorn some useful things, some seasonable, individual, or immediate ends ; yet it must incorporate itself in the most definite applications, in order to be clearly manifested. . . .

"But who then educates in nations and ages?—Both!—The living time, which for twenty or thirty years struggles unceasingly with men through actions and opinions, tossing them to and fro as with a sea of waves, must soon wash away or cover the precipitate of the short school years, in which only one man, and only words taught. The century is the spiritual climate of man, mere education the hot-house and forcing-pit, out of which he is taken and planted forever in the other. By century is here meant the real century, which may as often truly consist of ten years, as of ten thousand, and which is dated, like religious eras, only from great men. What can insulated words do against living present action ? The present has for new deeds also new words ; the teacher has only dead languages for the, to all appearance, dead bodies of his examples. The educator has himself been educated, and is already possessed, even without his knowledge, by the spirit of the age, which he assiduously labors to banish out of the youth (as a whole city criticises the spirit of the whole city). Only, alas ! every one believes himself to stand so precisely and accurately in the zenith of the universe, that, according to his calculation, all suns and nations must culminate over his head ; and he himself, like the countries at the equator, cast no shadow save into himself alone. . . . The spirit of the nation and of the age decides, and is at once the schoolmaster and the school ; for it seizes on the pupil to form him with two vigorous hands and powers ; with the living lesson of action, and with its unalterable unity. If—to begin with unity—education must be, like the Testament, a continuous endeavor to withdraw the force of interrupting mixtures, then nothing builds up so strong as the present, which ceases not for a moment, and eternally repeats itself ; and which, with joy and sorrow, with towns and books, with friends and enemies, in short, with thousand-handed life, presses and seizes on us. No teacher of the people continues so uniformly one with himself as the teaching people. Minds molten into masses lose something of their free movements : which bodies, for instance, that of the world, perhaps that of the universe, seem to gain by their very massiveness, and, like a heavy colossus, to move all the more easily along the old, iron-covered track. For however much marriages, old age, deaths and enmities, are in the individual case subject to the law of freedom, yet in a whole nation, lists of births and deaths can be made, by which it may be shown that in the canton of Berne (according to Mad. de Staël) the number of divorces, as in Italy that of murders, is the same from year to year. Must not, now, the little human being placed on such an eternally and ever similarly acting world, be borne as upon a flying earth, where the only directions that a teacher can give avail nothing, because he has first unconsciously received his line of movement upon it?

"Thence, in spite of all reformers and informers, nations, like meadows, reach ever a similar verdure ; thence, even in capital cities, where all school-books and schoolmasters, and even parents of every kind, educate, the spirit maintains itself unalterably the same. Repetition is the mother not only of study, but also of education. . . . Certainly one might say that also in families there educates, besides the popular masses, a pedagogic crowd of people ; at least, for instance, aunt, grandfathers, grandmothers, father, mother, god-parents, friends of the family, the yearly domestics, and at the end of all the instructor beckons with his forefinger, so that —could this force continue as long as it would gladly be maintained—a child, under these many masters, would resemble, much more than one thinks, an Indian slave, who wanders about with the inburnt stamps of his various masters. But how does the multitude disappear compared with the higher one, by which it was colored ; just as all the burnt marks of the slave yet cannot overcome the hot black coloring of the sun, but receive it as a coat of arms in a sable field? . . . The end desired must be known before the way. All means or arts of education will be, in the first instance, determined by the ideal or archetype we entertain of it. But there floats before common parents, instead of one archetype, a whole picture cabinet of ideals, which they impart bit by bit, and tattoo into their children. If the secret variances of a large class of ordinary fathers were brought to light, and laid down as a plan of studies, and reading catalogue for a moral education, they would run somewhat after this fashion :—In the first hour pure morality must be read to the child, either by myself, or the tutor ; in the second, mixed morality, or that which may be applied to one's own advantage ; in the third, ' Do you not see that your father does so and so ? ' in the fourth, ' You are little, and this is only fit for grown-up people ;' in the fifth, ' The chief matter is that you should succeed in the world, and become something in the state ;' in the sixth, ' Not the temporary, but the eternal, determines the worth of a man ;' in the seventh, ' Therefore rather suffer injustice, and be kind ;' in the eighth, ' but defend yourself bravely if any one attack you ;' in the ninth, ' Do not make such a noise, dear child ;' in the tenth, ' A boy must not sit so quiet ;' in the eleventh, ' You must obey your parents better ;' in the twelfth, ' and educate yourself.' So by the hourly change of his principles the father conceals their untenableness and one-sidedness. As for his wife, she is neither like him, nor yet like that harlequin who came on to the stage with a bundle of papers under each arm, and answered to the inquiry what he had under his right arm, ' orders,' and to what he had under his left, ' counter-orders ;' but the mother might be much better compared to a giant Briareus, who had a hundred arms, and a bundle of papers under each.

. . . The majority of educated men are, therefore, at present an illumination which burns off by fits and starts in the rain, shining with interrupted forms, and depicting broken characters. But the bad and impure spirits of educational systems are yet to be reduced into other divisions. Many parents educate their children only for themselves,—that is, to be pretty blocks, or soul-alarums, which are not set to move or sound when stillness is required. The child has merely to be that on which the teacher can sleep most softly or drum most loudly ; who, having something else to do and to enjoy, wishes to be spared the trouble of education, duly but most unreasonably expecting its fruits. . . . Related to those teachers who wished to be machine-makers are the educators for appearances and political usefulness. Their maxims, thoroughly carried out, would only produce pupils, or rather sucklings, passively obedient, boneless, well-trained, patient of all things,—the thick, hard, human kernel would give place to the soft, sweet fruit-pulp,—and the child's clod of earth, into which growing life should breathe a divine spirit, would be kept down and manured as though it were but a corn-field,—the edifice of the state would be inhabited by mere spinning-machines, calculating-machines, printing and pumping apparatus, oil-mills, and models for mills, pumps, and spinning-machines, &c.
. . . Education can neither entirely consist of mere unfolding in general, or, as it is now better called, excitement,—for every continued

existence unfolds, and every bad education excites, just as oxygen positively irritates,—nor in the unfolding of all the powers, because we can never act upon the whole amount of them at once ; as little as in the body susceptibility and spontaneity, or the muscular and nervous system, can be strengthened at the same time." (Richter, *Levana*, Preface, ix, and pp. 7–33. Boston. 1863.)

17. " A treatise on education does not include the theory of instruction, whose wide realm embraces the mistakes of all sciences and arts ; nor the theory of remedies, which would require libraries instead of volumes for the complication of mistakes, years, positions, and relations. At the same time no science is entirely disconnected from the rest ; the feet cannot move without the hands." (*Ibid.*, p. 390.)

18. The education that any one receives depends upon the ethical relations by which he is surrounded. But education must regard the nature and powers of the mind of him who is to be educated. Hence education, as a product, is founded upon ethical relations upon the one hand, and the nature of mind, or Psychology, upon the other. Education, in part, is dependent upon teaching or instruction as a means for securing its ends. Teaching, then, directly busies itself with the subject-matter that is to be learned, and with the mind which is to learn it.

19. " The educator of youth does not merely communicate so much instruction from year to year ; he develops the receptive and acquisitive tendencies of mind, which are afterwards to play their part in the intellectual activity of the nation. He trains the intelligence of those who are afterwards to be the teachers of others, as well as of those who are only to be interested inquirers after truth." (Calderwood, *On Teaching*, p. 49, ed. 1875, New York.)

III.

ON TEACHING.

20. Having briefly considered the notion of the terms Pedagogics and Education, the reader is directed to the conception of the term *Teaching*.

Thought is the modification of the activity called Intelligence, and Language is its Form. Language is the mirror which reflects the ideas that are in the mind of him who utters it. Language is a record of thought. Language, in its widest signification, is the instrument for perpetuating the life of a nation, or rather it is the life of a people perpetuated. Language is the form of the matter which once existed in the consciousness of the person who uttered it; it is a product of thought; perhaps more exactly it is thought itself. "It is only as there is a λoyos in the outer world, answering to the λoyos or internal reason of the parties, that men can come into a mutual understanding in regard to any thought-state whatever." (Grindon, *Life*, p. 349.)

"By Language we do not mean the mere art of speaking and writing according to some specific, arbitrary mode, which though intelligible in one country, is unintelligible in another. We mean that beautiful and inevitable flowering forth in speech of the inner, living intellect of man, which, older and more excellent than all prosody and spelling, is an integral work of nature ; and which, were .. possible for the accidental forms which it may hold at any given epoch, as English and French, Latin and Greek, to be suddenly and totally abolished, would in itself be unaffected, and speedily incarnate afresh, unchanged save in the extrinsic circumstances of costume." (*Ibid*, pp. 153, 154, third ed., London.) Nations differ in their language —these differences measure those differences that exist among the ideas or notions which are substantially common to many peoples. The content and extent of words having the same general meaning, when expressed in different languages, are hardly equivalent nor precisely identical. No two nations live and act exactly alike, and as language follows life, it is but in the harmony of things that this should occasion different notions of life and actions in the minds of the various peoples, and hence in language. Two or three examples will illustrate the case :

21. To indicate a certain notion, the Greeks used **deiknumi**, the English equivalents of which are : " To bring to light, to display, to portray, to represent to the life as in statuary, to shew, to point out, to make known by words, to tell, to explain, to teach, to prove, to offer, to proffer." Buttmann traces the prefix **deik** to a root **dek**, which contains the common notion of

stretching out the right hand either **to point, or to welcome.** (Liddell and Scott, *Greek-English Lexicon*, Oxford, 1871.) The essential idea seems to rest upon the action of pointing to, or towards, a thing. The Greeks cultivated the graces of action as well as the harmony of sounds, and it is not difficult to conceive the elders among the people pointing out, showing, portraying as artists, the things before them to the youth, much as a traveller would do at the present time to a youthful companion. The fact that Socrates was at so great pains to develop in his pupils the power to reason would argue that, in his opinion, before his time the powers of perception and memory of the youth had been recognized as of greater value in acquiring an education than the reflective powers. The word *teaching* also appears to exhibit some one as in the action of directing the attention of another to something through, or by means of, the gestures of his right hand—it does not so much seem to exhibit one as showing a thing, object, immediately and directly, as it shows indirectly through words and general gestures, and by illustrative sketches—it implies an exhortation to attend to this thing which is in mind as a philosophical truth. It would seem to indicate an explanation of memorized words. "When the children could read, and understand what they read, the works of the poets were put in requisition, to exercise their minds, and awaken their hearts to great and noble deeds. Plato, *Leg.* vii. p. 810, approves of this, and also recommends committing whole poems, or select passages, to memory ; and this method of instruction appears to have been universal. Above all, the poems of Homer were thought to contain, by precept and example, every thing calculated to awaken national spirit, and to instruct a man how to be beautiful and good." (Becker, *Charicles*, trans. by Frederick Metcalfe, ed. 1866, p. 233.)

22. The Latins conveyed a certain notion by **doceo,** which is rendered in English by : " To teach, to inform, to instruct, to show, to point out, to represent, to exhibit." It is compared with **edocere,** which means " to make one learn, to make acquainted with, more energetic than **docere." Perdocere** means " to teach perfectly, to instruct thoroughly." **Erudire** implies " to initiate in learning." Instruct, **in** and **struo,** means : To join together, to pile up, heap up, to erect, to build, to set in array, to join together, to construct. (Bullion, *Lat.-Eng. Dict.*, ed. 1869.) The essential idea with the Latins seems to be that of laying before one some matters as objects to be seen, handled, piled up in layers one upon another (instruct), to show as in an exhibition. The word pictures one as standing at work upon some visible objects, and calling the attention of another to these objects as he piles them up, one upon another. This sense is virtually different from the thought with the Greeks, who rather withdrew themselves from the presence of the things about which they discoursed, and crowded the thought home to the conviction of the hearer by words and exhortatory gestures of the right hand. This notion of **doceo** corresponds with the general characteristics of the Latins, who were a people pre-eminently skilful in the affairs of practical business. They regarded the objects of business directly, rather than through philosophy. Hence, the one would instruct a youth in law by exhibiting to him law practice in the courts, while the other would lecture the youth about the principles of law in the abstract, while seated in his stone chair, or while walking about the groves.

23. The Anglo-Saxons expressed a certain notion by the word **tǽcan**, which is rendered in English : " To teach, to instruct, to show, to direct, to command, to see to, to provide, to order, to convince, to prove." (Bosworth, *Anglo-Saxon and Eng. Dict.*, London, 1860.) In this case the notion has an element of *power* and *authority* in it ; it shows, with power to command attention ; it directs, but it is imperative about something towards somebody ; it does not simply exhort the attention of somebody towards an idea by the right hand in persuasion or welcome, as does the Greek **deiknumi**—nor does it call the attention of somebody to what the exhibitor has before him, piling it up in order, as do the Latin **doceo** and **instruo ;** but it shows something to somebody, meaning that this somebody shall attend to this something. This word **tǽcan** discloses the characteristic trait of the Anglo-Saxon life, the disposition to do something for another, and then to command him to respect what has been placed before him. The word regards with emphasis both what is provided, and him for whom it is provided.

24. These three instances illustrate the differences which exist among peoples when they express a notion that is ordinarily regarded as the same by them all. Each people has its own setting of thoughts which control the form, and assist in conserving the meaning of subsequent notions. These thoughts, notions, conserved in form, are language. The words "instruct" and "teach" are both in common use at this time, practically as synonyms. Following the lines of their ancestry, and considering the tendency of the present age, it is determined to use the word teaching rather than instruction in the expression *Methods of Teaching*. As illustrating the deep-seated element of authority which exists in the Anglo-Saxon notion of teaching, the following quotations are subjoined :

25. " I hope I may be excused for one remark on a tendency in education at present, more especially with regard to the modern subjects, to render the process interesting, as it is usually called, but amusing would probably be the more correct word. It would be absurd to recommend that any subject should be proposed in a purposely repulsive form to students, especially to youth ; but, on the other hand, it seems to me a most enervating practice to shrink from demanding even irksome attention whenever it is necessary. The lesson that success in any pursuit demands serious toil must be learned eventually, and like most lessons is learned with least pain in early years." (Todhunter, *Conflict of Studies and other Essays*, p. 21. London, 1873.)

26. " Parents and the public have little idea how close a resemblance there is between teaching and writing on the sands of the sea, unless either there is a distinct capacity for learning on the part of the pupil, or some system of examination and reward to force the pupil to apply." (Jevons, paper in *Mind*, p. 195, No. VI., April, 1877.) (Reinserted under Memory and " Cram," § 172.)

27. " Whatever the age and attainment of the pupils under charge, the first requisite for communicating instruction is to gain and keep their attention. Teaching, to be successful, must therefore be adapted to win attention. At the earlier stages of school life this is the one pressing requirement. Somehow, attention must be made possible even to the most restless little ones, to whom the first restraints of school life are irksome. Accustomed to have every new object attract their interest just as long as they recognized any thing attractive in it—permitted to change from one engagement to another as caprice dictated—they must be made familiar with restriction. They must begin to be regulated by the will of another. Taking this as self-evident, we are prone to say that they **must** do so, whether they will or not. This is one of our superficial current phrases which cover over many points needing careful consideration. Attention is not to be secured by mere exercise of authority. Authority has a great deal to do through the whole course of school life, but we cannot 'command' attention, as we say, by merely demanding that it be given. A radical mistake is made if a teacher lean on his authority in the school as the guarantee for attention by the scholars. He must consider the requirements of the undisciplined mind, and adapt himself to them. Children attend to what interests them. This must determine the kind of assistance to be given them in acquiring habits of attention. To help them in this is an obvious part of a teacher's work. . . . The master of a school in this respect shares a task which is common to all who essay to teach others. In this appears the true place and power of the profession." (Calderwood, *On Teaching*, pp. 47–49, ed. 1875.)

28. The conception of Teaching which prevails in these inquiries is limited to that assistance which one person (teacher) consciously gives to another person or thing (learner), when this latter is learning something. Teachers are not necessarily educators. Any thing educates the child that helps to mould its character, or that stimulates its self-control. Fire educates in an imperative manner, but it does not teach. The authority of the parent educates his child, while the child may be taught nothing in regard to the nature or source of authority. A teacher's personal influence may educate a school in ways of virtue, while he has taught them nothing about the nature of virtue. Teaching regards the purely intellectual capacities of Man. Education refers to all the capabilities of Mind. The intellect is taught by a person, and educated by persons and things. The will is educated by any power. Teaching sets the subject-matter, trusting the mind to accept the truth ; educating may exert a power without giving any reason or instruction. Teachers should be educators. Parents are educators—they may also be teachers. Good teaching and good educating put the mind of him who is taught or educated, into a frame which acknowledges and accepts testimony and authority from whatever source they spring. That teaching or educating is pernicious which leaves the mind of the learner in a state of undue skepticism towards testimony and authority. (See §§ 31-34.)

29. " The communication of knowledge in general is the common idea by which these words—*inform, instruct, teach*—are connected with each other. **Inform** is the general term ; the other two are specifick. To **inform** is the act of persons in all conditions ; to **instruct** and **teach** are the acts of superiours, either on one ground or another : one **informs** by virtue of an accidental superiority or priority of knowledge ; one **instructs** by virtue of superior knowledge, or superior station : one **teaches** by virtue of superiour knowledge, rather than station : diplomatick agents **inform** their governments of the political transactions in which they are concerned ; government **instructs** its different functionaries and officers in regard to their mode of proceeding ; professors and preceptors **teach** those who attend a publick school to learn.

" To **inform** is applicable to matters of general interest ; we may *inform* ourselves or others on every thing which is a subject of inquiry or curiosity ; and the *information* serves either to amuse or to improve the mind ; to **instruct** is applicable to matters of serious concern, or that which is practically useful ; it serves to set us right in the path of life. A parent *instructs* his child in the course of conduct he should pursue ; a good child profits by the **instruction** of a good parent to make him wiser and better for the time to come ; to **teach** respects matters of art and science ; the learner depends upon the **teacher** for the formation of his mind, and the establishment of his principles. Every one ought to be properly **informed** before he pretends to give an opinion ; the young and inexperienced must be **instructed** before they can act ; the ignorant must be **taught,** in order to guard them against errour. Truth and sincerity are all that is necessary for an **informant**; general experience and a perfect knowledge of the subject in question are requisite for the **instructer**; fundamental knowledge is requisite for **the teacher.** Those who give **information** upon the authority of others are liable to mislead ; those who *instruct* others in doing that which is bad, scandalously abuse the authority that is reposed in them ; those who pretend to **teach** what they themselves do not understand, mostly betray their ignorance sooner or later.

"To **inform** and to **teach** are employed for things as well as persons ; to **instruct** only for persons : books and reading **inform** the mind ; history or experience **teaches** mankind." (Crabb, *Synonyms*, ed. 1859.)

30. "**Inform** (Lat. **in** and **forma,** shape or form) relates only to matters of fact made known to one who could not have known them before. **Instruction** (Lat. **instruere, instructus**) relates to principles drawn from known facts. **Teaching** (A. S. **tǣcan,** to teach), as distinct from instruction, is applied to practice.(it may be the practice of an art or branch of knowledge). A child is instructed in grammar, and taught to speak a language. Teach has a purely mechanical application, which does not belong to instruct. A dog may be taught a trick ; but he could not be instructed in any thing. The two processes of teaching and instruction may thus go on simultaneously. In mathematics there is no information, because the propositions are not statements of fact, but are based upon principles assumed. Information is of new facts ; instruction is of undeveloped truths. Information extends knowledge ; instruction gives additional understanding ; teaching, additional power of doing. **Acquaint** (Fr. **accointer,** Lat. **accognitare,** from **cognosco, cognitus,** to know), **Apprise** (Fr. **appris,** from **apprendre,** the Lat. **apprehendere**), and **Advise** (Fr. **aviser,** Lat. **ad** and **videre, visus,** to see) closely resemble inform, inasmuch as they relate to the communication of matters of fact. I inform a man when I simply tell him a fact which he did not know before. I acquaint him with that of which I furnish him with all the details. So I inform him of the fact, and acquaint him with the particulars of it. I apprise him of what particularly concerns him to know, whether it be a good or an evil, or a danger, or a probability of any sort. I advise him of that which I impart to him formally, officially, or as in duty bound, of what occurs in due course." (Smith, *Syn. Discr.*)

IV.

ON AUTHORITIES.

31. " So in literature, men of established reputation, of classical merit, and known veracity, are quoted as **authorities** in support of any position." (Crabb, *Synonyms.*)

32. " Authority may come from superior knowledge or information, or from natural as well as social or professional relationship." (Smith, *Synonyms Discriminated.*)

33. "**The Principle of Authority.**—' The principle of adopting the belief of others, on a matter of opinion, without reference to the particular grounds on which the belief may rest.'

"**The Argument from Authority.**—It is an argument for the truth of an opinion that it has been embraced by all men, in all ages, and in all nations. *Quod semper, ubique, et ab omnibus,* are the morks of universality, according to Vincentius Lirinensis. 'This word is sometimes employed in its primary sense, when we refer to any one's example, testimony, or judgment ; as when, *e.g.*, we speak of correcting a reading in some book on the **authority** of an ancient MS., or giving a statement of some fact on the **authority** of such and such historians, etc. In this sense the word answers pretty nearly to the Latin **auctoritas**. It is a claim to **deference**. Sometimes, again, it is employed as equivalent to **potestas**, power, as when we speak of the **authority** of a magistrate. This is a claim to **obedience**.'

"**Consent**.—'Believing in the prophets and evangelists with a calm and settled faith, with that **consent** of the will, and heart, and understanding, which constitutes religious belief, I find in them the clear annunciation of the kingdom of God upon earth.'

"**Assent** is the consequence of a conviction of the understanding. **Consent** arises from the state of the disposition and the will. The one accepts what is **true**; the other embraces it as **true and good** and worthy of all acceptation. . . .

"' These things are to be regarded as **first truths**, the credit of which is not derived from other truths, but is inherent in themselves. As for **probable** truths, they are such as are admitted by **all** men, or by the **generality** of men, or by **wise** men; and among these last, either by all the wise, or by the generality of the wise, or by such of the wise as are of the highest authority.'

"**Assent** is that act of the mind by which we accept as true a proposition, a perception, or an idea. It is a necessary part of judgment; for if you take away from judgment affirmation or denial, nothing remains but a simple conception without logical value, or a proposition which must be examined before it can be admitted. It is also implied in perception, which would otherwise be a mere phenomenon which the mind had not accepted as true.

"**Assent** is **free** when it is not the unavoidable result of evidence, **necessary** when I cannot withhold it without contradicting myself. The Stoics, while they admitted that most of our ideas came from without, thought that images purely sensible could not be converted into real cognitions without a spontaneous act of the mind, which is just *assent* or belief. . . . '*Assent* of the mind to truth is, in all cases, the work not of the *understanding*, but of the *reason*. Men are not convinced by syllogisms; but when they believe a principle, or wish to believe, then syllogisms are brought in to prove it.'

"**Belief.**—' Belief, assent, conviction, are words which I do not think admit of logical definition, because the operation of mind signified by them is perfectly simple, and of its own kind. **Belief** must have an object. For he who believes must believe something, and that which he believes is the object of his **belief**. **Belief** is always expressed in language by a proposition wherein something is affirmed or denied. **Belief** admits of all degrees, from the slightest suspicion to the fullest assurance. There are many operations of mind of which it is an essential ingredient, as consciousness, perception, remembrance. We give the name of evidence to whatever is a ground of **belief**. What this evidence is, is more easily felt than described. The common occasions of life lead us to distinguish evidence into different kinds; such as the evidence of sense, of memory, of consciousness, of testimony, of axioms, and of reasoning. I am not able to find any common nature to which they may all be reduced. They seem to me to agree only in this, that they are all fitted by nature to produce **belief** in the human mind, some of them in the highest degree, which we call certainty, others in various degrees according to circumstances.'

" St. Austin accurately says, ' We **know** what rests upon **reason**; we **believe** what rests upon **authority**.' The original data of reason do not rest upon reason, but are necessarily accepted by reason on the authority of what is beyond itself. These data are, therefore, in rigid propriety, **beliefs** or **trusts**. Thus it is, that in the last resort, we must, perforce, philosophically admit, that **belief** is the primary condition of reason, and not reason the ultimate ground of **belief**. We are compelled to surrender the proud **Intellige ut credas** of Abelard, to content ourselves with the humble **Crede ut intelligas** of Anselm.

" To **believe** is to admit a thing as true, on grounds sufficient, **subjectively**; insufficient, **objectively**. The word **believing** has been variously and loosely employed. It is frequently used to denote states of consciousness which have already their separate and appropriate appellations. Thus it is sometimes said, I believe in my own existence and the existence of an external world, I believe in the facts of nature, the axioms of geometry, the affections of my own mind, as well as, I believe in the testimony of witnesses, or in the evidence of historical documents.

"Setting aside this loose application of the term, I propose to confine it, **first**, to the effect on the mind of the premises in what is termed probable reasoning, or what I have named contingent reasoning—in a word, the premises of all reasoning, but that which is demonstrative ; and, **secondly,** to the state of **holding true** when that state, far from being the effect of any premises discerned by the mind, is dissociated from all evidence. I propose to restrict the term **belief** to the assent to propositions, and demarcate it from those inferences which are made in the presence of objects and have reference to them. I would say, we **believe** in the proposition 'Fire burns,' but **know** the fact that the paper about to be thrust into the flame will ignite." (Fleming, *Vocab. of Phil.*)

34. " Another error is a conceit that of former opinions or sects after variety and examination the best hath still prevailed and suppressed the rest ; so as if a man should begin the labour of a new search, he were but like to light upon somewhat formerly rejected, and by rejection brought into oblivion : as if the multitude, or the wisest for the multitude's sake, were not ready to give passage rather to that which is popular and superficial, than to that which is substantial and profound ; for the truth is, that time seemeth to be of the nature of a river or stream, which carrieth down to us that which is light and blown up, and sinketh and drowneth that which is weighty and solid. . . . .

"Another error hath proceeded from too great a reverence, and a kind of adoration of the mind and understanding of man; by means whereof, men have withdrawn themselves too much from the contemplation of nature, and the observations of experience, and have tumbled up and down in their own reason and conceits. Upon these intellectualists, which are notwithstanding commonly taken for the most sublime and divine philosophers, Heraclitus gave a just censure, saying, **Men sought truth in their own little worlds, and not in the great and common world**; for they disdain to spell, and so by degrees to read in the volume of God's works: and contrariwise by continual meditation and agitation of wit do urge and as it were invocate their own spirits to divine and give oracles unto them, whereby they are deservedly deluded.

"Another error that hath some connexion with this latter is, that men have used to infect their meditations, opinions, and doctrines, with some conceits which they have most admired, or some sciences which they have most applied; and given all things else a tincture according to them, utterly untrue and improper. So hath Plato intermingled his philosophy with theology, and Aristotle with logic; and the second school of Plato, Proclus and the rest, with the mathematics. For these were the arts which had a kind of primogeniture with them severally. So have the alchymists made a philosophy out of a few experiments of the furnace; and Gilbertus our countryman hath made a philosophy out of the observations of a loadstone. So Cicero, when, reciting the several opinions of the nature of the soul, he found a musician that held the soul was but a harmony, saith pleasantly, **Hic ab arte sua non recessit, etc.** But of these conceits Aristotle speaketh seriously and wisely when he saith, **Qui respiciunt ad pauca de facili pronunciant.**

" Another error is an impatience of doubt, and haste to assertion without due and mature suspension of judgment. For the two ways of contemplation are not unlike the two ways of action commonly spoken of by the ancients: the one plain and smooth in the beginning, and in the end impassable; the other rough and troublesome in the entrance, but after a while fair and even: so it is in contemplation; if a man will begin with certainties, he shall end in doubts; but if he will be content to begin with doubts, he shall end in certainties.

" Another error is in the manner of the tradition and delivery of knowledge, which is for the most part magistral and peremptory, and not ingenuous and faithful; in a sort as may be soonest believed, and not easiliest examined. It is true that in compendious treatises for practice that form is not to be disallowed: but in the true handling of knowledge, men ought not to fall either on the one side into the vein of Velleius the Epicurean, **Nil tam metuens, quam ne dubitare aliqua de re videretur**; nor on the other side into Socrates his ironical doubting of all things; but to propound things sincerely with more or less asseveration, as they stand in a man's own judgment proved more or less.

"Other errors there are in the scope that men propound to themselves, whereunto they bend their endeavours; for whereas the more constant and devote kind of professors of any science ought to propound to themselves to make some additions to their science, they convert their labors to aspire to certain second prizes: as to be a profound interpreter or commenter, to be a sharp champion or defender, to be a methodical compounder or abridger, and so the patrimony of knowledge cometh to be sometimes improved, but seldom augmented.

"But the greatest error of all the rest is the mistaking or misplacing of the last or furthest end of knowledge. For men have entered into a desire of learning and knowledge, sometimes upon a natural curiosity and inquisitive appetite; sometimes to entertain their minds with variety and delight; sometimes for ornament and reputation; and sometimes to enable them to victory of wit and contradiction; and most times for lucre and profession; and seldom sincerely to give a true account of their gift of reason, to the benefit and use of men: as if there were sought in knowledge a couch whereupon to rest a searching and restless spirit; or a terrace for a wandering and variable mind to walk up and down with a fair prospect; or a tower of state, for a proud mind to raise itself upon; or a fort or commanding ground, for strife and contention; or a shop, for profit or sale; and not a rich storehouse for the glory of the Creator and the relief of man's estate. But this is that which will indeed dignify and exalt knowledge, if contemplation and action may be more nearly and straitly conjoined and united together than they have been; a conjunction like unto that of the two highest planets, Saturn, the planet of rest and contemplation, and Jupiter, the planet of civil society and action. Howbeit, I do not mean, when I speak of use and action, that end before-mentioned of the applying of knowledge to lucre and profession; for I am not ignorant how much that diverteth and interrupteth the prosecution and advancement of knowledge, like unto the golden ball thrown before Atalanta, which while she goeth aside and stoopeth to take up, the race is hindered. . . . .

"Neither is my meaning, as was spoken of Socrates, to call philosophy down from heaven to converse upon the earth; that is, to leave natural philosophy aside, and to apply knowledge only to manners and policy. But as both heaven and earth do conspire and contribute to the use and benefit of man; so the end ought to be, from both philosophies to separate and reject vain speculations, and whatsoever is empty and void, and to preserve and augment whatsoever is solid and fruitful." (Bacon, *Advancement of Learning*, pp. 39–43, ed. 1868.)

V.

RECAPITULATION.

35. This brief Introductory Discussion, recapitulated, exhibits the following synopsis:

I. PEDAGOGICS INCLUDES—
   1. Education,
   2. Ethics,
   3. Psychology.

II. EDUCATION RESTS UPON MATERIALS CONTAINED WITHIN—
   1. Ethics,
   2. Psychology.

III. EDUCATION, IN PART, DEPENDS UPON—
   1. Teaching.

IV. TEACHING ASSUMES A KNOWLEDGE OF THE TWO ELEMENTS—
   1. The mind that is to be taught—Psychology,
   2. The subject-matter that is to be learned, drawn from—
      (*a*) Ethics,
      (*b*) Psychology.

V. ON AUTHORITIES.

PART SECOND.

§§ 36-57.

ON METHOD IN GENERAL.

METHOD,	§§ 36–9.
SYSTEM,	§ 41.
ANALYSIS,	§ 43.
SEPARATION,	§ 44.
SYNTHESIS,	§ 45.
DEFINITION,	§ 46
ABSTRACTION,	§ 47.
RECONSTRUCTION,	§ 49.
GENERALIZATION,	§ 50.
CLASSIFICATION,	§ 51.
INDUCTION,	§ 52.
INTERPRETATION,	§ 53.
REPETITION,	§ 54.
DEDUCTION,	§ 55.
MANNER,	§ 56.
MODE,	§ 57.

ON METHOD IN GENERAL.

36. Method signifies literally the *way to seek after* a thing. The Greek philosophers used the word in this general sense, which has been retained to the present. Although writers agree substantially in assigning to the term the notion of way, a principle which determines direction, or orderly arrangement, yet the precise limitations of the way are not attributed with equal clearness and uniformity. By some, the term implies the only way in which a thing can be done. By others, Method is the only philosophical way of proceeding in an investigation, involving actually two operations, analysis and synthesis. Still others see in the word only a particular way of doing a given thing, which way may or may not depend upon the individuality of those who achieve the task. (See *Appendix A*, § 225.)

37. *Method in general* never has respect to the mind of the learner, but always has reference to the subject studied. It assumes intellectual activities and products. It is simply the way in which the mental products are utilized and unified into science. This field is that of logic. "I adopt the opinion of Mr. Herbert Spencer, that logic is really an objective science, like mathematics or mechanics." (Jevons, *Pri. Sci.*, p. 4, ed. 1877.)

38. The conception of Method resting upon substantial data at either end of the process, it is within the province of the term to speak of **methods of business,** when referring to this or that general way by which business transactions are accomplished. (See *Appendix A,* § 225.)

39. " The result has been half a century of steady and unprecedented material growth, accompanied with corresponding improvement in the structure of Government, which is probably unequalled to-day in the success with which scientific methods are made to work through popular forms." (*The Nation,* No. 700, p. 328, November 28, 1878.) " In a commercial country, which depends so much on the maintenance of credit, nothing is so important as that the credit should rest on solid foundations—not merely that the bases of the several transactions should be secure, but that the methods of business should be regular, legitimate, and trustworthy. The credit of an individual and of a bank depends much more on the known fact that the business done is done in a regular way, and with the habitual observance of certain rules of safe conduct, than upon a knowledge of the particular securities which accompany it. The one fact should be certified to the public in all possible ways, the other is in its nature private. (*Ibid.*, p. 330.)

40. In any investigation three distinct elements are presented to the inquirer : (1) The object-matter, which is the end of the inquiry ; (2) The way in which the activities of the examiner move forth and continue, while arriving at the end ; (3) The state or condition of the one who is putting forth the exertion to secure the end. A direct discussion suggests these questions : (1) Does Method regard immediately and solely the object-matter of the investigation, how it is finally left, or to be left, by the student, whether or not it shall be in an orderly arrangement, as of Classification ? (2) Or does it regard only the way in which the inquiry proceeds, as by Analysis, Synthesis, Induction, Deduction, Classification, or Generalization ? (3) Or does it consider especially the way in which the scholar, as as a particular individual, carries on his work, whether in this or that state of mind or body, or by means of these or those carefully chosen and utilized expedients and appliances which are peculiar to himself alone ?

That is, in recapitulation : (1) Does Method point sharply and first to the object investigated, in what shape, form, or condition it shall be left ? (2) Or does it indicate the direction, or way in, or over, which the energy of the mind moves in its activity ? (3) Or does it judge the characteristics which are the difference between the mind of the examiner and that of other men ? In order to answer these questions, it becomes necessary to attend to each in turn.

41. I. Consider the object-matter of study, whatever it may be, as arithmetic, botany, or grammar. The purposes of examining any object are to know it; to apprehend its parts, as single things; to discover the relations which exist among those parts; to rearrange its parts and relations, if thereby the mind can better seize, comprehend, or remember them, singly and collectively; to classify these parts into some new whole, which is the product solely of intellectual activity called thought, reflection, or simply reason. The student finds the object-matter of his attention in an apparently heterogeneous mass of disorder and confusion—he leaves it reduced into a congruous condition—he has been entirely unconscious of his own eccentricities, or individuality, or expedients, or ways in which his activities and energies have proceeded, whether by this or by that process or route—he has steadfastly and daily kept his attention upon the object-matter, as to what it is, and how he shall finally leave it adjusted, part to part, part to the whole, and the whole to other parts and wholes—himself and the ways by which his thought-powers went along in their work have dropped entirely out of consideration. In this case the idea of searching out is not found, because the attention rests exclusively upon the object-matter which incited and determined the action called **seeking after**—that is, the student considers the purposes attained, and not the routes or ways through or by which his powers brought forth those classified and organized ends. It follows, hence, that this is not a case of Method. The result or end spoken of is properly a **system, economy,** or **constitution.** (See § 124, and *Appendix B*, § 226.)

42. II. Consider exclusively the ways over which the activities of the intellect proceed when they are engaged in an investigation. These may be called **Modes of Method in General.**

43. (*a*) The faculties of observation are on the alert to discriminate the parts of the wholes of the object-matter of investigation, and the attributes or characteristics of those parts or wholes —these parts and attributes are likewise observed under the light of thought or reflection, called comparison, by which the analogous elements of similars are discovered. This way, by which the powers of the mind must pass in order to discover the individual Facts, known as elements, for the relations called similars and dissimilars, is properly denominated **Analysis.** (See *Appendix C*, § 227.)

44. A rigid distinction should be observed between analysis and **separation,** or **division.** Separation sets apart one thing from another—the thing set aside may be a part of that from which it is now placed, or it may be some other whole thing placed apart from the former. Division implies a taking asunder, and ordinarily refers to some whole which is cut into parts. In separation or division the process ends with the action, while in analysis these parts are not only made or found, but they are examined for the purpose of discovering similarities. Separation and division, having set apart the portions, give them no farther examination nor attention. An artisan takes a watch into its parts for the purpose of cleaning and repairing the time-piece. His examination of each part is to the sole end of discovering whatever particles of dust may be adhering to it. There is no examination in the interests of science or higher truth, either theoretical or practical. This is a case of separation, rather than of analysis.

45. (*b*) Assuming the foregoing analysis complete, the powers of thought apprehend the elements, which are to constitute the similars, and from them create a new intellectual product. In this process the unassimilative elements are rejected by the mind, and form no portion of the new products. The way or route by which the mind proceeds in creating these intellectual products is called **Synthesis**. (See *Appendix D*, § 228.)

46. Sometimes the elements of a synthesis are the products of **Definition**. (See *Appendix E*, § 229.)

47. The process of assorting and rejecting the analytical elements is known as **Abstraction**. (See *Appendix F*, § 230.)

48. "Analysis and synthesis, though commonly treated as two different methods, are, if properly understood, only the two necessary parts of the same method. Each is the relative and the correlative of the other. Analysis, without a subsequent synthesis, is incomplete; it is a mean cut off from its end. Synthesis, without a previous analysis, is baseless; for synthesis receives from analysis the elements which it recomposes." (Sir W. Hamilton, *Metaphysics*, p. 69, ed. 1871, Boston.)

49. Synthesis should be discriminated from **Reconstruction**—it is **Construction**. Reconstruction is the opposite of separation or division; it simply re-makes the whole by re-adjusting those elements or parts which were set aside from each other—it fashions no new whole. Synthesis is Construction; it fabricates an original product which essentially and materially differs in its nature from any and all of the wholes that were separated by analysis. In the supposition of the watch (§ 44), if the parts be restored to their former position, and the watch " put together " again, it is a case of reconstruction, rather than of synthesis. There is no new product created by the procedure.

50. (c) Analogous elements being assumed in the possession of the student, he proceeds by synthesis to " comprehend, under a common name, several objects agreeing in some point which he abstracts from each of them, and which that common name serves to indicate." This way of proceeding is usually known under the name of **Generalization**. (See *Appendix G*, § 231.)

51. (d) Generalization, in its ways of proceeding, is but another name for classification, although in the extent to which they are carried in science classification is the more comprehensive term. By some writers, generalization is used in reference to the object-matter of cause and effect, while investigation proceeding on the idea of observed resemblances, is the province of **Classification.** (See *Appendix H*, § 232.)

52. (*e*) When generalization or classification is complete in extension at any point in the ascending degrees, and the scholar, by his powers of thought, extends the generalization by inference so as to include objects which the preceding generalization does not cover in his experience or observation—thus making a new creation, known as a universal, sometimes as a general—the product is called an **Induction.** (See *Appendix I*, § 233.)

53. Induction should not be confounded with pure explanation, or what is known as *Mathematical Interpretation.* Induction creates a new inferential product, the elements of which are discovered only by the examination of many objects, and the inference extends over unexamined and unexplored territory. Interpretation places itself at the point of completion of a single observation, operation, or process, and retraces the steps over the way followed, and explains fully the meaning, extensive and intensive, of what is observed, predicting simply that all similar examples will be traced along the same way, and the same ends reached. Sciences founded upon general definitions instead of observation and experiment, are not inductive. The Pure Mathematical sciences are not properly inductive, and from their nature cannot be. What is usually called Mathematical Induction is Interpretation. The so-called Perfect Induction is hardly Induction in its nature, because no product is created

ON METHOD IN GENERAL. 63

beyond a generalization, or classification, and nothing is gained by using two terms for the same thing, when there are two notions to be distinguished from each other. (See *Appendix I*, § 233, Nos. 4, 5, and 7. Also *Appendix J*, § 234.)

54. Another point should be clearly outlined : The mere **Repetition** of examples, substantially identical, does not increase the force and certitude, nor extend the range, of an inference. One example covers the whole territory, and it, together with all others of the kind, does no more than illustrate the original principle established directly or indirectly by definition. In arithmetic, for example, repetition of examples adds nothing to the elements of which the "rule" is made—it simply serves to impress the way, the procedure, upon the mind of a learner, similarly to the repetition in the finger exercises upon the piano. (See §§ 204–7.)

It should be observed that there is a great variety of opinions among authors concerning the nature of Induction. The citations in the Appendix exhibit some of the views.

55. (*f*) If a scholar assume the possession of generals or universals, furnished either by Induction, by Definition, or by Intuition, and then use them with which to compare individual facts or truths, and by this means establish individual truths of like kind as an end of the process, the way of proceeding is known as **Deduction**. (See *Appendix K*, § 235.)

56. III. Consider the way in which the

individual student addresses himself to his tasks. He may be proceeding by any of the above-named modes, or ways, usually called Methods, and his own characteristics of disposition, habits, eccentricities, may be prominent. These may or may not be aids in securing valuable results of his labors. In any case, these are simply and solely individualities—they belong exclusively to the investigator—they are no necessary part of the mode or Method he is following—they are his **Manner**.

Critical discrimination should be made between what is necessary to a way, and what is purely incidental to the individual who is proceeding over that way. Indifference to this discrimination is followed by the pedantic assertion that each man can have a method of his own. Methods are ways which are independent of this or that man, and which are determined by the nature of the mind of man, or by the nature of the object-matter to be investigated. But Manner is his individuality when proceeding in a Method. (See § 123.)

57. When one's Manner is well ordered in its System, it is designated by the term **Mode**. (See § 123.)

PART THIRD.

§§ 58-216.

ON METHODS OF TEACHING.

I. ON THE THEORY OF METHODS OF TEACHING, ... §§ 58-143

II. ON THE PRACTICE OF METHODS OF TEACHING, ... §§ 144-216

    (A) On the Knowing Faculties of the Mind, ... §§ 144-187

    (B) On the Nature of Subject-Matter, ... §§ 188-210

    (C) On Discovering Methods of Teaching Special Subjects, . §§ 211-216

III. CONCLUDING REFLECTIONS, . §§ 217-224

I.

ON THE THEORY OF METHODS OF TEACHING.

58. " I am afraid it must be allowed, that no art, of equal importance to mankind, has been so little investigated scientifically as the art of teaching. · No art is in the hands of practitioners who are so apt to follow so blindly in the old paths. I say this with the full recollection that there has been great improvement in England lately, and that the books of teaching, most in use, have been purged of many gross errors both of statement and of method. But one line of enquiry there is which has never been sufficiently followed, though one would have thought it antecedently the most promising of all,—the study of the human mind through actual observation, and the study of the expedients by which its capacity for receiving and retaining knowledge may be enlarged. The field of investigation has been almost wholly neglected, and therefore it may just be that we are on the eve of great discoveries in education, and that the processes of these teachers are only a rough anticipation of the future. The fact that the methods of teaching followed in England are almost wholly empirical, that for the most part they entirely neglect individual differences of character and temperament, that they certainly work counter to the known laws according to which some of the mental faculties operate,—for example, the memory—all these facts seem to my mind to point at possibilities and chances of improvement, which a few persons, by expedients which, I frankly allow, seem even to me somewhat ignoble, have perhaps had the good fortune to realize beforehand." (Maine, *Village Communities and Miscellanies*, ed. 1876, pp. 285, 286.)

59. A complete discussion of the Theory of Methods of Teaching would include a full investigation of Psychology and of the nature of subject-matter to be taught—it would be an exhaustive examination of the relations which exist between the various faculties of the mind and the many kinds of objects to be learned. It would inquire, first, how mind acts as an original cause of activity, then what are the nature and character of its capacities, and lastly what are the products of its activity. This investigation is purely psychological, and lies anterior to the province of logic—it is supra-logical, and regards the function, nature, and character of the activities and faculties of the mind that learns, and that grows by introsusception.

60. By the **nature** of a faculty is meant not only its function, but that native endowment of its Potentiality out of which grow all those successive degrees of power that manifest themselves in a reality.

61. By the **character** of a faculty is designated the state in which it exists at any specified stage in its growth.

62. By Psychology is meant the introspective study of the experience of the mind itself.

63. " No student of Locke and Hume can read the psychological works of the present day without feeling anxiety for the future of the study of Mind or Experience. The modern psychologist is profoundly dissatisfied with his subject; the exact and the classificatory sciences, by the brilliance of their methods and results, fill him with envy; he is painfully conscious that mental phenomena are not definite enough to be the objects of a science; he must therefore connect them with other phenomena which are. Hence the ' Physiological Psychology ' of our day. But surely this is not psychology, or the study of experience, but physiology. Let us keep clearly before our minds that psychology is the study of experience. . . . . Psychology then, if we retain the word, is a **critique,** a Method, a certain thoughtful attitude in science, morals, and literature. It is the critical examination of my own adult opinions, desires and tastes in relation to present objects. . . . . . No amount of information respecting the evolution of belief or sentiment, and no amount of mental physiology can ever take the place of acquaintance with my own real opinions and desires. Modern works on mental science, with very few exceptions, forget this. The conditions of ideation, the origin of moral and æsthetic feelings, and such like, are fully discussed; but we look in vain for a home-question like this—'After all, do I really desire nothing for myself but Happiness.' Individualism—thoughtful reference to one's own experience—is indeed a rare quality now." (Stewart, *Psychology*, in *Mind*, pp. 445–451, No. IV, October, 1876.)

64. Methods of Teaching, having an acquaintance with Mind, consider the nature of intellectual products, show in what order they follow each other, reveal the way in which the activities of Mind proceed with these products, classify them, and build up Science out of them. This is the arena of Logic, and has reference to System, or subject-matter as such—it is infra-psychological. Succeeding this comes a thorough discussion of subject-matter that is to be learned by the mind of the student. A treatment so elaborate could not be concluded in one brief Study, were it desirable to attempt it. Another occasion must serve portions of this work, as it may occur. No more will be essayed at this time than to survey the line of the investigation as well as may be, by "blazing" the way, sometimes "doubling upon the track," so that others may follow and clear up the obscurities and remove the errors, that lie upon this intricate way, and enlarge the practical value which must result from a scientific research.

65. " Since the human mind must consciously reproduce what actually exists, the act of knowing is *conditioned in two ways:* a. **Subjectively,** by the essence and natural laws of the human mind, especially by those of the human powers of knowledge ; b. **Objectively,** by the nature of what is to be known. The constitutions and relations of what is to be known, so far as these require different ways of representation in the act of knowing, we call **forms of existence** (*e.g.*, subsistence and inherence). The notions of these forms of existence are the **metaphysical categories.** The different ways, corresponding to these forms of existence, in which what actually exists is taken hold of and copied in the act of knowledge, are the **forms of knowledge** (*e.g.*, the categorical judgment). The actual copy, the result of the activity of knowledge, is the **content of knowledge.** . . . The laws of knowing, as such, determine only the ways of representation (copying), or the forms of knowledge, not its contents. . . . These forms of knowledge correspond to the forms of existence, and they are conditioned by the objective reality." (Ueberweg, *Log. Doct.*, pp. 3, 4, ed. 1871.)

66. " The sense attached at the present day to the words **form** and **matter,** is somewhat different from, though closely related to, these (**form** and **law**). The **form** is what the mind impresses upon its perceptions of objects, which are the **matter; form** therefore means **mode of viewing** objects that are presented to the mind. When the attention is directed to any object, we do not see the object itself, but contemplate it in the light of our own prior conceptions. A rich man, for example, is regarded by the poor and ignorant under the **form** of a very fortunate person, able to purchase luxuries which are above their own reach ; by the religious mind under the **form** of a person with more than ordinary temptations to contend with ; by the political economist, under that of an example of the unequal distribution of wealth ; by the tradesman, under that of one whose patronage is valuable. Now, the object is really the same to all these observers ; the same rich man has been represented under all the different **forms.** And the reason that the observers are able to find many in one, is that they connect him severally with their own prior conceptions. The **form,** then, in this view, is **mode of knowing;** and the **matter** is the **perception,** or **object,** we have to know." (Thompson, *Outline of Laws of Thought,* p. 34, 2d ed.)

67. "**Form** is something which may remain uniform and unaltered, while the **matter** thrown into that form may be varied. Medals struck from the same dies have exactly the same form, but they may be of various matter, as bronze, copper, gold, or silver. A building of exactly the same form might be constructed either of stone or bricks ; furniture of exactly similar shape may be made of oak, mahogany, walnut wood, etc." (Jevons, *El. Les. Logic,* ed. 1878, pp. 4-5.)

68. "Distinction between Form and Matter.—This phraseology was introduced by Aristotle, who represented every thing as having in itself both matter and form. It had a new signification given to it by Kant, who supposes that the mind supplies from its own furniture a form to impose on the matter presented from without. The form corresponds to the **a priori** element, and the matter to the **a posteriori**. But the view thus given of the relation in which the knowing mind stands to the known object is altogether a mistaken one. It supposes that the mind in cognition adds an element from its own resources, whereas it is simply so constituted as to know what is in the object. This doctrine needs only to be carried out consequentially to sap the foundations of all knowledge,—for if the mind may contribute from its own stores one element, why not another? Why not all the elements? In fact, Kant did, by this distinction, open the way to all those later speculations which represent the whole universe of being as an ideal construction. There can, I think, be no impropriety in speaking of the original principles of the mind as forms or rules, but they are forms merely, as are the rules of grammar, which do not add any thing to correct speaking and writing, but are merely the expression of the laws which they follow. As to the word 'matter,' it has either no meaning in such an application, or a meaning of a misleading character." (McCosh, *Int. of Mind*, p. 312, ed. 1870.)

69. " The drift and meaning of a branch of knowledge varies with the company in which it is introduced to the student. If his reading is confined simply to one subject, however such division of labor may favor the advancement of a particular pursuit, a point into which I do not here enter, certainly it has a tendency to contract his mind. If it is incorporated with others, it depends on these others as to the kind of influnce which it exerts upon him. Thus the Classics, which in England are the means of refining the taste, have in France subserved the spread of revolutionary and deistical doctrines. In Metaphysics, again, Butler's *Analogy of Religion*, which has had so much to do with the conversion to the Catholic faith of members of the University of Oxford, appeared to Pitt and others, who had received a different training, to operate only in the direction of infidelity. . . It is not so much this study or that, as it is the setting into other studies that moulds the impression. In this is the notion of being liberally educated— that any subject is received without prejudice." (Newman, *Idea of A University*, p. 100, ed. 1873.)

70. " The policy of the present Minister of Public Instruction (Russia) has been to discountenance the study of natural science, as the source of mutiny and insubordination, and encourage that of the classics, as favorable to discipline and authority and to the state of religion." (*The Nation*, No. 704, Dec. 26, 1878, p. 393.)

" The generality of travellers enveloped forever in customs, habits, prejudices, and wants peculiar to themselves, move, as it were, in an atmosphere of their own, which divides them from the places through which they pass, as from so many different worlds. A Frenchman would fain carry all France along with him ; as soon as he misses the smallest of his accustomed conveniences, he overlooks its equivalent, and believes himself lost. Comparing continually what he sees with what he has quitted, he thinks it worse only because it is not the same, and cannot sleep in the Indies if his bed is not made as it was at Paris." (Rousseau, *Emilius*, vol. iv., pp. 226–7.)

71. "*Knowledge* is a general term which implies the thing *known:* **science, learning,** and **erudition,** are modes of **knowledge** qualified by some collateral idea : **science** is a systematick species of **knowledge** which consists of rule and order ; **learning** is that species of **knowledge** which one derives from schools, or through the medium of personal instruction ; **erudition** is scholastick **knowledge** obtained by profound research ; **knowledge** admits of every possible degree, and is expressly opposed to ignorance ; **science, learning,** and **erudition,** are positively high degrees of **knowledge.** . . . . *Learning* is less dependent on the genius, than on the will of the individual ; men of moderate talents have overcome the deficiencies of nature, by labour and perseverance, and have acquired such stores of **learning** as have raised them to a respectable station in the republick of letters. Profound *erudition* is obtained but by few ; a retentive memory, patient industry, and deep penetration, are requisites for one who aspires to the title of an *erudite* man." (Crabb, *Synonyms.*)

72. All knowledge that we possess must be

in some form—it would be well to say **shape**, if intellectual products or impressions could have shape. The term knowledge is sometimes used in two meanings : as completed thought, which is a product ; and as the action of the mind, the completion of which is a product. There is greater philosophical precision if the term be assigned only one signification—that of the noun, act or product. "Knowledge in its exactest definition is, in its positive form, **A Conscious identification of Attribute with its subject,** as in the affirmative proposition, **the sun is bright.** In its negative form, it is **A Conscious differencing of an Attribute from its subject,** as in the negative proposition, **the sun is not dark.**" (Day, *Outl. Ontolog. Science*, p. 32, ed. 1878.)

73. "Knowledge is the act or product of a rational nature. As such it ever tends to a system which is characterized by singleness of source and aim ; and this tendency is along the line which reason prescribes to a movement from a recognized source to the proposed end. There are different specific sources, as there are manifold specific aims in knowledge, indeed ; but reason is one and its field is one and its aim one, comprehensive of all special objects and all special aims. There is such a thing, therefore, as a method in all true rational knowledge." (*Ibid.*, p. 31.)

74. In these three distinct things—the *source,* the *end,* and the *way* of knowledge—the last is the **method of knowledge.** "The **aim** of knowledge is **Truth**. Knowledge arrived at the certainty of truth is **Science**. Material (or real) truth must be distinguished from (formal) correctness. Material truth in the absolute sense, or simply truth, is the agreement of the content (attributes) of knowledge with what actually exists. Material truth in the relative sense, or phenomenal truth, is the agreement of the mediately acquired content of thought with the immediate outer or inner perceptions which exist when the soundness of the mind and of the bodily organs is undisturbed, or would exist under the corresponding outer conditions." (Ueberweg, *Logical Doct.*, pp. 5, 6, ed. 1871.)

75. All these illustrations of the province of knowledge compel attention to the stages of the process of acquiring knowledge by the mind of the learner. (1) There is the source of the activity residing in the innate power of the mind to act responsively and intuitively at the presence of objects to be known. This innate power of the mind is called the ultimate **Cause of Knowledge**, or simply the Cause. (2) There is the rational way in which this activity proceeds, usually at the dictation of the power of the Will. This way is known as the **Method of Thought**. (3) There is, lastly, the end of the activity. This consummation of the process into completeness is known as the **act**, or **product of knowledge**, or simply Knowledge.

76. The preceding discussion relates, in the most general sense, to the consideration of knowledge as acquired by the learner. In ordinary acceptance the notion of learning is associated with two persons—the one an instructor or teacher of the other, who is called the learner, student, scholar, child, or pupil. When the pupil learns through the instrumentality of a *living teacher* he is said to be taught.

77. When he learns without this instrumentality, he is said to be *self-informed,* or *self-educated.* The self-informed student applies himself to understand whatever engages his attention, whether books, or objects of nature, or works of art ; he applies his powers of observation and of reason to the things that he finds scattered about him as a heterogeneous mass ; he constructs his own questions for himself, invents his own illustrations, creates his own hypotheses, and adjudges the validity of his own arguments and conclusions—that is, he alone pronounces upon the **form** and **matter** of his knowledge, and way of approaching it. In very many important matters he must leave it for time and experience to inform him whether his knowledge is correct in fact. The element of time spent in arriving at truth by the self-educated student is often great for the amount and quality of knowledge gained. The difficulties that present themselves to this learner are frequently sufficient to deter any but the most persevering and venturesome from attempting to surmount them. The fields of learning are so many and so extensive, and human life so short, that the imperative demands of our brief years give a practical value to some kinds of knowledge over others.

The exclusively self-informed student is not assured that his learning is best calculated to promote the welfare of himself and his fellow-man. A well-authenticated instance, related to the writer by Dr. J. Dorman Steele, will illustrate this statement: A young man of excellent parts entered college. He had adopted the theory that self-education is the only way to learning, and refused to consult or study books to prepare his lessons. He attended the recitations, observed closely what was said there, and depended upon his genius, or "inner consciousness," to evolve from himself the knowledge he possessed. In process of time he was graduated, and dropped into obscurity. After five or six years he suddenly appeared at the office of the president of the college. He desired to submit to the president a law in physics which he had discovered by his own unaided observations during the past six years. If approved by the president, he would publish his discovery. He had discovered "that heat expands metals, and cold contracts them." The president called his little daughter, and asked her, what is the "first law in Natural Philosophy"? She said, "That heat expands metals, and cold contracts them." Said the president, "You see how many valuable years you have lost by neglecting to study books as well as objects, depending entirely upon your own inner consciousness for your knowledge."

78. These considerations of reason and experience bring forward the idea of aiding the youth of the State by means of appropriating to their benefit the learning and experience of some of the older members of the State. Those who consciously and methodically aid the young in acquiring learning and experience are known as **Teachers.** The efforts, which they put forth to advance their pupils in knowledge, constitute the idea that is designated **Teaching**.

79. Teaching is consciously adjusting objects and acts to the proper faculties and capacities of the learner. "*Adjust* is to set right (Fr. **juste,** straight, right). Hence the word implies some relative order, shape, or standard, to which matters have to be brought, or some antecedent condition of **inherent** fitness to which they have to be reduced." (Smith, *Syn. Discr.*) The order in which objects are to be presented to the pupil is determined by the teacher. Nature, as the child finds her, presents objects to it in an unclassified, promiscuous mass. The pupil may see a cat, then an elephant, then a thunder-storm, all in one hour. The teacher would present objects in a sequence determined by previous study and classification. This order is artificial to the child, compared to the heterogeneous order in which Nature exhibits objects to it. From this view, it may be said that teaching is the conscious and philosophic adjustment of object-matter to the abilities of the pupil.

80. The teacher has other duties towards his pupil. He presents before the mind of the learner some entire object—Nature also usually does this, but she leaves the mind to struggle with the whole at once—the teacher, finding the whole too vast for the pupil, separates it, practically and virtually, into parts. This process of dissection may be accomplished by using the scalpel, the hammer, or by questions ; for questions are but knives that dissect out parts to display to the pupil, or they are colter-shares that cut out furrows in the turf, narrower or wider, for the pupil to turn over, according to his strength.

81. The teacher has still other duties in the case. He is to note both the *form and the matter of the knowledge* which the *learner acquires,* whether it stand in his mind correct in its impression and true in its essence. To secure these ends requires consummate skill of the teacher : his reason must be well trained and certain in its logical processes, his wit must be ready at analogies, his imagination must be fertile in illustration, his hands must be cunning in constructing, his understanding must be profound, and his knowledge must be overflowing in its quantity. Here lie the purely professional regions of teaching—here also are the processes called **Methods of Teaching.**

82. The teacher has now reached the great question of the Profession : **How to teach?** For it is in teaching and with teachers, as it is in Logic, " Where two conditions are found or assumed : Firstly, that there exist certain mental laws to which every sound thinker is bound to conform. Secondly, that it is possible **to**

transgress those laws, or to think unsoundly."
(Mansel, *Prolegomena Logica*, p. 16, ed. 1860.)

83. In order to answer this question, How to teach? even approximately, it is necessary to enter into a more critical examination of the conception of the word Teaching. To teach requires, obviously: (1) The mind of the learner, or the learner; (2) The mind of the instructor, or the teacher; (3) The objects, actions, or things to be learned by the student, which are commonly designated, collectively, as subjects, subject-matter, objects, or object-matter. The intellectual activities of the teacher proceed under certain fixed laws of mind. His intellectual faculties conform to spheres of activity into which they are necessitated or determined by their very nature. He cannot remember with his faculty of imagination, nor reason with memory. He must perceive with his senses, reason with his reflective powers, and retain by his memory. As with the teacher so with the learner, whose mental faculties and capabilities may differ from those of the teacher in original quantum of functional endowment, and in degrees of power, but not in kind or function.

84. This being true, the case resolves itself into this: (1) If the teacher knew subject-matter thoroughly he could arrange its parts into any order of dependence, or steps, or points, or classifications, that circumstances or exigencies might necessitate, or expediency demand. This would enable him to arrange and present his *system of subject-matter*. (2) If, in addition to this, he knew mind thoroughly, in its faculties, powers, capabilities, laws of growth—in short, in its nature and character, he would know exactly how to *adjust the subject-matter to be learned to the mind that is to learn it.* Varying circumstances of state or condition would not prevent this certainty of adjustment—it would be like the scientist adjusting the object that he is examining to the focus of his microscope so that his eye can see it in defined outline. (3) If, succeeding these two suppositions, the teacher now turns his attention for the time exclusively to consider the ways in which his system of subject-matter shall be set before, or in the presence of, those faculties which are the native ones to acquire learning from this system,—if he does this, he will be carrying on investigations in a province which is *original and peculiar to the Profession of Teaching.*

85. A recapitulation of these points presents: (1) The first field opened for the teacher-candidate is that of subject-matter to be taught by him, and that is to be learned by the student. This is the region of System,—of scholarship in the ordinary branches of learning as they are found in our schools, or as he may analyze and classify for presenting to his pupils. (2) The second field for the teacher-in-expectancy is also that of subject-matter, and is included within the range of our schools. It is special, however, to the Profession of Teaching, and is known by the name of Psychology, Mental Philosophy, or Intellectual Philosophy. (3) The third field is that of the science and art of adapting object-matter to the capabilities of the mind to be taught, that of adjusting objects to the focus of the intellectual vision of the pupil.

86. This is properly the **Province of Methods of Teaching**. This province is that of Principles—it is that of those Principles which exist in the constitution of things, and according to which certain subject-matter must be acquired by the mind in a certain fixed way, provided it ever becomes an actual knowledge within that mind. Some subject-matter is learned by one faculty, some by another. Intermediate between every kind of subject-matter and knowledge of it, there is the faculty which is native to the acquiring of that knowledge. If the proper faculty be not approached, true knowledge cannot be the product—from this conclusion there is no escape.

87. "A principle is that which being derived from nothing, can hold to nothing. . . . What is common to all first **principles** is that they are the **primary source from which any thing is, becomes, or is known.**" (Fleming, *Vocab. of Phil.*)

88. "**A Principle** is a central or representative truth in philosophy, science, art, religion, or morals, which is fundamental and general, and out of which other matters of a speculative or practical character flow, and become its practical illustration. 'He who fixes upon false **principles** treads upon infirm ground, and so sinks ; and he who fails in his deductions from right **principles** stumbles upon firm ground, and so falls.—**South.**" (Smith, *Syn. Discr.*, Doctrine.)

"**Principle** carries knowledge with it, and is applicable to action as a guide or basis of proceeding. A principle is a fundamental truth, or comprehensive law, from which others are derived, or on which they are founded. It may be observed, generally, that principles are last in the order of investigations, and first in the order of practice. They are arrived at by analysis, and when found become bases or starting-points for action or scientific inquiry." (*Ibid.*, Proverb.)

89. *Methods of Teaching are principles of adapting subject-matter to the capacities and powers of the pupil.* When the teacher says that this subject-matter should be presented for cognizance by this or that faculty of the mind, and in such and such quantities, according to the strength of those faculties, he is acting within the province of Methods of Teaching. But when the teacher says that this point or step of this subject-matter should succeed that or that step or point, he is acting within the scope of a System of subject-matter.

90. These two distinct operations are often confounded, or used indiscriminately, causing great confusion in the proper use of terms. In the following the word System is properly used: "The Gospel of St. John, adapted to the Hamiltonian System, by an Analytical and Interlineary Translation from the Italian, with full Instructions for its use, even by those who are wholly ignorant of the language. For the Use of Schools. By James Hamilton, Author of the Hamiltonian System, London, 1825." (Sydney Smith, *Essays*, p. 74, late ed.) In the expression, "Grube's Method of Teaching Number," the word Method is improperly used. It should be "Grube's System," because the author arranges the subject-matter in such a way that the processes of addition, subtraction, multiplication, and division, must be taught in such and such a sequence of order, and in such and such an order of steps. The teacher in this case is not investigating what faculties are to be incited to learn these steps, nor in what quantities the subject-matter shall be set to those faculties, as Methods require. The same remarks apply to the so-called "A, B, C Method" of teaching children to read, the "Word Method," and all similar expressions, where Method is used improperly for System.

91. The questions relating to what branches shall be taught or studied, do not belong, in strict analysis, to the Province of Methods of Teaching. They are questions of Ethics and of Psychology,—of the relations of the individual to the Family, the Society, and the State, of which he is a member and a part, according to the estimate of these relations by each people or nation for itself. They also are within the field of the development of man as man, in his subjective condition—that is, in his psychological estate. They belong to the wider field of Pedagogics, or Education, or to what Mr. J. S. Mill calls " Ethology, the science of which education is the art." (Chamb. Encycl., article **Education**.)

92. " Ethics may be defined as the Science of Practice or Conduct : the latter term is preferable, as Practical Science is more conveniently used to include along with Ethics the cognate studies of Jurisprudence and Politics.

" All three alike are distinguished from speculative sciences by the characteristic that they attempt to determine not the actual but the ideal : what ought to exist, not what does exist. An objection is sometimes taken to the application of the term ' Science ' to such studies as these. It is said that a Science must necessarily have some department of actual existence for its subject-matter : and there is no doubt that the term ' Moral Sciences ' is frequently—perhaps more frequently—used to denote studies that deal with the actually existent : viz. Psychology, or a portion of it ; what Mr. Mill calls Ethology, or the inquiry into the laws of the formation of character ; and Sociology, or (as it has also been termed) the Physiology of Society." (Sidgwick, *The Methods of Ethics*, p. 1, ed. 1874, London.)

93. Voluntary and conscious instruction and teaching are the handmaids of education, and are ways of approaching mind, setting before that mind those branches of study which Ethics and Psychology determine are best.

94. Those principles of Ethics and Psychology

according to which peoples, families, or individuals, determine what branches of study shall be pursued in schools and elsewhere, are properly denominated **Methods of Pedagogics**. The term Education being used by English and American authors as nearly or quite the equivalent of the German Pedagogics, **Methods of Education** will be used instead of Methods of Pedagogics. Methods of Education regard the future man as a member of a given society; they consider what the child is to become; they are subjects of choice by nations, communities, families, or individuals, because they determine the uses to be made of the learning and discipline which nations or families require of the young. In Germany, Methods of Education are determined by the condition of the body-politic, and are well established. In France, the Methods of Education differ from those of Germany, in so far as the purposes of the government differ from those in Germany. In England, Methods of Education still vary, as also they do in the United States. Whatever purposes Methods of Education propose for the young, they always point distinctly to the end that these young persons, when grown up, shall be good and loyal citizens of that Community or State. Methods of education in France are not calculated to produce good citizens for Germany, but for France. It is the same with every nation. Families adopt Methods of Education which aim at giving specific direction to the energies of the children in those families, referring immediately to the positions which these chlidren shall come to occupy, as professional, diplomatic, or governmental. These Methods inquire what is to be studied by the learner, in order that he may attain a certain end desired. Methods of Teaching are concerned in Methods of Education only so far as to ask in what way shall the branches determined by the family or the nation be presented to the mind. Methods of Teaching know no nationality nor family ; Methods of Education preserve nationality and family attainments. To elaborate the subject of Methods of Education would require an extended treatise, and must be set aside until a more convenient time shall present itself for the work.

95. In the following quotation the province of Methods of Teaching is not discriminated from that of Methods of Education, although the notion of Method in general is very clearly outlined :

" **The Methodick** :—(1) The Educator must **guide** the pupil to knowledge of the outer world by aiding him to acquire it for himself in accordance with the **natural operation, successive movements or procedure** of Intelligence ;— that is to say, according to the way or method whereby Intelligence proceeds and must proceed. These processes, as we have seen, are, in the first instance, Analytic, but have Synthesis and Induction for their end. When ascertained, they yield the doctrine of Method in Education—The Methodick of Education.

" (2) The Educator must perform the same

task with reference to the higher feelings and emotions, with a view to constitute them habitual motives. In things of sense or of thought the learner learns by truly knowing: in things of action the learner learns through the action of others, and by his own action. The doctrine of The Methodick of Education is to be called **Methodology,** and embraces the application of Method to every subject of intellectual study and to every stage of ethical training alike (page 16). . . .

"The **way** of carrying out the Educative process to a successful issue, both intellectual and ethical, is, as we have seen, **The Methodick** of Education (p. 18.) . . . How must I convey instruction so as to insure assimilation by the pupil? . . . The answer to this question contains the Doctrine of Method, and rests on the **process** of the Will in its movements towards knowledge. Dependent on this are—**Particular Methods.**" (Laurie, *Synopsis of Lect.*, p. 20, 1877.)

96. Methods of Education have regard for the growth of mind as an end or habit unto itself, an object to be attained for itself, and also for knowledge or matter, as an *end*. (1) "What subjects of instruction must I teach in order to give to the future man the materials of right judgment? (The Real.) This leads us into a discussion of subjects of Instruction generally and their relative values. (2) How must I instruct so as most effectually to exercise the intelligence of the pupil in making those distinctions on which the rightness of judgment depends? (The Senses. The Formal as Will-power in reference to Intelligence.) The answer to the first of these questions contains the Doctrine of **the Real** with reference to the outer world—the substance of Knowledge. The answer to the second questions contains the Doctrine of Formal discipline in its intellectual relations." (Laurie, *Synopsis of Lect.*, p. 20, 1877.)

97. "It is a physiological law, first pointed out by M. Isidore St. Hilaire, and to which attention has been drawn by Mr. Lewes in his essay on **Dwarfs and Giants**, that there is an antagonism between **growth** and **development**. By growth, as used in this antithetical sense, is to be understood **increase of size;** by development, **increase of structure.** And the law is, that great activity in either of these processes involves retardation or arrest of the other. A familiar illustration is furnished by the cases of the caterpillar and the chrysalis. In the caterpillar there is extremely rapid augmentation of bulk; but the structure is scarcely at all more complex when the caterpillar is full-grown than when it is small. In the chrysalis the bulk does not increase; on the contrary, weight is lost during this stage of the creature's life; but the elaboration of a more complex structure goes on with great activity. The antagonism, here so clear, is less traceable in higher creatures, because the two processes are carried on together. But we see it pretty well illustrated among ourselves by contrasting the sexes. A girl develops in body and mind rapidly, and ceases to grow comparatively early. A boy's bodily and mental development is slower, and his growth greater. At the age when the one is mature, finished, and having all faculties in full play, the other, whose vital energies have been more directed towards increase of size, is relatively incomplete in structure ; and shows it in a comparative awkwardness, bodily and mental. Now this law is true not only of the organism as a whole, but of each separate part. The abnormally rapid advance of any part in respect of structure involves premature arrest of its growth ; and this happens with the organ of the mind as certainly as with any other organ. The brain, which during early years is relatively large in mass but imperfect in structure will, if required to perform its functions with undue activity, undergo a structural advance greater than is appropriate to the age ; but the ultimate effect will be a falling short of the size and power that would else have been attained. And this is a part cause—probably the chief cause—why precocious children, and youths who up to a certain time were carrying all before them, so often stop short and disappoint the high hopes of their parents." (Herbert Spencer, *Education*, pp. 271, 272, ed. 1870.)

"To **grow** is the process of which to **increase** is the result or manifestation. Trade has been growing for years past, and is now considerably increased. To increase, however, does not necessarily imply to grow ; rapid expansion or dilatation of parts will produce increase in bulk; but the process of growth implies either an accretion of parts by external apposition, or an assimilative power from within, as in the vital force. The snowball grows by accretion, and so increases as it rolls. The tree grows by its own vitality, and increases also in size." (Smith, *Syn. Discr.*)

98. Methods of Teaching consider the growth of the faculties of the mind, and the quantity of knowledge, not as ends, but as ***necessary knowledge*** from which to project anew procedures in teaching while the mind of the learner is growing. This is essential in order that the teacher may set to this learner, at any stage of his growth, the maximum quantity of subject-matter which the present attainments and powers of the learner can master; to set less than this amount to a pupil is puerile, and to set more is to prevent his powers from comprehending it. Yet the faculties of mind grow into powers far more rapidly by attempting to comprehend the unknown, the mysterious, by trying to enlarge the maximum degrees of efforts, than by resting contentedly with efforts near the minimum of degrees. "Mental dyspepsia" comes from starvation, as well as from plethora of subject-matter. "A well-regulated course of study will no more weaken the mind than hard exercise will weaken the body; nor will a strong understanding be weighed down by its knowledge, any more than an oak is by its leaves, or than Samson was by his locks. He whose sinews are drained by his hair, must already be a weakling." (Grindon, *Life*, p. 197.) "If the child of eight years old finds his improved language understood by a child of three, why should you contract yours to his vocabulary? Always employ a language some years in advance of the child (men of genius in their books speak to us from the vantage-ground of centuries) : speak to the one-year-old child as though he were two, and to him as though he were six ; for the difference of progress diminishes in the inverse proportion of years. Let the teacher, especially he who is too much in the habit of attributing all learning to teaching, consider that the child already carries half his world, that of mind,—the objects, for instance, of moral and metaphysical contemplation,—ready formed within him ; and hence that language, being provided only with physical images, cannot give, but merely illumine, his mental conceptions." (Richter, *Levana*, pp. 347–8.)

99. In this immediate connection it will be profitable to give a brief attention to the popular expression, "Teachers should teach pupils how to learn, how to use their faculties in order that they shall be able to continue their mental activities by themselves, in subsequent years." It is a plain fact in psychological phenomena, that nearly all the faculties of mind grow, "increase in size," by exercise. This is emphatically true of the faculties of Thought and Attention, which are energies of the Will. Education is a habit. Hence no one can be said to know how to command his faculties, who has not the habit of it, called education. This state is attained by those, and those only, who actually exert their faculties to the maximum degrees, so that this state becomes habitual. Methods of Teaching regard these degrees as their bases in Mind. Mere Theory will never produce these habits. All teaching of pupils " how to study," which does not demand of them their maximum efforts in practice, is a delusion, and a fatal deception to the learners. The arm of the smith does not grow strong by his standing at the forge and looking at the sledge-hammer, but by wielding it. Intellectual growth comes not by thinking how to study, but by mental application in studying up to the measure of the highest degrees.

100. So far as Methods of Teaching are concerned, the matter taught may be in itself, either *error* or *truth*. Methods take whatever subjects, in whatever form of text-books or objects, that are set to them, and convey them into the presence of the corresponding faculties that are to learn these subjects—this conveying, if according to a philosophical principle, is teaching; for no power external to the mind of the learner can learn for that mind, nor compel it to learn. The learning is a matter within the exclusive province of the mind that is to learn, or to be taught.

101. Methods of Teaching are not concerned with what is popularly called "waking up mind," for if Methods assume any thing pre-eminently, it is that subject-matter, when set before mind according to the principles of adaptation, will incite the mind to activity, intuitively and spontaneously. "To wake up mind," implies, in practice, the false notion that the children are to be excited or astonished at the manner of the teacher, and at the irrelevancy of the points he presents, rather than at the value of the subject-matter set before them to be learned. This is mere charlatanism. Emotional excitement, with dissipation of thought, can never take the place of calm, deliberate, intense attention and continued thinking, when sound learning is sought. Nothing is more pernicious to good habits of thought than the introduction into class-rooms of what is called "variety," as the term is practically exemplified. The only "variety" permissible, is that which follows upon progress, pointedly, into additional subject-matter of the lesson, not into this or that subject which has no direct and close relationship to the recitation, and which permits attention and power to be dissipated, not concentrated. The mind of childhood is always awake—it may need to be centred on this subject.

102. "Bonnet calls attention the mother of genius, but she is in fact her daughter; for whence does she derive her origin, save from the marriage contracted in heaven between the object and the desire for it? Hence attention can really be as little preached or flogged into a person as ability. . . . A very important distinction must be drawn between the power of attention diffused among the generality of men, and that appertaining solely to men of genius. The latter can only be recognized, protected, and cherished, but not created. . . . On the other hand, common every-day attention needs not so much to be aroused, as to be distributed and condensed; even careless, inattentive children possess the faculty, but it is dissipated upon all passing objects. . . . In what manner can you arouse the innate desire of mental progress? The impulses of the senses excite and then stupefy, but help not to produce it. To overwhelm the mind with lessons, that is, with mere summaries of accounts, resembles the Siberian custom of giving the sacrament of the Lord's Supper to infants. . . . Philosophy begins with what is highest and most difficult; mathematics, with what is nearest and easiest. . . . What, then remains? The metaphysics of the eye; the knowledge forming the boundary between experience and abstraction." (Richter, *Levana*, pp. 353-9.)

103. "To **Excite** (Latin, **excitare**) is to call out into greater activity what before existed in a calm or calmer state, or to rouse to an active state faculties or powers which before were dormant. The term is also used of purely physical action. We excite heat by friction. **Awaken** (A. S., **awaccian, awecian**) is to rouse from a state of sleep, or, analogously, to rouse any thing that has lain quiet, and, as it were, dormant, as to awaken suspicion, and is applicable only to intelligent subjects. **Rouse**

(A. S., **rasian**) is to awaken in a sudden or startling manner, so as to bring into an energetic state by a strong impulse. To **incite** (Latin, **incitare**) is to excite to a specific act or end which the inciter has in view. To **stimulate** is to quicken into activity (**stimulus**, a spur) and to a certain end. Men are incited when their passions are roused; they are stimulated when they are induced to make greater exertions, as by a hope of reward or any other external impulse. They are awakened out of indifference, roused out of lethargy and torpor, incited by the designing influences of others, stimulated by new motives of action. Men are incited to what otherwise they would not have given their efforts. They are commonly stimulated to something which they are pursuing, or intending to pursue, but with want of energy." (Smith, *Syn. Discr.*)

104. As to the **Form** in which knowledge is left in the mind, when all the circumstances attending the presentation have been rigidly based upon the nature of the case, Methods of Teaching have no responsibility—that ends when the presentation is completed. The mind, as a cause unto itself, and its prior state of knowledge, are responsible for the form or impression, in which the matter, under these conditions, exists within itself. If this form lacks certitude, or "material truth in the absolute sense," it can only be corrected by presenting to the learning mind other subject-matter. But what this subject-matter shall be is no concern of Methods

METHODS OF TEACHING. 99

of Teaching, as has been shown in a previous section of this investigation. If the subject-matter be not properly separated into parts, and those parts sharply freed from adventitious matter, so that it may be brought boldly and unequivocally into the conscious presence of the corresponding faculties—if there be a want here, it is the fault of the System of the teacher. Methods of Teaching demand only that the *principles of adaptation be not violated.* The Methods assume the subjects placed in the hands of the teacher. The teacher has two important things to do : (1) To consider if his System of subject-matter is so constructed that it is capable of being presented to this individual learner ; (2) To reflect upon the principles which underlie the actual procedure of teaching. He must attend to System and then to Method.

105. In connection with Methods of Teaching one often hears the expressions, " Develop the idea in the mind of the learner," " Lead the mind gradually up to the idea." To simple perception there can be no development work, for perception is intuitive, and is ultimate in its authority, upon the presence in consciousness of the object. Development exists within the Province of Thought.

Notions, or conceptions, or ideas, are aggregations of simpler elements, which constitute the group or Unit of notions. When the faculties of the mind are too feeble to comprehend the unit group, the elements of the unit are separated and set before the mind of the learner in succession until all are seen as one. The process (Mode), called "development," is that by which the teacher analyzes and presents the notion that is to be taught, and the synthetical process by which the learner apprehends, and combines or reconstructs, the elements into a notion that is similar to that possessed by the teacher.

106. The process by which a student is inducted into a prehension and a comprehension of an aggregation of ideas, which bear an intimate and necessary relation to each other, is called **Thoroughness**. A student who is thoroughly taught surveys from the centre, a group of ideas which constitute a structure created by Thought.

107. " To **Develop** is to open out what was contained in another thing, or the thing itself (Fr. **développer**). In develop these **two** ideas are inherent, the gradual opening of the whole containing, and the gradual exhibition of the particular contained. So we might say, ' Time developed his character,' or ' circumstances developed the cruelty which was latent in his character.' Unlike **Unfold**, develop is not used of purely physical processes. We speak of the development of plans, plots, ideas, the mind ; and also of the development of the body in growth ; but these are scientific terms involving other ideas, as of the vital functions in growth. We should never speak of the development of a flag or a tablecloth. In other words, it is not used of manual or mechanical unfolding. On the other hand, in the sense of the mechanical process of gradually opening, unfold is used as well as in the other; but in this latter develop expresses far more than unfold, and relates to the laws of expansion by which a thing unfolds in definite sequence of expansion, and in conformity with principles which conserve the type developed. Hence we speak of a true and a vicious development. To **Unravel** (old German, **reffen**, to pluck) is purely a mechanical effort of separating what is complicated, whether naturally or accidentally, and expresses simple disentanglement, not growth or expansion. As the former indicate ordinary processes of nature or art, so the latter indicates extraordinary and counteractive processes, and commonly implies the abnormal state of that which needs to be unravelled.

" ' Then take him to *develop* if you can,
And hew the block off and get out the man.'
Pope.

" ' Several pieces of cloth, the largest we had seen being fifty yards long, which they **unfolded** and displayed so as to make the greatest show possible.'—*Cook's Voyages.*

" ' What riddle's this? **Unfold** yourself, dear Robin.'—*Ben Jonson.*

" ' That great chain of causes which, linking one to another, even to the throne of God Himself, can never be **unravelled** by any industry of ours.'—*Burke.*" (Smith, *Syn. Discr.*, ed. 1878, *Develop.*)

108. Methods of Teaching must have reference to the ways according to which the learner's faculties proceed *when he is applying himself to study.* Unless this be understood, the faculties of the pupil will be embarrassed in their normal activities. This will cause discouragement to both teacher and pupil.

109. " There exist nevertheless certain general modes of treating any subject which can be clearly distinguished by the student. Logic cannot teach him exactly how and when to use each kind of method, but it can teach him the natures and powers of the methods, so that he will be more likely to use them rightly. We must distinguish:

" 1. The method of discovery,
" 2. The method of instruction.

" The **method of discovery** is employed in the acquisition of knowledge, and really consists in those processes of inference and induction, by which general truths are ascertained from the collection and examination of particular facts. The second method only applies when knowledge has already been acquired and expressed in the form of general laws, rules, principles or truths, so that we have only to make ourselves acquainted with these and observe the due mode of applying them to particular cases, in order to possess a complete acquaintance with the subject.

" A student, for example, in learning Latin, Greek, French, German, or any well-known language, receives a complete Grammar and Syntax setting forth the whole of the principles, rules and nature of the language. He receives these instructions, and takes them to be true on the authority of the teacher, or the writer of the book ; and after rendering them familiar to his mind he has nothing to do but to combine and apply the rules in reading or composing the language. He follows, in short, the method of Instruction. But this is an entirely different and opposite process to that which the scholar must pursue who has received some writings in an unknown language, and is endeavoring to make out the alphabet, words, grammar, and syntax of the language. He possesses not the laws of grammar, but words and sentences obeying those laws ; and he has to detect the laws if possible by observing their effects on the written language. He pursues, in short, the method of discovery consisting in a tedious comparison of letters, words, and phrases, such as shall disclose the more frequent combinations and forms in which they occur. The process would be a strictly inductive one, such as I shall partially exemplify in the Lessons on Induction ; but it is far more difficult than the method of Instruction, and depends to a great extent on the happy use of conjecture and hypothesis, which demands a certain skill and inventive ability.

"Exactly the same may be said of the investigation of natural things and events. The principles of mechanics, of the lever, inclined plane, and other Mechanical Powers, or the Laws of Motion, seem comparatively simple and obvious as explained to us in books of instruction. But the early philosophers did not possess such books; they had only the Book of Nature, in which is set forth not the laws, but the results of the laws, and it was only after the most patient and skilful investigation, and after hundreds of mistakes, that those laws were ascertained. It is very easy now to understand the Copernican system of Astronomy, which represents the planets as revolving round the sun in orbits of various magnitude. Once knowing the theory we can readily see why the planets have such various movements and positions, and why they sometimes stand still; it is easy to see, too, why in addition to their own proper motions they all go round the earth apparently every day in consequence of the earth's diurnal rotation. But all these changes were exceedingly puzzling to the ancients, who regarded the earth as standing still.

"**The method of discovery** thus begins with facts apparent to the senses, and has the difficult task of detecting those universal laws or general principles which can only be comprehended by intellect. It has been aptly said that the method of discovery thus proceeds **from things better known to us,** or our senses (**nobis notiora**), to those which are more simple or **better known in nature (notiora naturae).** The method of Instruction proceeds in the opposite direction, beginning with the things **notiora naturae,** and proceeding to show or explain the things **nobis notiora.** The difference is almost like that between **hiding** and **seeking.** He who has hidden a thing knows where to find it; but this is not the position of a discoverer, who has no clue except such as he may meet in his own diligent and sagacious search.

"Closely corresponding to the distinction between the methods of Discovery and Instruction is that between the methods of **Analysis** and **Synthesis.** It is very important indeed that the reader should clearly apprehend the meanings of these terms in their several applications. Analysis is the process of separating a whole into its parts, and synthesis the combination of parts into a whole. The analytical chemist, who receives a piece of mineral for examination, may be able to separate completely the several chemical elements of which it is composed and ascertain their nature and comparative quantities; this is chemical analysis. In other cases the chemist mixes together carefully weighed quantities of certain simple substances and combines them into a new compound substance; this is chemical synthesis. Logical analysis and synthesis must not be confused with the physical actions, but they are nevertheless actions of mind of an analogous character.

"In **logical synthesis** we begin with the simplest possible notions or ideas, and combine them together. We have the best possible example in the elements of Geometry. In Euclid we begin with certain simple notions of points, straight lines, angles, right angles, circles, &c. Putting together three straight lines we make a triangle; joining to this the notion of a right angle, we form the notion of a right-angled triangle. Joining four other equal lines at right angles to each other we gain the idea of a square, and if we then conceive such a square to be formed upon each of the sides of a right-angled triangle, and reason from the necessary qualities of these figures, we discover that the two squares upon the sides containing the right angle must together be exactly equal to the square upon the third side, as shewn in the 47th Proposition of Euclid's first book. This is a perfect instance of combining simple ideas into more complex ones.

"We have often, however, in Geometry to pursue the opposite course of **Analysis**. A complicated geometrical figure may be given to us, and we may have, in order to prove the properties which it possesses, to resolve it into its separate parts, and to consider the properties of those parts each distinct from the others.

"A similar distinction between the analytical and synthetic methods can be traced throughout the natural sciences. By keeping exact registers of the appearance and changes of the weather we may readily acquire an immense collection of facts, each such recorded fact implying a multitude of different circumstances occurring together. Thus in any storm or shower of rain we have to consider the direction and force of the wind; the temperature and moistness of the air; the height and forms of the clouds; the quantity of rain which falls, or the lightning and thunder which occur with it. If we proceed by analysis only to explain the changes of the weather we should have to try resolving each storm or change of weather into its separate circumstances, and comparing each with every other to discover what circumstances usually go together. We might thus ascertain no doubt with considerable certainty what kinds of clouds, and what changes of the wind, temperature, moisture, &c., usually precede any kind of storm, and we might even in time give some imperfect explanation of what takes place in the atmosphere.

"But we might also apply with advantage the synthetical method. By previous chemical investigations we know that the atmosphere consists mainly of the two fixed gases, oxygen and nitrogen, with the vapour of water, the latter being very variable in quantity. We can try experimentally what takes place when portions of such air of various degrees of moistness are compressed or allowed to expand, or are mixed together, as often happens in the atmosphere. It is thus discovered that whenever moist air is allowed to expand cloud is produced, and it may be drops of rain. Dr. Hutton, too, found that whenever cold moist air is mixed with warm moist air cloud is again produced. We can safely argue from such small experiments to what takes place in the atmosphere. Putting together synthetically, from the sciences of chemistry, mechanics, and electricity, all that we know of air, wind, cloud and lightning, we are able to explain what takes place in a thunderstorm far more completely than we could do by merely observing directly what happens in the storm. We are here however anticipating the methods of inductive investigation, which we must consider in the following lessons. It will appear that **Induction** is equivalent to analysis, and that the deductive kinds of reasoning which we have treated in prior lessons are of a synthetic character.

"It has been said that the synthetic method usually corresponds to the method of instruction and the analytic method to that of discovery. But it may be possible to discover new truths by synthesis and to teach old ones by analysis. Sir John Herschel in his well-known *Outlines of Astronomy* partially adopts the analytic method; he supposes a spectator in the first place to survey the appearances of the heavenly bodies and the surface of the earth, and to seek an explanation; he then leads him through a course of arguments to show that these appearances really indicate the rotundity of the earth, its revolution about its own axis and round the sun, and its subordinate position as one of the smaller planets of the solar system. Mr. Norman Lockyer's *Elementary Lessons in Astronomy* is a clear example of the synthetic method of instruction; for he commences by describing the sun, the centre of the system, and successively adds the planets and other members of the system, until at last we have the complete picture; and the reader who has temporarily received everything on the writer's authority, sees that the description corresponds with the truth. Each method, it must be allowed, has its own advantages. (Jevons, *Lessons in Logic*, ed. 1878, pp. 202–208.)

110. Methods of Teaching must respect that inherited and national "cast of mind" which exhibits itself so prominently that it forms an important element in teaching. Those national bents of mind, traits of disposition, and survival of tendencies, constitute a "prior knowledge," or setting, which gives form to the knowledge presented by the teacher. The Italian mind inherits peculiar adaptations for music. The German mind, as revealed in the language, is disposed to aggregate and accumulate conceptions. The native tendency with the French mind, in language, is towards separation and analysis. The English mind, in language, evidently has its form in directness, neither cumulative nor over analytical. With some nations, gesticulation forms a prominent inheritance of the people. The United States, being peopled from all nations, present a multitude of national peculiarities to the teacher, who, herein, has a more delicate work before him than teachers who labor with a single nationality. This element, although subtle, is powerful in any place where the schools are composed of children of many nationalities. While the psychological faculties are the same in kind and function among all peoples, yet the native quality of these faculties, or the bent for giving form to knowledge, varies with the peoples. These native qualities or bents are not the differences in degrees of the same capacities of people of the same nationality. They are powers or forces which necessarily modify the form of the same matter which is set before all alike. This is done unconsciously to the children who are taught.

111. Methods of Teaching are difficult to suit, "as an object to a quality," in their daily application, by reason of the intricacy and evanescence of psychological phenomena. But the province is established. The very delicacy and mutability of the modifications of Mind lend a zest to Methods, and consequently to teaching, that must emphatically and forever banish all tendencies to mere routine and formalism, when teachers fully grasp the Spirit of Methods. Genuine Methods of Teaching, from their nature, must be universally successful for accomplishing their objects. A principle can never become spiritless—the application of it may, if it be an unintelligent one, but the principle must be as constant and as enduring as the subjects to which it relates, or out of which it springs.

112. Methods of Teaching are not, in the present state of psychological science, absolutely invariable. The one element in the foundations, that of subject-matter, is firm, as science is firm. The other element in the foundations, that of psychology, is less firm, perhaps, because the Science of Mind is not so well established in its fullness as are most other sciences which are pursued in schools. No science or art is more stable or lasting than its foundations. However, the main principles of the science of psychology are very thoroughly established, as they appear to-day rising up out of hundreds of years of diligent study by the philosophers of the past and the present. "In mental philosophy the general statements have commonly a genuine fact, but mixed with this there is often an alloy. The error may not influence the spontaneous action of the primitive principle, but it may tell disastrously or ludicrously in the reflex application." (McCosh, *Int. of Mind*, p. 60, ed. 1870.)

113. What are ordinarily denominated " classdrill " and " examinations," are no legitimate elements in the conception of Methods of Teaching. They are no new things—they are mere repetitions. The value of repetition is purely a psychological problem, not belonging to subject-matter and mind, as do the problems of Methods. " Repetition, else the mainspring of instruction, is the chief destroyer of attention ; because, in order to give attention to what is repeated, you must first have found it worthy of a still greater exertion of that faculty." (Richter, *Levana*, p. 356.)

114. Methods of Teaching, from their nature, forbid the so-called Individuality of any teacher to enter into them, as a constituent part of their essence. The foundations of the Methods being the principles of adaptation between subject-matter and mind, the eccentricities, idiosyncrasies, or peculiarities of any one mind form no factor in the Science and Art of Methods of Teaching. " Every mind is more or less like every other mind ; there is always a basis of similarity, but there is a superstructure of feelings, impulses, and motives which is distinctive for each person." (Jevons, *Princ. of Science*, p. 733, ed. 1877.)

115. Teachers have their individuality, which shows itself in greater or less degrees in their school-room practice, while applying philosophical Methods of Teaching. This individuality is exhibited in the way that one teacher illustrates a point differently from another—in the way he speaks—in the way he looks—in the way he thinks, it may be—in the way in which his questions are conceived—in the impromptu expedients which he devises—in what, in general, is called "his way of doing things." This individuality of the teacher is known as **Manner**. Misapprehension of the true province of scientific Methods of Teaching has led many to apply the term to any peculiar experiment or expedient which may be selected, which things are in fact but examples of Manner. The familiar expressions so often heard—"my method is thus and so," "my method is not that, but this," "I illustrate by this method, using a bundle of sticks instead of kernels of corn"—are simply examples of Manner.

116. A teacher has his own Manner of Teaching—*he can not have his Method*, because Methods are general or universal principles, which are beyond the exclusiveness of the individual. Mannerisms can be affected or imitated, or devised, or invented; but Methods of Teaching, existing originally in the native constitution of things, can not be invented—they must be discovered. Being discovered, they are no more his who discovers them, than the principle of gravity is the property of Newton because he discovered its nature and laws.

117. This conception of Methods of Teaching should not be confused with that of Methods in general, which are ways of procedure in the investigations of subject-matter only—they do not aim at mind. Such expressions as "Horner's Method of Approximation," and the like, correctly use the word Method.

118. In the subjoined quotation the terms Manner and Method are not sufficiently discriminated in demarcation—each includes portions of the conception of Mode.

"Perhaps this difference between method and manner will appear better if we use an illustration which is supported by the etymology of the word method : Suppose it is proposed to establish a connection between two cities, for this purpose a road is made ; this road will be used by all that go from one city to the other, and by all kinds of individuals ; it is the same road for all and not liable to be changed by individual whims or notions. But the manner in which the road is used varies very much ; some will walk, others will run, and others still will ride. The road in our illustration represents the method in pedagogics ; it may be used by the most widely different individualities ; the way in which people make use of it is the manner. Manner cannot be thoroughly specified or defined. Here the utmost freedom must be allowed to teachers and pupils to develop their own individualities." (Soldan, art. *Method and Manner*, Nat. Ed. Ass. Proceedings, 1874, p. 249.)

119. When the Manner of a teacher has "method in it,"—when it is more or less determined into a System—when it has become a somewhat systematized exposition or application of the principle of adaptation, *i.e.*, of Methods of Teaching,—when Manner has assumed this state, it is called **Mode.**

120. Methods of Teaching are fundamental and general principles " out of which other matters of a speculative or practical character flow, and become its practical illustrations"— they must be discovered, if known. They can be investigated in their nature—they can not be copied, imitated, or assumed—they can only be stated as principles, which can be illustrated or exemplified in practice in certain ways called Modes, and sometimes Manners. Manner is the term which contains prominently the individuality of the teacher. Mode refers to the systematic application or illustration of Methods—it has little of the notion of individuality in it. Manner can be imitated, but hardly taught. Mode can be imitated and taught. If a teacher writes out a lesson in a methodical order, point by point, and question by question, such lesson is his Mode —and it may partake of his Manner. The more nearly teachers comprehend the nature of subject-matter as related to knowing mind, and the mind itself, the more nearly will their Modes be identical when teaching the same subject-matter to classes of similar attainments—and the less of mannerisms will be exhibited by the teachers.

121. If perfection of knowledge and of adaptation were possible, it is extremely probable that all *perfect teaching* would set the same subjects to the same pupils in exactly the same Mode, which would then reach a perfect illustration of Method of Teaching.

122. The failure to discriminate the provinces of Methods of Teaching, Modes, and Manners, has led to considerable abuse of the former expression. Mode and Manner can be imitated by those even who do not comprehend the principle which is illustrated; supposing a principle involved in the case, which principle is sometimes wholly imaginary in actual practice. This being the state of affairs, teachers who rest satisfied with copying another's Mode or Manner must fail, because they do not apprehend the animating principle, the Method of Teaching, which underlies the Mode imitated. Those teachers are dealing with the mere dress, lifeless forms, of Methods. Methods are life, enduring as mind. Modes have a portion of the life of Methods, and a portion from that of the teacher. Manner has only the life of the teacher whose it is.

123. " While **Mode** (Lat. *modus*) is also applicable to way of **being, Manner** (Fr. *manière*) denotes way of **action.** Manner, too, is casual; mode, systematic. Mode might be defined regular manner. Hence manner of action implies voluntariness on the part of the agent;

mode of action, uniformity in the thing acting. Modes of existence. Manners of conduct or operation." (Smith, *Syn. Discr.*, Mode.) "In consequence of the authorship—there being a large number of different writers—there is great variety in the modes of treatment." (*The Nation*, No. 700, p. 340, Nov. 28, 1878.) "We all remember how rapidly the theory grew up that in the greenbacks we had stumbled, by a happy accident, on a new mode of acquiring wealth and avoiding financial convulsions, and how rapidly, too, in many minds, they began to wear the air of weapons of war, like a grandfather's sword or musket, hallowed by associations, and unfit subjects for scientific examination or treatment." (*Ibid.*, No. 704, p. 394, Dec. 26, 1878.) "Washburn's *Outlines of Criminal Law*. A Manual of Criminal Law, including the Mode of Procedure by which it is enforced." (*Ibid.*, No. 704, Dec. 26, 1878.)

124. "**System** (Gr. $\sigma\nu\sigma\tau\eta\mu\alpha$, from $\sigma\nu\nu\iota\sigma\tau\alpha\nu\alpha\iota$, to place together) regards fixed **subjects** which have rational dependence or connection. **Method** (Gr. $\mu\varepsilon\tau\alpha$, after, and $\dot{o}\delta\dot{o}s$, a way) regards fixed **processes**. System is logical or scientific collocation. Method is logical or scientific procedure. But, inasmuch as a mode of procedure may be itself harmonized, system is frequently used in place of method. We sometimes say, ' to go systematically to work,' meaning methodically. Method lays down rules for scientific inquiry, and is the way which leads to system. 'All method,' says Sir

W. Hamilton, ' is a rational progress—a progress toward an end.' When Watts says, ' The best way to learn any science is to begin with a regular **system**, or a short and plain scheme of that science well drawn up into a narrow compass,' he is recommending a **method**." (Smith, *Syn. Discr.*, art. *System*.) "**System** is a connected body of knowledge." (Jevons, *El. Les. Logic*, p. 346.)

125. In the following quotation, the definitions are not strictly accurate, although they express the outlines :—" In pedagogy, **method** is the way chosen, the order followed by the teacher to put his own thought, his intelligence, in relation with the intelligence of his pupils ; **mode** is the way of organizing the school according as it is desired to convey lessons directly or indirectly to the pupils ; and **procedures** are the secondary means, ordinarily mechanical, which are used to assure the success of the method. They depend generally on the mode adopted." (L. Mariotti, *Conférences de Pédagogie*, p. 146, ed. 1873, Paris.)

126. In the following quotation (*b*), or "Applied," under both the **general** and the **special**, contains the conception of Mode.

"**Definition of Method.**

"**General:** (*a*) **Theoretical** :—The laws according to which the tendency to acquire knowledge, exerts itself, arranged so as to show their natural order and relations.

(b) **Applied:**—The same laws translated into rules, and arranged in the same order.

"**Special:** (a) **Theoretical:**—The laws according to which the tendency to acquire a knowledge of Physics, Logic, &c., exerts itself, arranged so as to show their natural order and relations.

(b) **Applied:**—The same laws translated into rules, and arranged in the same order."
(The late J. W. Armstrong, D.D.—*A Paper on Method.*)

127. "The tendency of any power or force to act in any particular way is called a **Principle**. The particular way in which a tendency operates is called a **Law**. The statement of a law in such form as will adapt it to the solution of problems is called a **Rule**." (*Ibid.*)

128. (a) Method, Mode, and Manner of Teaching, may be illustrated and contrasted, perhaps not inaptly, by the following supposition: Suppose an engineer desires to span a stream by a bridge—(1) he rears his abutments on either side—(2) he places the main timbers or "stringers" from abutment to abutment across the chasm —(3) he lays a roadway of planks upon the stringers—(4) he travels across the gulf upon the bridge. In the analogy, (1) rearing the abutments corresponds to the acquisition of a knowledge of subject-matter (say arithmetic), and of mind of the learner (Psychology), by the teacher —(2) throwing the stringers across the stream illustrates the process of discovering the principles of adjusting subject-matter to the mind of the learner, which is the Method of Teaching—(3) covering these stringers (which represent the principles of connection) with a flooring of whatever nature, suggests the invention of a Mode of Teaching—(4) the general or the particular "air," or "style," or "bearing," of the teacher while teaching (crossing the bridge) indicates his Manner of Teaching. Manner also includes a little of the notion of the flooring, as that a part of it is laid of wood, a part of iron, according to the fancy of the engineer.

(*b*) Another illustration :—"Another thing—at Hillard on the Pacific railway—on the use of which Eastern people venture queer conjectures, is a high, narrow tressel-work bridge supporting a V-shaped trough—an object familiar enough to residents of the Pacific Coast. This is a 'flume,' and the wood used in the kilns is floated through it for a distance of twenty-four miles from the mountains. Over 2,000,000 feet of lumber were necessary in its construction, and from its mouth it falls 2,000 feet, the stream rushing through it and sweeping the logs on its bosom with a rapidity and ease that makes us wonder why people ever haul wood in cumbersome waggons." (D. Appleton & Co., *The Art Journal*, New Series, No. 27, p. 71.)

In this illustration, the principle of conveyance is known in popular language as the "buoying up power of water," the relative specific gravity. This is the Method,—by floating on water. The contrivance, a V-shaped trough, instead of the surface of a river, exhibits the Mode of applying the principle or Method. Whatever is peculiar, or individual about the trough, or the preparation of the wood, or the letting of the water into the flume, indicates the Manner involved in the case.

(c) Another illustration :—"A railroad has been constructed to the mines of Summit Hill, about nine miles W. of the town (Mauch Chunk —Mawk Chunk'—in Pennsylvania). The cars, loaded with coal, descend by their own gravity to the landing, and after being emptied have been heretofore drawn up the plane by mules. But now the labors of the mules are superseded. A 'back track' has been constructed, which is regarded as a master piece of bold and successful engineering. From the chutes where the coal cars are unloaded at the town of Mauch Chunk, they return by their own weight to the foot of Mount Pisgah. They are then drawn to the top of that mountain on an inclined plane by means of a stationary engine. From the head of this plane they pass by their own gravity along a railway of 6 miles, to the foot of another inclined plane. To the top of this they are again raised by steam, and thence descend to the different mines, where they are filled with coal, and again descend by their own weight to the chutes." (J. Thomas, *Lippincott's Pronouncing Gazetteer*, ed. 1868, Mauch Chunk.)

In this illustration, three principles of motive power are introduced—gravity, animal-power, and steam. They are the Methods of transportation. The principle of gravity is utilized by carriages on wheels, instead of carriages on runners; the principle of animal-power was utilized by using mules, instead of horses; the principle of steam-power is utilized by means of a stationary, instead of a movable, engine. The carriages on wheels, the mules, and the stationary engine, are objects which are used to apply the Methods, and are Modes of transportation. Whatever is individual, or peculiar, in any of these—not necessary, used instead of something else in form, rate of motion, or way of application, or in construction,—exhibits Manner.

(*d*) Another illustration :—A gentleman employs a span of horses to draw his carriage. Horse-power is the principle involved in conveying—it is the Method of transporting the carriage. A carriage on wheels is used, instead of a sleigh, or "carriage on runners," as the way of showing the application of the principle of horse-power—this represents the Mode of conveyance used by the gentleman. His particular kind of carriage is a landau, instead of a wagonette—this notion, together with whatever of "style," or "air," he may choose to introduce, exhibits his Manner of riding in his landau. (See, also, Mill's use of these terms in § 224.)

129. Mr. Page uses Mode correctly in this:

"Right Modes of Teaching--Pouring-in Process, or lecturing; Drawing-out Process, or questioning." (*Theory and Practice of Teaching*, p. 5, *Contents*, ed. 1853.)

130. The subjoined illustrates Mode, Manner, and the idea of "leading" the pupil:

"The class were puzzled to understand the **resistance of the various media.** 'I do not know as I understand what **media** means,' said one of the boys. 'A medium is that in which a body moves,' read the teacher from a book. '**A medium?**' 'Yes; we say **medium** when we mean but one, and **media** when we mean more than one.' After a time, the pupil still gaining no light, the regular teacher approached: 'John,'—taking his watch in his hand—'would this watch continue to go, if I should drop it into a pail of water?' 'I should think it would not long.' 'Why not?' 'Because the water would get round the wheels and stop it, I should think.' 'How would it be if I should drop it into a quart of molasses?' The boys smiled. 'Or into a barrel of tar?' 'Suppose I should force it, while open, into a quantity of lard.' John said, 'The watch would not go in any of the articles.' '**Articles**, why not say **Media?**' 'Oh, I understand it now.'" (*Ibid.*, pp. 319–321.)

131. In the annexed extract, the author uses "Manner" properly, but substitutes Method for Mode: "The agreeable talents are too much confined to method. They are rendered too abstracted by being reduced to maxims and precepts; and hence those things which should constitute the amusement of young people, are made disgusting to them, as the study of an art. I cannot conceive any thing more ridiculous, than to see an old singing or dancing-master, approach a young, lively, giggling girl, with a frigid and formal air; and assume, in teaching his frivolous science, a more pedantick and magisterial tone, than if he were teaching her the catechism. Is it that the art of singing, for instance, depends on the knowledge of written musick? Is it not possible to acquire a just command of voice, to learn to sing with taste, and even to accompany an instrument, without knowing a single note? Is the same manner of singing adapted to all voices? Doth the same method of teaching suit equally every genius? It is impossible to make me believe, that the same attitudes, the same steps, the same motions and gestures, or even the same dances, are equally proper for a little, lively, sharp-eyed brunette, and a tall beauty with languishing eyes and flaxen hair. When I see a dancing-master give the same lesson, therefore, indiscriminately to both, I say to myself, this man follows the customs of his profession, but he understands nothing of his art." (Rousseau, *Emilius*, vol. 3, p. 205, ed. 1783, London.)

132. In the extract following, the Socratic Mode, often improperly called Method, is illustrated: " Now a guide, when he has found a man out of the road leads him into the right way: he does not ridicule or abuse him and then leave him. Do you also show the illiterate man the truth, and you will see that he follows. But so long as you do not show him the truth, do not ridicule him, but rather feel your own incapacity. How then did Socrates act? He used to compel his adversary in disputation to bear testimony to him, and he wanted no other witness. Therefore he could say, 'I care not for other witnesses, but I am always satisfied with the evidence (testimony) of my adversary, and I do not ask the opinion of others, but only the opinion of him who is disputing with me.' For he used to make the conclusions drawn from natural notions so plain that every man saw the contradiction (if it existed) and withdrew from it (thus): Does the envious man rejoice? By no means, but he is rather pained. Well, do you think that envy is pain over evils? and what envy is there of evils? Therefore he made his adversary say that envy is pain over good things. Well then, would any man envy those who are nothing to him? By no means. Thus having completed the notion and distinctly fixed it he would go away without saying to his adversary, Define to me envy; and if the adversary had defined envy, he did not say, You have defined it badly, for the terms of the definition do not correspond to the thing defined— These are technical terms, and for this reason disagreeable and hardly intelligible to illiterate men, which terms we (philosophers) cannot lay aside. But that the illiterate man himself, who follows the appearances presented to him, should be able to concede any thing or reject it, we can never by the use of these terms move him to do. Accordingly being conscious of our own inability, we do not attempt the thing; at least such of us as have any caution do not. But the greater part and the rash, when they enter into such disputation, confuse themselves and confuse others; and finally abusing their adversaries and abused by them, they walk away.

" Now this was the first and chief peculiarity of Socrates, never to be irritated in argument, never to utter any thing abusive, any thing insulting, but to bear with abusive persons and to put an end to the quarrel. If you would know what great power he had in this way, read the Symposium of Xenophon, and you will see how many quarrels he put an end to. Hence with good reason in the poets also this power is most highly praised,

'Quickly with skill he settles great disputes.'
HESIOD, *Theogony*, v. 87.

Well then; the matter is not now very safe, and particularly at Rome; for he who attempts to do it, must not do it in a corner, you may be sure, but must go to a man of consular rank, if it so happen, or to a rich man, and ask him, Can you tell me, Sir, to whose care you have entrusted your horses?—By all means.—Well then; can you tell me to whom you entrust your gold or silver things or your vestments? I don't entrust even these to any one indifferently. Well; your own body, have you already considered about entrusting the care of it to any person?—Certainly.—To a man of experience, I suppose, and one acquainted with the aliptic, or with the healing art?—Without doubt.—Are these the best things that you have, or do you also possess something else which is better than all these?—What kind of a thing do you mean?—That I mean which makes use of these things, and tests each of them, and deliberates.—Is it the soul that you mean?—You think right, for it is the soul that I mean.—In truth I do think that the soul is a much better thing than all the others which I possess.—Can you then show us in what way you have taken care of the soul? for it is not likely that you, who are so wise a man and have a reputation in the city, inconsiderately and carelessly allow the most valuable thing that you possess to be neglected and to perish.—Certainly not.—But have you taken care of the soul yourself; and have you learned from another to do this, or have you discovered the means yourself?—Next, if you persist in troubling him, there is danger that he may raise his hands and give you blows. I was once myself also an admirer of this mode of instruction until I fell into these dangers." (Epictetus, *Discourses*, chap. xii.)

133. In the following extract the conceptions of Mode and Manner of Teaching are not distinguished from that of Methods of Teaching. "Another ' peccant humour' which at present infects the body of education is the employment of **Mechanical Methods.** These methods were perhaps not at first mechanical ; they have become so by degeneration in the hands of merely imitative persons. If a method is not thoroughly assimilated by the teacher so as to become a living part of his own mind, if it does not marry itself willingly to his own thought and his own habits, if it is adopted as a mere plan for saving himself trouble and for escaping from his usual amount of work, it has a tendency to degenerate into a kind of machine, into something that cannot call forth thought and mental activity from his pupils. The essential requisite of a method is that it shall be living and possess the adaptability of life, and that it shall not interfere with but promote the spontaneous interest which the pupil may be inclined to feel in his subject. But our ancient and standing enemy—routine—is at hand here also, and is always ready to turn the best method into a monotonous device, or a crank-like exercise of activities. Man is by nature a hunting animal, and the heuristic method in teaching is one of the most potent for developing the mental powers. But in the degeneration which is natural to all human things, unless the breath that created them at first breathes through them again, among the destructive powers which produce this degeneration, there is none more potent than the habit of imitation. Question and answer—from the pupil as well as from the teacher—is one of the best ways of searching out truth that are given to human faculties. But no sooner is this perceived than some one writes a book on what he calls this method, and the life is killed out of the method by the very process which seemed to preserve it—it is strangled in the grasp of stereotype. And there are now hundreds of books, used mostly in ladies' schools, in which this base-born plan is still followed, to the irretrievable loss of those who are subjected to the process. An eminent Cambridge mathematician at present trains all his pupils on this heuristic method—and without book; and his success at the university as well as in school is marked and solid. But if he were to give a sketch of his method in writing, it would be ignobly stuck to and slavishly followed—to the death of the very method he had been endeavouring to set forth and recommend. If we could only train all our teachers to the use and constant practice of the heuristic method, we should make them themselves more strong in thought and purpose, more firm and real in their intellectual life, and more capable of firing their pupils with a single and undivided zeal for truth. . . . We are in fact overdone with machinery; our education is choked by the means we use to promote it; and the informing spirit is too often absent. . . .

". . . Our mechanical methods blind us to the necessity of seeking to analyse our subjects in the fullest manner, and so to arrange the steps that the children may go up with ease and pleasure. We are constantly giving knowledge prematurely; we are every day anticipating results which the child will reach for himself; and all over our pupils suffer in their brains from the malady of the day—imperfect digestion." (Meiklejohn, *Inaug. Address, Bell Chair of Education*, pp. 33-36, 1876.)

134. The expressions "**Methods of Nature,**" "**Nature's Methods,**" "Consult Nature for Methods of Education and Teaching," are heard from time to time. It may be profitable to examine this conception a little. What is Nature? How does she work? Where shall we find her? We find her about us everywhere, as a wild, incongruous, heterogeneous, restless mass of objects and activities. The most natural things in the world, probably, are a swamp and barbarism, for they are "fresh from the hand of Nature." The most natural road across the swamp is a corduroy road. The most natural action of a boy is to kick another boy when he dislikes him. The most natural way to occupy land is to tent upon it, and by force keep others away from it, as the nomadic peoples do. The most natural of plows is the Asiatic—the fork of a tree. The most natural apple is that which grows from the natural seed, not the welcome fruit of the graft. We also say that these works of art, all high art, are natural. What, then, is Nature? Nature is not simply the fact that is presented to man—she is not alone an object formed without the help of man—she is not a single objective thing by itself. Nature is a term for **Capacities** and **Possibilities**, whether of matter or of mind. We speak of capacities of the human mind, all of which are natural ;

and the developments of them are all natural. Nothing can be produced which is outside of the range of possibilities, and, hence, that is outside of Nature. But by way of distinction, those things which man himself has been instrumental in directing and controlling are called **Artificial**. If the swamp and the barbarian are very natural, drained meadows and civilization are very artificial. Yet in all these cases man never can go beyond what his own natural powers can naturally do. No man ever constructs a bridge or paints a madonna that his natural powers do not naturally accomplish. It is all of Nature, and all natural—just as natural as it was for Demosthenes to stammer or, subsequently, to move all Greece by his eloquence. One man uses his right hand familiarly, another his left, and still another both with equal facility —which is the natural one? An Icelander naturally resists cold—an African naturally resists heat—an American resists both heat and cold. Which is the natural case? A honey bee gathers honey in temperate zones, but, moved southward, ceases—what is the naturalness in the case? In these cases one is just as natural as another—they all are so because of native endowments, capacities, or possibilities. What is the most natural language to speak, for a child, English, French, or Italian? "Man, by nature, is formed to suffer with patience, and die in peace. It is the physicians with their prescriptions, the philosophers with their precepts, and the clergy with their prayers and exhortations, that have debased the heart of man, and made him ignorant how to die." (Rousseau, *Emilius*, vol. 1, p. 47.) In the following, which is the natural stage of relationship, compared to that now established by law and custom in the United States at the present time? "We shall endeavour to establish the following propositions:—1. That the most ancient system in which the idea of blood-relationship was embodied, was the system of kinship through females only. 2. That the primitive groups were, or were assumed to be, homogeneous. 3. That the system of kinship through females only tended to render the exogamous groups heterogeneous, and thus to supersede the system of capturing wives. 4. That in the advance from savagery the system of kinship through females only was succeeded by a system which acknowledged kinship through males also; and which, in most cases, passed into a system which acknowledged kinship through males only. 5. That the system of kinship through males tended to rear up homogeneous groups, and thus to restore the original condition of affairs—where the exogamous prejudice survived—as regards both the practice of capturing wives and the evolution of the form of capture. 6. That a local tribe, under the combined influence of exogamy and the system of female kinship, might attain a balance of persons of different sexes regarded as being of different descent, and that thus its members might be able to intermarry with one another, and wholly within the tribe, consistently with the principle of exogamy. 7. That a local tribe, having reached this stage and grown proud through success in war, might decline intermarriage with other local tribes and become a caste. 8. That on kinship becoming agnatic, the members of such a tribe might yield to the universal tendency of rude races to eponomy, and feign themselves to be all derived from a common ancestor, and so become endogamous. And 9. That there is reason to think that some endogamous tribes became endogamous in this same manner. . . . The earliest human groups can have had no idea of kinship. . . . The idea must be regarded as a growth. . . . Individuals had been affiliated not to persons, but to some group. . . . As distinguished from men of other groups, they would be the group-stock, and named after the group." (McLennan, *Primitive Marriage*, pp. 118-123, ed. 1876, London.)

135. The question is really, not what is natural? but what is *artificial?* If the word has any proper signification and scope, they must be something like this :—Artificial things include all those products and results which have been developed from the capacities and possibilities of Nature by the direct agency of man. Under this definition come all that man has ever done in civilization and in history—*i.e.*, in civilization. "**Culture** or Civilization, taken in its wide ethnographic sense, is that complex whole which includes knowledge, belief" (religious and otherwise), "art, morals, law, custom, and any other capabilities and habits acquired by man as a member of society." (Tylor, *Primitive Culture*, vol. i., p. 1, ed. 1874, New York.) In so far as the faculties of the mind are native to the mind, they are natural—but in so far as they are developed into power by this or that kind of life, or by this or that branch of knowledge, and for this or that purpose, the developed powers and the resulting products of effort, although quite natural, are known as *artificial.* Methods of Education are artificial. Modes of Teaching are artificial, yet, if based upon principles, they are naturally founded upon the native powers of the learning mind and the subject-matter to be learned. This subject-matter is both natural and artificial, although all produced by the capacities of Nature. Methods of Teaching, being founded upon the innate nature of things, are natural.

136. It is also true that the term "natural," as commonly understood when applied to the human conditions, means the general idea or notion that people acquire as an induction from experience. An action is pronounced natural in proportion as it approaches spontaneous favor from the greatest number of observers. In proportion as it diverges from this it is called "affected," "false," "sham," "unnatural," "monstrous." Still all these phases of experience and observation are within the capacities of Nature, and hence natural. A broad discrimination should be made between the term natural as applied to one individual, and as applied in the sense of the inductive general idea. The author who can gather up the sense of the greatest number of people into one picture or character, or trait of experience, is called the most life-like and natural in his writings. But he is no more natural than the man who stammers, or squints, or says, as the child, "I be going."

137. "But the only distinct meaning of that word (natural) is, **stated, fixed,** or **settled;** since what is natural as much requires and presupposes an intelligent agent to render it so, *i.e.* to effect it continually, or at stated times, as what is supernatural or miraculous does to effect it once." (Butler, *Analogy*, Malcom's ed., 1860, p. 94.)

138. "According to its derivation, nature (**natura—nascitur**) means that which is born or produced—**the becoming**; that which has a beginning and an end; that which has not the cause of its existence in itself, and the cause of which must be sought in something antecedent to and beyond itself—that is, nature is **the phenomenal.** This the word expresses in the strongest manner. That which begins to be, as the necessary consequence of antecedent conditions, is **natural.** The co-existence, resemblance, and succession of phenomena constitute the **order of nature;** and the uniformity of these relations among phenomena are the **laws of nature.** . . . The word 'nature' is also employed to denote the essential properties of matter, and the various forms of energy, potential and kinetic." (Cocker, *Theistic Conception of the World*, pp. 193–4, ed. 1875.)

139. "**Nature** is the aggregate or totality of all material or physical phenomena. **A Law of Nature** is the statement of a certain uniformity observed in the relations among phenomena. The laws of nature are ' simply expressions of phenomenal uniformities, having no **coercive** power whatever.' (Carpenter.)

140. "**The Uniformity of the Order of Nature** may mean either ' uniformity of co-existence ' or ' uniformity of succession.' ' Uniformity of co-existence ' means that the same substances must always have the same essential properties and the same permanent relations to other substances. . . . The constancy of the **course** of nature or the uniformity of causation is not a self-evident and necessary truth. In so far as it is a scientific truth it is purely an induction from experience, an experience which is necessarily limited, and therefore does not warrant a universal conclusion. . . . It is an immediate fact of consciousness that the will is a cause which is adequate to the production of a diversity of effects. . . . Physical science itself does not teach that the course of nature is absolutely uniform. . . . ' Nature,' says Dr. Cohn, of Breslau, ' is an equation with very many unknown quantities. It is the work of natural science to determine the value of these quantities.' " (*Ibid.*, pp. 325-33.)

141. " According to its derivation, **nature** should mean that which is produced or born ; but it also means that which produces or causes to be born. . . . The term **nature** is used sometimes in a wider, sometimes in a narrower extension. When employed in its most extensive meaning, it embraces the two worlds of mind and matter. When employed in its more restricted signification, it is a synomym for the latter only, and is then used in contradistinction to the former. In the Greek philosophy, . . . the word was general in its meaning; and included not only the sciences of matter, but also those of mind. With us, the term **nature** is more vaguely extensive than the terms **physics, physical, physiology**, or even than the adjective **natural**; whereas, in the philosophy of Germany, **natur** and its correlatives, . . . are, in general, expressive of the world of matter in contrast to the world of intelligence.

"**Nature** as opposed to **art**, all physical causes, all the forces which belong to physical beings, organic or inorganic. The **nature** or essence of any particular being or class of beings, that which makes it what it is.

" ' The word **nature** has been used in two senses,—viz., actively and passively; energetic (= **forma formans**), and material (= **forma formata**). In the first it signifies the inward principle of whatever is requisite for the reality of a thing as **existent**; while the **essence**, or essential property, signifies the inner principle of all that appertains to the **possibility** of a thing. Hence, in accurate language, we say the essence of a mathematical circle or geometrical figure, not the **nature**, because in the conception of forms, purely geometrical, there is no expression or implication of their real existence. In the second or material sense of the word **nature**, we mean by it the sum total of all things, as far as they are objects of our senses, and consequently of possible experience—the aggregate of phenomena, whether existing for our outer senses, or for our inner sense. The doctrine concerning **nature**, would therefore . . be more properly entitled phenomenology, distinguished into its two grand divisions, somatology (= doctrine of the general properties of bodies or material substances), and psychology.' (*Coleridge.*)

" ' There is no such thing as what men commonly call the **course of nature**, or the **power of nature**. The **course of nature**, truly and properly speaking, is nothing else but the **will of God** producing certain effects in a continued, regular, constant, and uniform manner ; which course or manner of acting, being in every movement perfectly **arbitrary**, is as easy to be **altered** at any time as to be **preserved**.' (*Clarke.*)

" ' All things are artificial,' said Sir Thomas Browne, ' for **nature** is the **art** of God.' The antithesis of **nature** and **art** is a celebrated doctrine in the peripatetic philosophy. Natural things are distinguished from artificial, inasmuch as they have, what the latter are without, an intrinsic principle of formation. (*Arist.*)

" Dr. Reid said that **nature** is the name we give to the efficient cause of innumerable effects which fall daily under observation. But if it be asked what **nature** is ? whether the first universal cause or a subordinate one ? whether one or many? whether intelligent or unintelligent?— upon these points we find various conjectures and theories, but no solid ground upon which we can rest. And I apprehend the wisest men are they who are sensible that they know nothing of the matter." (Fleming, *Vocab. of Phil.*)

142. " When he was visited by one of the magistrates, Epictetus inquired of him about several particulars, and asked if he had children and a wife. The man replied that he had ; and Epictetus inquired further, how he felt under the circumstances. Miserable, the man said. Then Epictetus asked, In what respect, for men do not marry in order to be wretched, but rather to be happy. But I, the man replied, am so wretched about my children that lately, when my little daughter was sick and was supposed to be in danger, I could not endure to stay with her, but I left home till a person sent me news that she had recovered. Well then, said Epictetus, do you think that you acted right? I acted naturally, the man replied. But convince me of this that you acted naturally, and I will convince you that everything which takes place according to nature takes place rightly. This is the case, said the man, with all or at least most fathers. I do not deny that.: but the matter about which we are inquiring is whether such behaviour is right ; for in respect to this matter we must say that tumours also come for the good of the body, because they do come ; and generally we must say that to do wrong is natural, because nearly all or at least most of us do wrong.

Do you show me then how your behaviour is natural. I cannot, he said; but do you show me how it is not done according to nature, and is not rightly done." (Epictetus, *Discourses*, Book I., Chap. XI., Long's trans.)

143. "The object of what we commonly call education—that education in which man intervenes and which I shall distinguish as artificial education—is to make good these defects in Nature's methods; to prepare the child to receive Nature's education, neither incapably nor ignorantly, nor with wilful disobedience; and to understand the preliminary symptoms of her displeasure, without waiting for the box on the ear. In short, all artificial education ought to be an anticipation of natural education. And a liberal education is an artificial education, which has not only prepared a man to escape the great evils of disobedience to natural laws, but has trained him to appreciate and to seize upon the rewards, which Nature scatters with as free a hand as her penalties. . . . Ignorance is visited as sharply as wilful disobedience—incapacity meets with the same punishment as crime." (Huxley, *Lay Sermons*, p. 34, ed. 1870.)

II.

ON THE PRACTICE OF METHODS OF TEACHING.

(A) ON THE KNOWING FACULTIES OF THE MIND.

144. In discussing these Elements of Methods of Teaching, no attempt is made to present a systematic view of Psychology. To do this would require a volume by itself, and must be reserved for another occasion as opportunities shall permit. Sufficient data are introduced to serve as bases for Methods of Teaching. Without endeavoring to classify the matter inserted, it is used as it best serves the scope of the investigation. This matter is also very valuable to the student for its suggestiveness, even when it does not bear directly upon the line of the inquiry. Those professional students, who are already familiar with some system of Psychology, will need to be delayed only a short time on this division of the volume.

145. Adapting from Sir William Hamilton's *Metaphysics*, Murray's text, edition of 1874, pp. 39–66, psychological phenomena of consciousness are classified under three great divisions: (1) Cognitions, or the faculties which have the power to know ; (2) Feelings, or sensibilities, those which are susceptible of giving pain or pleasure ; (3) Conations, which are "tendencies to action, and are divisible into classes, as such tendencies are either blind and fatal, or deliberate and free. The former are **desires**, the latter, **volitions**, (p. 226). For present purposes it is necessary to elaborate only the first division, cognitions, including consciousness.

146. (*a*) "Consciousness is the recognition by the thinking subject of its own acts or affections. It is an actual and not a potential knowledge. It is an immediate, not a mediate knowledge. It supposes a contrast, a discrimination—as the ego and non-ego, the discrimination of states or modifications of the internal subject or self from each other, and the distinction between the parts and qualities of the outer world. It involves judgment, or the mental act by which one thing is affirmed or denied of another. It is conditioned upon memory, for without this our mental states could not be held fast, compared, distinguished from each other, and referred to self. Consciousness in its simplicity necessarily involves three things,—(1.) a recognizing or knowing subject, ego ; (2.) a recognized or known modification ; and (3.) a recognition or knowledge by the subject of the modification (pp. 39–42).

(*b*) "Comparison requires a **tertium quid**, a locus—call it what you will—in which the two outward existences may meet on equal terms. This forum is what is known as a consciousness.

Even sensations cannot be supposed, simply as such, to be aware of their relations to each other. A succession of feelings is not (as James Mill reiterates) one and the same thing with a feeling of succession, but a wholly different thing. The latter feeling requires a self-transcendency of each item, so that each not only is in relation, but knows its relation, to the other. This self-transcendency of data constitutes the conscious form. Where we suppose it to exist we have mind ; where mind exists we have it. . . . Thus, then, the words Use, Advantage, Interest, Good, find no application in a world in which no consciousness exists. Things there are neither good nor bad ; they simply are or are not. Ideal truth to exist at all requires that a mind also exist which shall deal with it as a judge deals with the law, really creating that which it professes only to declare. . . . This category (of consciousness, or personality) might be defined as the mode in which data are brought together for **comparison with a view to choice.** Both these points, comparison and choice, will be found alike omnipresent in the different stages of its activity. The former has always been recognized ; the latter less than it deserves. Many have been the definitions given by psychologists of the essence of consciousness. One of the most acute and emphatic of all is that of Ulrici, who in his *Leib und Seele* and elsewhere exactly reverses the formula of the reigning British school, by calling consciousness a discriminating activity. But even Ulrici does not pretend that consciousness creates the differences it becomes aware of in its objects. They pre-exist and consciousness only discerns them ; so that after all Ulrici's definition amounts to little more than saying that consciousness is a faculty of cognition—a rather barren result. I think we may go farther and add that the powers of cognition, discrimination and comparison which it possesses, exist only for the sake of something beyond themselves, namely, Selection. Whoever studies consciousness, from any point of view whatever, is ultimately brought up against the mystery of **interest** and **selective attention.** There are a great many things which consciousness **is** in a passive and receptive way by its cognitive and registrative powers. But there is one thing which it **does, suâ sponte,** and which seems an original peculiarity of its own ; and that is, always to choose out of the manifold experiences present to it at a given time some one for particular accentuation, and to ignore the rest. And . . from its simplest to its most complicated forms, it exerts this function with unremitting industry." (James, *Article* in *Mind,* No. XIII., January, 1879, pp. 6–9.)

147. " I. In the first place, as we are endowed with a faculty of Cognition, or Consciousness in general, and since it cannot be maintained that we have always possessed the knowledge which we now possess, it will be admitted that we must have a faculty of acquiring knowledge. But this acquisition of knowledge can only be accomplished by the immediate presentation of a new object to consciousness; in other words, by the reception of a new object within the sphere of our cognition. We have thus a faculty which may be called the **Acquisitive,** or the **Presentative,** or the **Receptive.** Now, new or adventitious knowledge may be either of things external or of things internal. If the object of knowledge be external, the faculty receptive or presentative of the qualities of such object will be a consciousness of the non-ego. This has obtained the name of **External Perception,** or of **Perception** simply. If, on the other hand, the object be internal, the faculty receptive or presentative of the qualities of such subject-object, will be a consciousness of the ego. This faculty obtains the name of **Internal** or **Reflex Perception,** or of **Self-consciousness.** By the foreign psychologists this faculty is termed also the **Internal Sense.**" (Hamilton.)

"The two classes of sense-perceptions thus characterized are **the original** and **the acquired.** They are thus defined: an original perception is one that is performed by a single sense, when exercised alone. Whatever the mind knows in this way, either of an object or of its relations, is known directly and by an original endowment of man. It is a pure work or operation of nature, and cannot be traced to art. An acquired perception is one which we gain by experience or exercise. We use the knowledge given directly by one sense, as the sign or evidence of the knowledge which we might, but do not, in this particular case, gain by another." (Porter,

The Human Intellect, p. 159, ed. 1869.) Continuing from Hamilton :—

148. " II. In the second place, inasmuch as we are capable of knowledge, we must be endowed not only with a faculty of acquiring, but with a faculty of retaining or conserving it when acquired. We have thus, as a second necessary faculty, one that may be called the **Conservative** or **Retentive.** This is **Memory**, strictly so denominated.

149. " III. But, in the third place, if we are capable of knowledge, it is not enough that we possess a faculty of acquiring, and a faculty of retaining it in the mind, but out of consciousness. We have a reproductive power. This **Reproductive** faculty is governed by the laws which regulate the succession of our thoughts,—the laws, as they are called, of Mental Association. If these laws are allowed to operate without the intervention of the will, this faculty may be called **Suggestion, or Spontaneous Suggestion;** —whereas, if applied under the influence of the will, it will properly obtain the name of **Reminiscence, or Recollection.** By reproduction, it should be observed, that I strictly mean the process of recovering the absent thought from unconsciousness, and not its representation in consciousness.

150. " IV. In the fourth place, as capable of knowledge, we must not only be endowed with a presentative, a conservative, and a reproductive faculty ; there is required for their consummation a faculty of representing in consciousness, and of keeping before the mind the knowledge presented, retained, and reproduced. We have thus a **Representative** faculty ; and this obtains the name of **Imagination** or **Phantasy**.

151. " V. In the fifth place, all the faculties we have considered are only subsidiary. They acquire, preserve, call out, and hold up, the materials, for the use of a higher faculty which operates upon these materials, and which we may call the **Elaborative** or **Discursive** faculty. This faculty has only one operation,—it only compares. It may startle you to hear that the highest function of mind is nothing higher than comparison ; but, in the end, I am confident of convincing you of the paradox. From this mere act of Comparison, there are created the intellectual products known as **Collective Notions, Abstractions, Generalizations, Judgments**, and **Reasoning**.

152. " VI. But, in the sixth and last place, the mind is not altogether indebted to experience for the whole apparatus of its knowledge. What we know by experience, without experience we should not have known ; and as all our experience is contingent, all the knowledge derived from experience is contingent also. But there are cognitions in the mind which are not contingent,—which are necessary,—which we cannot but think,—which thought supposes as its fundamental condition. These cognitions, therefore, are not mere generalizations from experience. But if not derived from experience, they must be native to the mind. These native cognitions are the laws by which the mind is governed in its operations, and which afford the conditions of its capacity of knowledge. These necessary laws, or primary conditions of intelligence, are phenomena of a similar character ; and we must, therefore, generalize or collect them into a class ; and on the power possessed by the mind of manifesting these phenomena we may bestow the name of the **Regulative** faculty. (*Lect. on Metaph.*, XX.)

153. "The following is a tabular view of the distribution of the Special Faculties of Knowledge.

COGNITIVE FACULTIES.

I. Presentative { 1. External—Perception.
2. Internal—Self-consciousness.
II. Conservative—Memory.
III. Reproductive { 1. Without will—Suggestion.
2. With will—Reminiscence.
IV. Representative—Imagination or Phantasy.
V. Elaborative—Comparison, or the Faculty of Relations.
VI. Regulative—Reason or Common Sense."

154. "Some writers on education call the desire of intellectual progression the faculty of obtaining knowledge,—that is to say, they call painting seeing,—or the intellectual powers, and think of the senses and the memory as also exerting an educational influence ; or they speak of the development of spontaneous activity, as if the will itself were not such a developing power. . . . The will reproduces itself only, and acts only within, not without, itself ; for external action is as little the new act of the particular volition, as are the words signifying it of the particular thought. The desire of mental progress, on the contrary, enlarges its world for the reception of new creatures, and is as dependent on objects as the pure will is independent of them. The will could reach its ideal, but finds a strange opposition to it,—whereas no power stands opposed to thought,—but only the difference between its steps, and the impossibility of seeing whither they reach. . . . The mental desire of advancement which, in a higher sense than the physical, works by means of, and in accordance with, the will, that is to say, creates new ideas out of old ideas, is the distinguishing characteristic of man. No will restrains the order of a beast's actions. In our waking moments we are actually conscious that we think; in our dreams we receive, if I may so express it, that consciousness. In the man of genius the formation of ideas appears actually creative; in ordinary men, merely recollective and necessary." (Richter, *Levana*, pp. 342–4.)

155. "The Intelligence reaches its end according to a certain way, process, or method. . . . The Formal movements of intelligence accordingly fall under two heads, thus :—(*a*) Will-power. (*b*) Process or Method of reaching Knowledge." (Laurie, *Syn. of Lectures*, p. 10, ed. 1877.)

156. "No act of intelligence can be performed without some determination of the Ego, no act of determination without some cognition, and no act of the one or the other without some amount of feeling being mingled in the process. Thus, while each mental state may have its distinctive characteristics, there is unity at the root —the **identical Ego, spirit,** *Will* (p. 36). . . . When, therefore, it is asked, What causes the will to effect one volition rather than another? our answer is, **Nothing whatever**! Of its own effect, *Will,* in its proper conditions, is not a partial, but a full and adequate cause." (Cocker, *Theistic Conception of the World,* p. 391.)

157. In continuation of what has been said there is added the following, adapted from Porter on the Imagination : " The imagination has various applications. (*a*) The **poetic** imagination is that creative power which is employed for the gratification of the emotional nature in the production of pictures more or less elevating in their associations, which are fixed and expressed by means of rhythmical language.

158. (*b*) " The **philosophic** imagination is that without which philosophic invention and discovery are impossible. To invent or discover, is always to recombine. It is to adjust in new positions, objects or parts of objects which have never been so connected before. The discoverer of a new solution for a problem, or a new demonstration for a theorem in mathematics, the inventor of a new application of a power of nature already known, or the discoverer of a power not previously dreamed of, the discoverer of a new argument to prove or deduce a truth or a new induction from facts already accepted, the man who evolves a new principle or a new definition in moral or political science—must all analyze and recombine in the mind things, acts, or events, with their relations, in positions in which they have never been previously observed or thought of. This recombination is purely mental. If there be a discovery or invention, there has never before been such a juxtaposition of the materials nor of their parts in the world of fact or in the thoughts of men. These objects and parts are now for the first time brought together in the mind—*i.e.*, the imagination of the discoverer. Every discovery is, in fact, a work of the creative imagination. . . . In the communication of scientific truth there can be no question that a large measure of imagination is of essential service. He that would amply illustrate, powerfully defend, or effectively enforce the principles and truths of science, is greatly aided by a brilliant imagination. This, of all other gifts, delivers him from that tendency to the dry and abstract, to the general and the remote, to which the expounder of science is continually exposed from his familiarity with principles which are strange to his pupils and readers, and which need to be continually explained and illustrated by fresh and various examples. The philosophic writer or teacher who is gifted with imagination is more likely to be clear in statement, ample in illustration, pertinent in his application and exciting in his enforcement of the truths with which his science is conversant, whatever may be the subject-matter with which the science is concerned.

159. " (c) The **practical** or **ethical** uses of the imagination are numerous and elevated. These are sufficiently obvious from the single consideration, that the law of duty is and must be an ideal law : for whether it is or is not fulfilled, it must precede the act which reaches or falls short of itself. Every ethical rule must be a mental creation, an ideal formed by the creative power, and held before the soul as a guide and law.

160. " (d) The relation of the imagination to **religious faith** is interesting and important. The objects of our faith, by their very definition, have never been subjected to direct or intuitive knowledge. Neither sense-perception nor self-consciousness, have confronted them directly or brought report of them. And yet the imagination pictures these objects as real and most important." (*Human Intellect*, pp. 366–73, ed. 1869.)

161. " The fact is, that the educated Native mind requires hardening. That culture of the imagination, that tenderness for it, which may be necessary in the West, is out of place here ; for this is a society in which, for centuries upon centuries, the imagination has run riot, and much of the intellectual weakness and moral evil which afflict it to this moment, may be traced to imagination having so long usurped the place of reason. What the Native mind requires, is stricter criteria of truth ; and I look for the happiest moral and intellectual results from an increased devotion to those sciences by which no tests of truth are accepted, except the most rigid." (Maine, *Village Communities*, pp. 275–6, ed. 1876, *Address* to University of Calcutta, March, 1866.)

162. Concerning the subject of memory more should be said, because it is a faculty which performs so lasting and important a part in the existence of man. Various views of memory are expressed by writers who study Psychology ; the prevailing notion appears to be that it is a faculty which retains and reproduces in Consciousness the mental products that formerly were there. Another view of memory is this : Memory is that endowment of the Mind by which it is able to reproduce its previous modifications. "**Modification** is properly the bringing a thing into a certain mode of existence." (Hamilton, *Metaphysics*, Murray, p. 33.)

163. Regarding the nature of memory as a factor in the conception of teaching, the following opinions are appended :—" With regard to younger boys, he said, 'It is a great mistake to think that they should **understand** all they learn; for God has ordered that in youth the memory should act vigorously, independent of the understanding—whereas a man cannot usually recollect a thing unless he understands it.' " (*Life of Dr. Tho. Arnold*, pp. 133–4, ed. 1870, Boston.)

164. " Imagination, Memory, and Hope, are psychologically one and the same faculty. In

Imagination, the presence of the image is necessarily accompanied by a conviction of the **possible** existence of the corresponding object in an intuition. Memory is the presence of the same image, accompanied by a conviction of the fact, that the object represented has actually existed in a **past** intuition. Hope, in like manner, is the presence of the same image, together with an anticipation, more or less vivid, of the actual existence of the object in a **future** intuition.

Imagination, memory, and hope, are thus (whether formed by a reflective process or not) in their actual results partly **presentative,** partly **representative.** They are presentative of the image, which has its own distinct existence in consciousness, irrespectively of its relation to the object which it is supposed to represent. They are representative of the object, which that image resembles, and which, either in its present form or in its several elements, must have been presented in a past act of intuition. Thus there is combined an immediate consciousness of the present with a mediate consciousness of the past. An immediate or presentative consciousness of the past or the future, as such, is impossible. Imagination, being representative of an intuition, is, like intuition, only possible on the condition that its immediate object should be an **individual.** . . . On the other hand, my **notion of a man in general** can attain to universality only by surrendering resemblance ; it becomes the indifferent representative of all mankind, only because it has no special likeness to any one in particular. This distinction must be carefully borne in mind in comparing imagination with the cognate process of conception. . . . Memory is sometimes considered as the result of a process of thought." (Mansel, *Metaphysics*, pp. 128–9, ed. 1871.)

165. " ' The resuscitation of thoughts which in some shape or other have previously occupied the mind,' is nothing more or less than a prelude to what will unquestionably form a chief part of our intellectual experience of futurity; namely, the inalienable and irrepressible recollection of the deeds and feelings played forth while in the flesh, providing a beatitude or a misery forever. Ordinarily, this resuscitation is of such a medley and jumbled character, that not only is the general product unintelligible, but the particular incidents are themselves too fragmentary and dislocated to be recognised. But it is not always so. There must be few who have not experienced in their sleep, with what peculiar vividness, unknown to their waking hours, and with what minute exactitude of portraiture, events long past and long lost sight of, will not infrequently come back, shewing that there is something within which never forgets, and which only waits the negation of the external world, to leap up and certify its powers. . . . That which so vividly remembers is the Soul; and if in the sleep which refreshes our organic nature, it utters its recollections brokenly and indistinctly, it will abundantly compensate itself when the material vesture which clogs it shall be cast away. Much of the indistinctness of dreams probably arises from physical unhealthiness. If a sound body be one of the first requirements to a sound mind, in relation to its waking employments, no less must it be needful to the sanity and precision of its sleeping ones. Brilliant as are the powers and functions of the spiritual body, the performance of them, whether sleeping or waking, so long as it is investured with flesh and blood, is immensely, perhaps wholly, contingent on the health of the material body." (Grindon, *Life*, pp. 290–291, 3d ed., London.)

166. "Memory, a receptive, not a creative faculty, is subjected to physical conditions more than all other mental powers; for every kind of weakness (direct and indirect, as well bleeding as intoxication) impairs it, and dreams interrupt it; it is not subject to the will, is possessed by us in common with the beasts; and can be most effectually strengthened by the physician: a bitter stomachic will increase it more than a whole dictionary learnt by heart. For if it gained strength by what it receives, it would grow with increasing years, that is, in proportion to its wealth in hoarded names; but it can carry the heaviest burdens most easily in unpracticed youth, and it holds those so firmly that they appear above the gray hairs of age as the evergreens of childhood." (Richter, *Levana*, pp. 370–1.) . . .

"No one has a memory for everything, because no one feels an interest in everything. And the physical powers set bounds even to the strengthening influence of desire on the memory;

—think of that when with children,—for instance, if a Hebrew bill of exchange for a thousand pounds were promised, on condition of demanding its payment in the very words of the document, as once read aloud, everybody would try to remember them, but, unless he were a Jew, the words and the form would fail him. . . . I myself, however, would not choose any of these proposed methods of catching and yoking attention (artificial arts of memory), but would adopt that of steady industry. I do believe that a rod would help a creeping child to walk better than crutches under his arms, which at first carry, but afterwards are carried by him. Yea yea, nay nay, are the best double watchwords for children. . . . Fear cripples the memory, both by producing physical weakness and mental irritation; the frost of cold fear chains every living power which it approaches." (Richter, *Levana*, pp. 374–6.)

167. "It is incomprehensible to me, how people fancy they can teach children to read or write the letters easily by pointing out their resemblances, and laying before them at once **i y, c e**, or, in writing, **i r, h k**, &c. The very opposite plan ought to be pursued; **i** should be placed next **g**, **v** next **z**, **o** next **r**; the contrast, like light and shadow, make both prominent; until reflected lights and half shades can separate them anew from each other. The fast-rooted dissimilarities serve at last to hold fast the resemblance that exists among them. So the old plan of teaching spelling by lists of words alphabetically arranged is bad, on account of the difficulty of distinguishing similar sounds; whereas that of classing together derivations from the same Latin or Greek word assists the remembrance, because the radical word does not alter." (Richter, *Levana*, pp. 375-6.)

168. "There is not a man living, whom it would so little become to speak of memory as myself, for I have none at all; and do not think that the world has again another so treacherous as mine. My other faculties are all very ordinary and mean; but in this I think myself very singular, and to such a degree of excellence, that (besides the inconvenience I suffer by it, which merits something) I deserve methinks, to be famous for it, and to have more than a common reputation: though, in truth the necessary use of memory consider'd, Plato had reason when he call'd it a great and powerful Goddess. In my country, when they would decypher a man that has no sense, they say, such a one has no memory." (Montaigne, *Essays*, p. 33, third ed., London.)

169. "I am oblig'd to fortune for having so oft assaulted me with the same sort of weapons; she forms and fashions me by usance, hardens and habituates me so, that I can know within a little for how much I shall be quit. For want of natural memory, I make one of paper; and as any new symptom happens in my disease, I set it down; from whence it falls out, that being now almost past all sorts of examples, if any astonishment threaten me, tumbling over these little loose notes, as the Sibyls leaves, I never fail of finding matter of consolation from some favourable prognostick in my past experience." (*Ibid.*, p. 652.)

"Memory is a faculty of wonderful use, and without which the judgment can very hardly perform its office: for my part I have none at all: what any one will propose to me, he must do it by parcels, for to answer a speech consisting of several heads, I am not able. I could not receive a commission by word of mouth, without a note-book: and when I have a speech of consequence to make, if it be long, I am reduc'd to the miserable necessity of getting it word for word what I am to say by heart; I should otherwise have neither fashion nor assurance, being in fear that my memory would play me a slippery trick. But this way is no less difficult to me than the other. I must have three hours to learn three verses. And besides, in a work of a man's own, the liberty and authority of altering the order, of changing a word, incessantly varying the matter, makes it harder to stick in the memory of the author. The more I mistrust it, the worse it is, it serves me best by chance, I must negligently sollicit it, for I press it, 'tis astonish'd, and after it once begins to stagger, the more I sound it, the more it is perplex'd; it serves me at its own hour, not at mine. And the same defect I find in my memory, I find also in several other parts. I fly command, obligation and constraint. That which I can otherwise naturally and easily do: if I impose it upon myself by an express and strict injunction, I cannot do it. Being once in a place where it is look'd upon as the greatest discourtesie imaginable not to pledge those who drink to you, though I had there all liberty allowed me, I try'd to play the good fellow, out of respect to the ladies that were there, according to the custom of the country; but there was sport enough, for this threatning and preparation, that I was to force myself contrary to my custom and inclination, did so stop my throat, that I could not swallow one drop; and was depriv'd of drinking so much as to my meat. I found myself gorg'd, and my thirst quench'd by so much drink as my imagination had swallow'd. This effect is most manifest in such as have the most vehement and powerful imagination: but it is natural notwithstanding, and there is no one that does not in some measure find it. They offer'd an excellent archer, condemn'd to dye, to save his life, if he would shew some notable proof of his art, but he refused to try, fearing least the too great contention of his will would make him shoot wide, and that instead of saving his life, he should also lose the reputation he had got of being a good marks-man. A man that thinks of something else, will not fail to take over and over again the same number and measure of steps, even to an inch, in the place where he walks: but if he makes it his business to measure and count them, he will find that what he did by nature and accident, he cannot so exactly do by design. My library, which is of the best sort of country libraries, is situated in a corner of my house ; if anything comes into my head that I have a mind to look on or to write ; lest I should forget it in but going cross the court, I am fain to commit it to the memory of some other. If I venture in speaking to digress never so little from my subject, I am infallibly lost, which is the reason that I keep myself in discourse strictly close. I am forc'd to call the men that serve me either by the names of their offices, or their country ; for names are very hard for me to remember. I can tell indeed that there are three syllables, that it has a harsh sound, and that it begins or ends with such a letter, but that's all : and if I should live long, I do not think but I should forget my own name, as some others have done. Messela Corvinus, was two years without any trace of memory, which is also said of Georgius Trapezuntius. For my own interest, I often meditate what a kind of life theirs was, and if, without this faculty, I should have enough left to support me with any manner of ease, and prying narrowly into it, I fear that this privation, if absolute, destroys all the other functions of the soul.

Plenus rimarum sum, hac atque illac perfluo.
Ter. Eun. act. 1. fc. 2.
" I'm full of chinks, and leak out every way."

It has befall'n me more than once to forget the word I had three hours before given or receiv'd, and to forget where I had hid my purse, whatever Cicero is pleas'd to say : I help myself to lose what I have a particular care to lock safe up, 'Memoria certe non modo philosophiam, sed omnis vitæ usum, omnesque artes, una maxime continet.'—**Cicero**. 'The memory is the receptacle and sheath of all science;' and therefore mine being so treacherous, if I know little, I cannot much complain ; I know in general the names of the arts, and of what they treat, but nothing more. I turn over books, I do not study them ; what I retain I do not know to be anothers, and is only what my judgment has made its advantage of ; discourses and imaginations in which it has been instructed. The author, place, words, and other circumstances, I immediately forget, and am so excellent at forgetting, that I no less forget my own writings and compositions than the rest. I am very often quoted to myself, and am not aware of it ; and whoever should enquire of me where I had the verses and examples that I have here huddled together, would puzzle me to tell him, and yet I have not borrow'd them but from famous and known authors, not satisfying myself that they were rich ; if I moreover had them not from rich and honourable hands, where there is a concurrence of authority as well as reason. It is no great wonder if my book run the same fortune that other books do, and if my memory lose what I have writ as well as what I have read, and what I give, as well as what I receive. Beside the defect of memory, I have others which very much contribute to my ignorance ; I have a slow and heavy wit, the least cloud stops its progress, so that, for example, I never propos'd to it any never so easie a riddle that it could find out. There is not the least idle subtility, that will not gravel me. In games, where wit is requir'd, as chess, draughts, and the like, I understand no more but the motions of the men, without being capable of anything of design. I have a slow and perplex'd apprehension, but what it once apprehends, it apprehends well, for the time it retains it." (*Ibid.*, pp. 404–406.)

170. " But the objection which is commonest, and which most intimately concerns us here, is, that the knowledge communicated by the subordinate Colleges and verified by this University is worthless, shallow, and superficial. The course of the University of Calcutta is sometimes said to be in fault, and it is alleged, to use a term at once expressive and fashionable, that it encourages ' cramming.' Now there are some things in our Calcutta course, of which I do not altogether approve. But it was settled after long discussion, shortly after I became Vice-Chancellor, and it would be absurd to be perpetually changing that which of all things ought to be fixed and permanent, on account of small defects which are, after all, disputable. I wish, however, to say something of the whole class of objections implied in that one word ' cramming.' If there is anything in them, you know, I suppose, that they have a far wider application than their application to this University. They are constantly urged against the numerous competitive systems which are growing up in England, and in particular against the system under which the Civil Service of India, probably the most powerful official body in the world, is recruited, and will be recruited.

"The discredit which has been successfully attached to certain systems by this word is a good illustration of the power of what a famous writer called dyslogistic expression, or, to put it more simply, of giving a thing a bad name. And here I must say, that the habit Englishmen have of importing into India these common-place censorious opinions about systems and institutions, is a great misfortune for the Natives. Even in the mouths of Englishmen who invented them, they generally have very little meaning, for they are based on a mere fragment of truth ; when passed about among the multitude, they have still less ; and, at last, when exported hither, and repeated by the Natives in a foreign tongue, they have simply no meaning at all.

"As far as I understand the word, it means nothing more than the rapid communication of knowledge,—communication, that is to say, at a rate unknown till recently. Some people, I know, would add something to the definition, and would say that cramming is the rapid communication of superficial knowledge ; but the two statements will generally be found identical, and that they mean by superficial knowledge, knowledge which has been rapidly acquired. The true point, the point which really has to be proved is, whether knowledge rapidly acquired is more easily forgotten than knowledge which has been slowly gained. The point is one upon which, to some extent, everybody can judge for himself or herself. I do not assert the negative, but I am rather surprised at the readiness with which the affirmative has been usually taken for granted ; no doubt, if it be true, it is a curious psychological fact, but surely there are some reasons for questioning the reality. It might plausibly be argued that knowledge slowly acquired, has been acquired at the cost of frequent intervals of inattention and forgetfulness. Now everybody knows that inattention and forgetfulness tend to become habits of the mind, and it might be maintained that these habits would be likely to recur, in association with a subject of thought, even when that subject has for once been successfully mastered. On the other hand, it might be contended that knowledge rapidly acquired has been necessarily acquired under a certain strain and tension of the mental faculties, and that the effects of this tension are not likely to be so readily lost and dissipated.

"The simple truth is, that under the strong stimulus applied by that system of examinations by which the entrance to almost every English profession is now barred, there has sprung up an active demand for knowledge of a more varied description than was once coveted, and above all, for knowledge rapidly imbibed and mastered. To meet this demand, a class of teachers has sprung up who certainly produce remarkable results with remarkable rapidity. I hear it said, that they are men of a lower order of mind and accomplishment than the teachers who follow the old methods. It may be so; but that only renders the probability greater, that some new power has been brought into play." (Maine, *Village Communities and Miscellanies*, pp. 282–5, ed. 1876, *Address* to Univ. of Calcutta, March, 1866.)

171. " I have had some opportunity myself of making a comparison, and my judgment is decidedly in favour of the present system (of competitive examinations). I am aware that many persons think the matter is settled by asserting that all we do by our examination system, is to encourage **cram**; but unfortunately no definition is given of what is reprobated by this much employed word. It seems to me that at least one very prominent tendency of the competitive system is extremely valuable; namely, that of securing from the teacher attention to the progress of his pupils individually." (Todhunter, *Conflict of Studies*, ed. 1873, pp. 63–4.)

172. " Fortunately, too, for the opponents of examination, an admirable 'cry' has been found. Examination, they say, leads to 'cram,' and 'cram' is the destruction of true study. People who know nothing else about examination know well enough that it is 'cram.' The word has all the attributes of a perfect **question-begging epithet**. It is short, emphatic, and happily derived from a disagreeable physical metaphor. Accordingly, there is not a respectable gentleman distributing prizes to a body of scholars at the end of the session, and at a loss for something to say, who does not think of this word ' cram,' and proceed to expatiate on the evils of the examination-system.

"I intend in this article to take up the less popular view of the subject and say what I can in favour of examinations. I wish to analyse the meaning of the word 'cram,' and decide, if possible, whether it is the baneful thing that so many people say. There is no difficulty in seeing at once that 'cram' means two different things, which I call 'good cram' and 'bad cram.' A candidate, preparing for an important competitive examination, may put himself under a tutor well-skilled in preparing for that examination. This tutor looks for success by carefully directing the candidate's studies into the most 'paying' lines, and restricting them rigorously to those lines. The training given may be of an arduous, thorough character, so that the faculties of the pupil are stretched and exercised to their utmost in those lines. This would be called 'cram' because it involves exclusive devotion to the answering of certain examination-papers. I call it 'good cram.'

"'Bad cram,' on the other hand, consists in temporarily impressing upon the candidate's mind a collection of facts, dates, or formulæ, held in a wholly undigested state and ready to be disgorged in the examination-room by an act of mere memory. A candidate, unable to apprehend the bearing of Euclid's reasoning in the first book of his **Elements**, may learn the propositions off by heart, diagrams, letters and all, like a Sunday scholar learning the collects and gospels. Dates, rules of grammar, and the like, may be 'crammed' by mnemonic lines, or by one of those wretched systems of artificial memory, teachers of which are always going about. In such ways it is, I believe, possible to give answers which simulate knowledge, and no more prove true knowledge, than the chattering of a parrot proves intellect.

"I am far from denying the existence of 'bad cram' of this character, but I hold that it can never be advantageously resorted to by those who are capable of 'good cram.' To learn a proposition of Euclid by heart is far more laborious than for a student of moderate capacity to master the nature of the reasoning. It is obvious that all advantages, even in an examinational point of view, are on the side of real knowledge. The slightest lapse of memory in the bad 'crammer,' for instance the putting of wrong letters in the diagram, will disclose the simulated character of his work, and the least change in the conditions of the proposition set will frustrate his mnemonic devices altogether. If papers be set which really can be answered by mere memory, the badness is in the examiners.

"Thorough blockheads may be driven to the worst kind of 'cram,' simply because they can do nothing better. Nor do the blockheads suffer harm; to exercise the memory is better than to leave the brain wholly at rest. Some qualities of endurance and resolution must be called into existence, before a youth can go through the dreary work of learning off by heart things of which he has no comprehension. Nor with examiners of the least intelligence is there any reason to fear that the best directed 'bad cram' will enable a really stupid candidate to carry off honours and appointments due to others. No examination-papers even for junior candidates should consist entirely of 'book-work,' such as to be answered by the simple reproduction of the words in a text-book. In every properly conducted examination, questions are, as a matter of course, set to test the candidate's power of applying his knowledge to cases more or less different from those described in the books. Moreover good examiners always judge answers by their general style as well as by their contents. It is really impossible that a stupid slovenly candidate can by any art of 'cramming' be enabled to produce the neat, brief, pertinent essay, a page or two long, which wins marks from the admiring examiners.

"If we may judge from experience, too, 'bad cram' does not pay from the tutor's point of view. That this is so we may learn from the fact that slow ignorant pupils are ruthlessly rejected by the great 'coaches.' Those who have their reputation and their living to make by the success of their candidates cannot afford to waste their labor upon bad material. Thus it is not the stupid who go to the 'cramming' tutors to be forced over the heads of the clever, but it is the clever ones who go to secure the highest places. Long before the critical days of the official examination, the experienced 'coach' selected his men almost as carefully as if he were making up the University boat. There is hardly a University or a College in the kingdom which imposes any selective process of the sort. An entrance or matriculation examination, if it exists at all, is little better than a sham. All comers are gladly received to give more fees and the appearance of prosperity. Thus it too often happens that the bulk of a college class consists of untutored youths through whose ears the learned instructions of the professor pass, harmlessly it may be, but uselessly. Parents and the public have little idea how close a resemblance there is between teaching and writing on the sands of the sea, unless either there is a distinct capacity for learning on the part of the pupil, or some system of examination and reward to force the pupil to apply.

"For these and other reasons which might be urged, I do not consider it worth while to consider 'bad cram' any further. I pass on to inquire whether 'good cram' is an objectionable form of education. The good 'cramming' tutor or lecturer is one whose object is to enable his pupils to take a high place in the list. With this object he carefully ascertains the scope of the examination, scrutinises past papers, and estimates in every possible way the probable character of future papers. He then trains his pupils in each branch of study with an intensity proportioned to the probability that questions will be asked in that branch. It is too much to assume that this training will be superficial. On the contrary, though narrow it will probably be intense and deep. It will usually consist to a considerable extent in preliminary examinations intended both to test and train the pupil in the art of writing answers. The great 'coaches' at Cambridge in former days might be said to proceed by a constant system of examination, oral instruction or simple reading being subordinate to the solving of innumerable problems. The main question which I have to discuss, then, resolves itself into this:—whether intense training directed to the passing of certain defined examinations constitutes real education. The popular opponents of 'cram' imply that it does not; I maintain that it does.

"It happened that, just as I was about to write this article, the Home Secretary presided at the annual prize-distribution in the Liverpool College, on the 22d December, 1876, and took occasion to make the usual remarks about 'cram.' He expressed with admirable clearness the prevailing complaints against examinations, and I shall therefore take the liberty of making his speech in some degree my text. 'Examination is not education,' he said. 'You require a great deal more than that. As well as being examined, you must be taught. . . . In the great scramble for life, there is a notion at the present moment of getting hold of as much general superficial knowledge as you can. That to my mind is a fatal mistake. On the other hand, there is a great notion that if you can get through your examination and ' cram up ' a subject very well, you are being educated. That, too, is a most fatal mistake. There is nothing which would delight me so much, if I were an examiner, as to baffle all the ' cramming ' teachers whose pupils came before me ' (laughter).

" Let us consider what Mr. Cross really means. Examination, he says, is not education ; we require a great deal more ; we must be taught as well as be examined. With equal meaning I might say, ' Beef is not dinner ; we want a great deal more ; we must have potatoes, bread, pudding, and the like.' Nevertheless beef is a principal part of dinner. Nobody, I should think, ever asserted or imagined that examination alone was education, but I nevertheless hold that it is one of the chief elements of an effective education. As Mr. Cross himself said in an earlier part of his speech, ' the examination is a touchstone and test which shows the broad distinction between good and bad. . . . You may manage to scramble through your lessons in the ' half,' but I will defy you to get through your examinations if you do not know the subjects.'

" Another remark of Mr. Cross leads me to the main point of the subject. He said—' It is quite necessary in the matter of teaching that whatever is taught must be taught well, and nothing that is taught well can be taught in a hurry. It must be taught not simply for the examination, but it must sink into your minds, and stay there for life.' Both in this and his other remarks Mr. Cross commits himself to the popular but wholly erroneous notion that what boys learn at school and college should be useful knowledge indelibly impressed upon the mind, so as to stay there all their lives, and be ready at their fingers' ends. The real point of the objections to examination commonly is, that the candidate learns things for the examination only, which, when it is safely passed, he forgets again as speedily as possible. Mr. Cross would teach so deliberately and thoroughly that the very facts taught could not be forgotten, but must ever after crop up in the mind whatever we are doing. I hold that remarks such as these proceed from a wholly false view of the nature and purposes of education. It is implied that the mind in early life is to be stored with the identical facts, and bits of knowledge which are to be used in after life. It is, in fact, Mr. Cross and those who think with him, who advocate a kind of 'cram,' enduring it is true, but still 'bad cram.' The true view of education, on the contrary, is to regard it as a course of training. The youth in a gymnasium practises upon the horizontal bar, in order to develop his muscular powers generally ; he does not intend to go on posturing upon horizontal bars all through life. School is a place where the mental fibres are to be exercised, trained, expanded, developed, and strengthened, not 'crammed' or loaded with 'useful knowledge.'

"'The whole of a youth's subsequent career is one long course of technical 'cramming' in which any quantity of useful facts are supplied to him

nolens volens. The merchant gets his technical knowledge at the clerk's desk, the barrister in the conveyancer's offices or the law courts, the engineer in the workshop and the field. It is the very purpose of a **liberal education,** as it is correctly called, to develop and train the plastic fibres of the youthful brain, so as to prevent them taking too early a definite 'set,' which will afterwards narrow and restrict the range of acquisition and judgment. I will even go so far as to say that it is hardly desirable for the actual things taught at school to stay in the mind for life. The source of error is the failure to distinguish between the **form** and the **matter** of knowledge, between the facts themselves and the manner in which the mental powers deal with facts.

" It is wonderful that Mr. Cross and those who moralise in his strain do not perceive that the actual facts which a man deals with in life are infinite in number, and cannot be remembered in a finite brain. The psychologists, too, seem to me to be at fault in this matter, for they have not sufficiently drawn attention to the varying degrees of duration required in a well organised memory. We commonly use the word Memory so as to cover the faculties of Retention, Reproduction and Representation, as described by Hamilton, and very little consideration will show that in different cases we need the powers of retention, of suggestion and of imagination in very different degrees. In some cases we require to remember a thing only a few moments, or a few minutes; in other cases a few hours or days; in yet other cases a few weeks or months: it is an infinitesimally small part of all our mental impressions which can be profitably remembered for years. Memory may be too retentive, and facility of forgetting and of driving out one train of ideas by a new train is almost as essential to a well-trained intellect as facility of retention.

"Take the case of a barrister in full practice, who deals with several cases in a day. His business is to acquire as rapidly as possible the facts of the case immediately before him. With the powers of representation of a well-trained mind, he holds these facts steadily before him, comparing them with each other, discovering their relations, applying to them the principles and rules of law more deeply graven on his memory, or bringing them into connection with a few of the more prominent facts of previous cases which he happens to remember. For the details of laws and precedents he trusts to his text writers, the statute book, and his law library. Even before the case is finished his mind has probably sifted out the facts and rejected the unimportant ones by the law of obliviscence. One case done with, he takes up a wholly new series of facts, and so from day to day, and from month to month, the matter before him is constantly changing. The same remarks are even more true of a busy and able administrator like Mr. Cross. The points which come before him are infinite in variety. The facts of each case are rapidly brought to his notice by subordinates, by correspondence, by debates in the House, by deputations and interviews, or by newspaper reports. Applying well-trained powers of judgment to the matter in hand, he makes a rapid decision and passes to the next piece of business. It would be fatal to Mr. Cross if he were to allow things to sink deep into his mind and stay there. There would be no difficulty in showing that in like manner, but in varying degrees, the engineer, the physician, the merchant, even the tradesman or the intelligent artisan, deal every day with various combinations of facts which cannot all be stored up in the cerebral framework, and certainly need not be so.

"The bearing of these considerations upon the subject of examinations ought to be very evident. For what is 'cram' but the rapid acquisition of a series of facts, the vigorous getting up of a case, in order to exhibit well-trained powers of comprehension, of judgment, before an examiner? The practised barrister 'crams' up his 'brief' (so called because, as some suppose, made **brief** for the purpose) and stands an examination in it before a judge and jury. The candidate is not so hurried; he spends months or it may be two or three years in getting up his differential calculus or his inorganic chemistry. It is quite likely that when the ordeal is passed, and the favourable verdict delivered, he will dismiss the equations and the salts and compounds from his mind as rapidly as possible; but it does not follow that the useful effect of his training vanishes at the same time. If so, it follows that almost all the most able and successful men of the present day threw away their pains at school and college. I suppose that no one ever heard of a differential equation solving a nice point of law, nor is it common to hear Sophocles and Tacitus quoted by a leading counsel. Yet it can hardly be denied that our greatest barristers and judges were trained in the mathematical sciences, or if not, that their teachers thought the classics a better training ground. If things taught at school and college are to stay in the mind to serve us in the business of life, then almost all the higher education yet given in this kingdom has missed its mark. I come to the conclusion, then, that well-ordered education is a severe system of well-sustained 'cram.' . . . We cannot consider it the work of teachers to make philosophers and scholars and geniuses of various sorts : these, like poets, are born not made. Nor, as I have shown, is it the business of the educator to impress indelibly upon the mind the useful knowledge which is to guide the pupil through life. This would be ' cram ' indeed. It is the purpose of education so to exercise the faculties of mind that the infinitely various experience of after-life may be observed and reasoned upon to the best effect. What is popularly condemned as ' cram ' is often the best devised and best conducted system of training towards this all-important end." (Jevons, '*Cram*,' art. in *Mind*, pp. 193–207, No. VI., April, 1877.)

173. " The act of knowing is that activity of the mind by means of which it consciously reproduces in itself what actually exists. The act of knowing is partly immediate or outer and inner perception, partly mediate or thinking. The regulative laws (injunctions, prescriptions) are those universal conditions to which the activity of knowledge must conform in order to attain to the end and aim of knowledge." (Ueberweg, *Hist. Log. Doct.*, p. 1, ed. 1871.)

174. "**Knowledge,** in the wider sense in which we here use the word, comprehends both **cognition,** which rests on perception (and on the evidence transmitting perceptions of which we are ignorant), and also **knowledge in the stricter sense**, which is attained by thinking.

175. "The act of knowing, in so far as it is the copying in the human consciousness of the essence of the thing, is an **after-**thinking of **the** thoughts which the divine creative thinking has built into things. In **action** the preceding thought determines what actually exists, but in **knowing** the actual existence, in itself conformable to reason, determines the human thought." (*Ibid.*, p. 2.)

176. "1. The objective existence to be known consists not merely of natural objects, but also (as in history, etc.) of mental contents. 2. The mirroring in consciousness, although reproduction, cannot be accomplished without a peculiar activity of the mind. 3. The whole activity of the mind is not exhausted in knowledge. There is besides the creative power of the phantasy, reforming and refining what is given in the conception, and ethical action." (*Ibid.*, pp. 2–3.)

177. "Knowledge of fact is knowledge by onlook; knowledge inferred is knowledge of one thing through means of another; knowledge of first principles is knowledge by insight into truth higher than fact." (Calderwood, *Hand Book, Moral Phil.*, p. 39, ed. 1879.)

178. In giving the difference between Thought, properly so called, and other phenomena of the mind, I cannot do better than to quote the following : " Every state of consciousness necessarily implies two elements at least : a conscious subject, and an object of which he is conscious. In every exercise, for example, of the senses, we may distinguish the object seen, heard, smelt, touched, tasted, from the subject seeing, hearing, smelling, touching, tasting. In every emotion of pleasure or of pain, there is a certain affection, agreeable or disagreeable, existing within me, and of this affection I am conscious. In every act of volition, there takes place a certain exercise of my will, and I am conscious that it takes place. . . . But to constitute an act of **Thought,** more is required than the immediate relation of subject to object in consciousness. Every one of the above states might exist in a mind totally incapable of thought. Let us suppose, for example, a being, in whose mind every successive state of consciousness was forgotten as soon as it had taken place. Every individual object might be presented to him precisely as it is to us. Animals, men, trees, and stones, might be successively placed before his eyes; pleasure, and pain, and anger, and fear, might alternate within him ; but, as each departed, he would retain no knowledge that it had ever existed, and consequently no power of comparison with similar or dissimilar objects of an earlier or later consciousness. He would have no knowledge of such objects **as referred to separate notions**; he could not say, this which I see is a man, or a horse ; this which I feel is fear, or anger. He would be deficient in the distinctive feature of Thought, the concept or general notion resulting from the comparison of objects. Hence arises the important distinction between **Intuitions**, in which the object is immediately related to the conscious mind, and **Thoughts**, in which the object is mediately related through a concept gained by comparison. . . . By Intuition is meant to include all the products of the perceptive (external and internal) and imaginative faculties ; every act of consciousness, in short, of which the immediate object is an **individual**, thing, act, or state of mind, presented under the condition of distinct existence in space or time. It is necessary to distinguish between the act of thought and its product—the former is designated by the term **conception**, the product by **concept**. . . . Intuition contains two elements only, the subject and the object standing in present relation to each other. Thought contains three elements, the thinking subject, the object about which he thinks, and the concept mediating between the two. Thus even the exercise of the senses upon present objects, in the manner in which it is ordinarily performed by a man of mature faculties, does not consist of mere intuition, but is accompanied by an act of thought. In mere intuition, all that is simultaneously presented to the sense appears as one whole ; but mere intuition does not distinguish its several parts from each other under this or that notion. I may see at once, in a single panorama, a ship upon the sea, an island lying behind it, and the sky above it. To mere intuition this is presented only in confusion, as a single object. To distinguish its constituent portions, as sea and land, ship and sky, requires a comparison and classification of them relatively to so many separate concepts existing in the mind ; and such classification is an act of Thought.

In every act of Consciousness the ultimate object is an **individual.** But in intuition this object is **presented** to the mind directly, and does not imply the existence, past or present, of anything but itself and the mind to which it is presented. In thought, on the other hand, the individual is **represented** by means of a concept, which contains certain attributes applicable to other individuals of the same kind. This implies that there have been presented to the mind prior objects of intuition, originating the concept or general notion to which subsequent objects are referred. Hence arises another important distinction. All intuition is direct and presentative ; all thought is indirect and representative. . . . By representation are here included the concept, which is representative of many individuals, and the image, which is representative of one. . . . Perception is employed to denote all those states of Consciousness which are presentative only, not representative. It will thus include all intuitions except those of Imagination. . . . The office of the faculty of Imagination, whose office is the production of images representative of the several phenomena of Perception, internal as well as external. . . . Imagination, regarded as a product, may be defined, the consciousness of an image in the mind resembling and representing an object of intuition. It is thus at the same time **presentative** and **representative.** It is presentative of the image which has its own distinct existence in consciousness, irrespective of its relation to the object which it is supposed to represent. It is representative of the object which that image resembles ; and such resemblance is only possible on the condition that the image be, like the object, **individual.** . . . The distinguishing feature of a concept is, **that it cannot in itself be depicted to sense or imagination.** It is not the sensible image of one object, but an intelligible relation between many. A second important characteristic of all concepts is, that **they require to be fixed in a representative sign,** which is language." (Mansel, *Prolegomena Logica,* pp. 20–6, ed. 1860.)

179. "In a psychological point of view, to enumerate separate mental faculties and operations, as giving rise to the various products of thought, is, to say the least, to encumber the science with unnecessary and perplexing distinctions. It will be sufficient to refer them to the single faculty of **thought** or **reflection**, the operation of which is, in all cases, **comparison**. The unit of thought is always a judgment, based on a comparison of objects ; and the several operations of thought are, in ultimate analysis, nothing more than judgments derived from different data. In order to exhibit this in special instances, it will be convenient to adopt provisionally the logical classification, and to examine the phenomena of thought under the several heads of Conception, Judgment, and Reasoning." (Mansel, *Metaphysics*, pp. 176-7, ed. 1871, New York.)

180. " In a psychological point of view, to enumerate separate mental faculties, as giving rise to the various products of thought, is, to say the least, to encumber the science with unnecessary and perplexing distinctions. It will be sufficient to refer them to the single faculty of **Thought**, the operation of which is in all cases Comparison (see Hamilton, *Lect. on Metaphysics, Lect. xxxiv.*). But the faculty of **Thought**, though uniform in its own nature and in the manner of its operation, may yet give rise to different products, according to the diversity of the materials upon which it operates ; and this difference forms the basis of the classification usually adopted in Logic. Extending the terms Apprehension and Judgment beyond the region of Thought proper (into Psychology), it may be laid down, as a general canon of Psy-

chology, that the unit of consciousness is a **judgment**; in other words, that every act of consciousness, intuitive or discursive, is comprised in a conviction of the presence of its object, either internally in the mind or externally in space. The result of every such act must thus be generally stated in the proposition, "This is here." Consequently, at least with reference to the primary and spontaneous, as distinguished from the secondary and reflex acts of consciousness, it is more correct to describe Apprehension as the analysis of Judgments, than Judgment as the synthesis of Apprehensions. In a psychological point of view, therefore, it is incorrect to describe Simple Apprehension as the first operation of the mind. In one sense, indeed, the relation of prior and posterior is altogether out of place : Chronologically, inasmuch as every Apprehension is simultaneous with a Judgment, and every Judgment with an Apprehension ; and logically, inasmuch as Judgment cannot exist without Apprehension, nor Apprehension without Judgment. In another sense, however, we may properly say that Judgment is prior to Apprehension ; meaning that the subject and the object are first given in their mutual relation to each other, before either of them can itself become a separate object of attention. But when a corresponding division is adopted of the operation of Thought, properly so called, the same order of priority cannot be observed. Every operation of thought is a judgment, in the psychological

sense of the term; but the psychological judgment must not be confounded with the logical. The former is the judgment of a relation between the conscious subject and the immediate object of consciousness; the latter is the judgment of a relation which two objects of thought bear to each other. The former cannot be distinguished as true or false, inasmuch as the object is thereby only judged to be present at the moment when we are conscious of it as affecting us in a certain manner; and this consciousness is necessarily true. The latter is true or false according as the relations thought as existing between certain concepts are actually found in the objects represented by those concepts or not. The logical judgment necessarily contains two concepts (products of thought), and hence must be regarded as logically and chronologically posterior to the conception (act of thought), which requires one only. The psychological judgment is coeval with the first act of consciousness, and is implied in every mental process, whether of intuition or of thought. It cannot, therefore, be called prior or posterior to any other mental operation, for there is no mental operation in which it does not take place; but the judgments of intuition are logically and chronologically prior to the judgments of thought. Conception is a psychological judgment, but not a logical one, and is properly ranked as the first operation of Thought, inasmuch as it is the simplest. . . .
 . . Conceiving has been already explained as the individualizing of certain attributes compre-

hended in a general notion and expressed in a general term ; the representation, namely, of such attributes as coëxisting in a possible object of intuition. Language is, . . . in its earliest operations, a sign, not of concepts, but of intuitions. Its earliest terms are employed as the proper names of individual objects. Conception does not take place till after we have learned to give the same name to various individuals presented to us with certain differences of attributes, and hence we associate it with a portion only, not with the whole, of what is presented in each. This may be distinguished as **Abstraction**, a spontaneous, though not always a voluntary act, the concentration of the mind on certain portions only of a given object in relation to its name. This must not be treated . . as a conscious process of thought, being only a preliminary condition to thinking, taking place in the majority of cases unconsciously, during the gradual acquisition of speech. Our names thus gradually acquire a signification, being transformed from proper names to appellatives. Finally, the act of conception consists in contemplating the attributes thus combined in the signification of a name as coëxisting, along with individual features, in a possible object of intuition, and hence, apart from the individual features, as indifferently representing all such objects. This representative collection of attributes, combined by means of a sign, is a **Concept**. . . . As in Conception a single general notion is considered in its relation to a possible object of intuition, so in Judgment two such notions are considered as related to a common object. When I assert that A is B, I do not mean that the attributes constituting the concept A are identical with those constituting the concept B,—for this is only true in identical judgments,—but that the object in which the one set of attributes is found is the same as that in which the other set is found. . . . The common language and common thought of mankind assume, whether they explain it or not, that a certain smell and color and form, which are distinct attributes, are in some way related, as parts or qualities, to some one thing which we call a rose ; and that, when I assert that the rose is fragrant, I imply that the thing which affects in a certain way my power of sight is in some manner identical (Identity) with that which affects in a certain way my power of smell. . . . Reasoning is the most complex of the three operations, as in it two concepts are determined to be in a certain manner related to each other, through the medium of their mutual relations to a third concept. This operation is therefore treated last in order. The several relations asserted in the premises and deduced in the conclusion, are of the same nature as those implied in Judgment. . . . It will be sufficient to attempt . . a definition of the products of the several acts of Thought, the Concept, the Judgment, and the Syllogism, the legitimate objects of Formal Logic. 1. A Concept is a collection of attributes, united by a sign, and representing a possible object of intuition. 2. A Judgment is a combination of two concepts, related to one or more Common objects of possible intuition. 3. A Syllogism is a combination of two judgments, necessitating a third judgment as the consequence of their mutual relation." (Mansel, *Prolegomena Logica*, pp. 62-9, ed. 1860.)

181. "The mental powers employed in the acquisition of knowledge are probably three in number. They are substantially as Professor Bain has stated them (*Senses and Intellect*, 2d ed., pp. 5, 325, etc.):—1. The Power of Discrimination; 2. The Power of Detecting Identity; 3. The Power of Retention. We exert the first power in every act of perception. Hardly can we have a sensation or feeling unless we discriminate it from something else which preceded. Consciousness would almost seem to consist in the break between one state of mind and the next, just as an induced current of electricity arises from the beginning or the ending of the primary current. We are always engaged in discrimination; and the rudiment of thought which exists in the lower animals probably consists in their power of feeling difference and being agitated by it. Yet had we the power of discrimination only, Science could not be created. To know that one feeling differs from another gives purely negative information. It cannot teach us what will happen. In such a state of intellect each sensation would stand out distinct from every other; there would be no tie, no bridge of affinity between them. We want a unifying power by which the present and the future may be linked to the past ; and this seems to be accomplished by a different power of mind. Lord Bacon has pointed out that different men possess in very different degrees the powers of discrimination and identification. It may be said indeed that discrimination necessarily implies the action of the opposite process of identification ; and so it doubtless does in negative points. But there is a rare property of mind which consists in penetrating the disguise of variety and seizing the common elements of sameness ; and it is this property which furnishes the true measure of intellect. The name of ' intellect ' expresses the interlacing of the general and the single, which is the peculiar province of mind. (Max Müller, *Lect. Sci. Lang.*, 2d series, Vol. II., p. 63). . . . Plato said of this unifying power, that if he met the man who could detect **the one in the many,** he would follow him as a god." (Jevons, *The Princ. of Science,* pp. 4-5, ed. 1877.)

" LAWS OF IDENTITY AND DIFFERENCE.

182. " At the base of all thought and science must lie the laws which express the very nature and conditions of the discriminating and identifying powers of mind. These are the so-called Fundamental Laws of Thought, usually stated as follows :—

1. The Law of Identity. **Whatever is, is.**
2. The Law of Contradiction. **A thing cannot both be and not be.**

3. The Law of Duality. **A thing must either be or not be.**

"The first of these statements may perhaps be regarded as a description of identity itself, if so fundamental a notion can admit of description. A thing at any moment is perfectly identical with itself, and, if any person were unaware of the meaning of the word 'identity,' we could not better describe it than by such an example.

"The second law points out that contradictory attributes can never be joined together. The same object may vary in its different parts; here it may be black, and there white; at one time it may be hard and at another time soft; but at the same time and place an attribute cannot be both present and absent. Aristotle truly described this law as the first of all axioms—one of which we need not seek for any demonstration. All truths cannot be proved, otherwise there would be an endless chain of demonstration; and it is in self-evident truths like this that we find the simplest foundations.

"The third of these laws completes the other two. It asserts that at every step there are two possible alternatives—presence or absence, affirmation or negation. Hence I propose to name this law the Law of Duality, for it gives to all the formulæ of reasoning a dual character. It asserts also that between presence and absence, existence and non-existence, affirmation and negation, there is no third alternative. As Aristotle said, there can be no mean between opposite assertions : we must either affirm or deny." (*Ibid.*, *pp.* 5–6.)

183. " The primitive and essential gradation of thought we have indicated to be the Judgment. In accordance with what has been said, a Judgment may be defined to be **a recognition of the identity or non-identity between any two objects presented to the Faculty of Thought.** As expressed in words, a Judgment is called a **Proposition**, or in grammatical nomenclature, a **Sentence**.

" Besides the Judgment, there are two other products of thought, both derivatives from the Judgment. The one is the **Concept,** which is derived from several Judgments by an act of **Conceiving**—taking together, in other words, by an act of synthesis. The other is the **Reasoning,** which is derived from one or more Judgments by an act of analysis or separation. As all thought is essentially a movement in Quantity, and as variations in Quantity can be affected only in the one or the other of these two directions, synthesis and analysis, the Concept and the Reasoning are the only conceivable derivatives from a Judgment, except such as consist only in variations of form, that do not affect the identity of the thought.

" In explication of this definition of a Judgment, it will be necessary simply to recall what has been already said in the exposition of the general nature of thought. As we have seen, a judgment necessarily supposes two objects ;

and its essential characteristic, as an act of Intelligence, consists in this : that it is a cognition of this particular relation of identity or non-identity between the two objects. These two objects of a judgment are given to it by some other faculty of the Intelligence, as of Perception, Intuition; Memory, or by the Discursive Faculty itself, in some previous exercise. It may be some object of Perception, as **Bucephalus.** As thus given by the Perceptive Faculty, the cognition is of an object by itself, without relation either to other objects or to the parts of the object itself. Color is not in the perception itself distinguished from figure ; neither color nor figure from the position or the time in which it is perceived ; and neither of these from the useful qualities of the object. All the perceptible qualities are given together without distinction in the presentation itself of the object. But when thus given, the mind at once, and by a kind of necessity of its being as essentially active and reflective, exerts its activity on it, first, by apprehending it as a part of a multiplicity of objects around, to each of which it stands in relation, and also, as a whole, containing parts in itself. This is the primitive and conditional gradation in all thought—the apprehension of an object as a part or as a whole—in other words, in the relation of Quantity. Simultaneously with this, it apprehends some other object of thought given to it by Perception, or by some other Faculty of the Intelligence, or in some previous exercise of the

Judgment, and thus comes to view the two objects thus given in relation to each other, as the same or not the same. Its act then becomes complete ; and a perfected product of thought, a Judgment, is the result. Thus the second object may be given in the Perception itself, as **black,** or **four-footed,** and the Judgment recognizes this color or this form as belonging to Bucephalus—that is, as identical with one of the parts or characters that make up the whole perception. Or the second object may be given by the Regulative Faculty, or Faculty of Intuition, as of Being, of Space, of Time, or other idea of the proper Reason ; and then the Judgment identifies Bucephalus with Existence, with some part of Space, of Time ; or in other words, affirms Bucephalus **to be, to be in such a place, at such a time,** and the like. The second object of thought may, in like manner, be given to the Judging Faculty by the Memory. We may identify Bucephalus as now perceived with the Bucephalus perceived yesterday ; with the black color, the four-footed figure, before perceived in some other object.

" The essential nature of a Judgment, thus, is seen to be an identification of one object with another, either totally or partially—in some one or in all respects. It is accordingly a **relative** cognition ; and in the relation which it involves are necessarily contained three elements : 1. The object of thought identified with some other. 2. The object with which it is identified, either in whole or in part. And, 3. The mental act which identifies. The first two constitute **the matter of thought**, the **datum**; the last is the Thought itself, the identifying cognition—the Judgment.

"To the several parts, or to different aspects of the complex procedure in all Thought as thus exemplified in one of its gradations—the Judgment—Psychology has assigned distinctive names, which it may not be inexpedient here to recall. Inasmuch as the original **datum** or object of thought is given in an indefinite vagueness as one and undivided, and as, in order to be cognized in thought, it must be viewed in relation to some part, it becomes necessary to loosen up, to analyze or separate it as a whole into its parts. This part of the process is called **Analysis**.

"The next step is to select the part out of the whole for separate apprehension, and to draw it away, as it were, to abstract it from the other parts. This part of the movement in Thought is called **Abstraction**. The term, however, it is proper to add, is applied in various ways by different writers or on different occasions, but with the same result. Thus it may be applied to the mind itself; so that in Abstraction the mind, when confining its view to certain parts of an object, is regarded as being abstracted or drawn away from the parts that are to be excluded from view; and this, it may be observed, is in strictness the most correct view. But in a looser sense the term may be applied to the part itself that is selected, and then such part is regarded as being abstracted from the other parts. Or, in the third place, it may be applied to those other excluded parts themselves, and then they are regarded as being abstracted or drawn away either from the other parts or from the mind's consideration. The result is the same in any view, that one part is separated from the other parts for exclusive consideration, and it is therefore a matter of indifference, so far as the result is concerned, which of these different views is entertained.

" When thus one part is separated from the rest for exclusive consideration by the mind, the act of mind in which it concentrates its notice upon it is called **Attention.**

" In the next place, the two objects are brought up and viewed face to face with each other in order that their identity or non-identity may be apprehended. This part of the process is called **Comparison.**

" Finally, the last part of the complex process, in which the thought is perfected by bringing together the two objects attended to into one relative cognition, is called an act of **Synthesis.**

" All Thought thus begins with an Analysis, it proceeds by Abstraction, Attention, and Comparison, it ends with a Synthesis. And this is to be understood in a sense more or less full and complete, in modes varying with the nature of the particular gradation of all the acts of thought, whether in judging, conceiving, or reasoning. The two essential elements of thought are analysis and synthesis. With one it necessarily begins, with the other it necessarily ends. For its very function is to lead to truth, to a unity in the intelligence, which supposes an undistinguished manifold as its condition, and a gathering into a unity as its result. The other parts of the complex process, abstraction, attention, and comparison, are the means by which the mind passes from the multiform given in the analysis to the unity in the synthesis. . . .

"Of the two objects of thought identified in a Judgment, one is necessarily viewed as the primitive which is to be identified with the other, or is determined by it. This so viewed primitive or determined object is called the **Subject**; which may be defined to be that of which we judge. The other, viewed as the determining element, is called the **Predicate**, which may be defined to be that which is judged of the subject. The Subject and the Predicate make up the matter of thought or the **datum** to thought. They are called the **Terms** of a Proposition (termini). The act of thought itself which recognizes the identity between the two terms is called the **Copula**, which may be defined to be the identification of two objects of thought. It was called by Aristotle, in reference to the two terms, an **Interval**." (Day, *Ele. of Logic*, pp. 31–5, ed. 1868.)

184. "The Second gradation of Thought is the **Concept**. It is derived from the primitive product, the Judgment, by an act of synthesis or composition. It accordingly presupposes two or more Judgments, and, if a valid product of

Thought, can always be resolved back into them. It can, in fact, be verified only by being thus referred back to the Judgments from which it is derived. It is formed either by the synthesis of the Subjects of two or more Judgments, or by a synthesis of their Predicates—an alternative which gives rise to the two fundamental classes of Concepts. It may conduce to clearness to exemplify the process of forming the Concept in these two ways separately.

"First, then, if we synthesize the subjects, the procedure will be as follows: The Judgments, out of which the Concept is to be formed, we will assume to be—**Socrates is rational; Cicero is rational; James is rational.** By uniting the subjects, we have **Socrates** and **Cicero** and **James**, and marking the union by a single term which shall embrace them all in one, we will say, **man**, we have the union signalized in language. This union of the differing subjects of several propositions having a common predicate is called a **Concept**; in this case a Concept in Extensive Quantity. The formula for the formation of all Concepts of this class is, accordingly: The Judgments, **B is A, C is A**, give the Concept (**B + C**), or when signalized in language by one term, the Concept **D**; or in brief: The Judgments **B is A, C is A**, give **B + C =** the Concept **D**.

"The procedure in forming Concepts of the other class is analogous. Here the Subject remains the same, and the Concept arises from the synthesis of the Predicates which differ. Thus, the Predicates in the Judgments, **Socrates is rational, Socrates is animal**, being united, we have **rational and animal**, or signalizing the union by a single term, we have the Concept, **Man.** The term **Man** here, it will be observed, means a complement of attributes, as **rational, animal**, not, as before, of subjects, as **Socrates**, &c. This is a concept in Comprehensive Quantity; the formula of which is: The Judgments **A is B, A is C**, give, by synthesis of the differing Predicates, the aggregate (**B + C**), which signalized as one in Language is expressed by **D**. Or the Judgments **A is B, A is C**, give Concept (**B + C**) = **D**.

"**A Concept** may be defined, accordingly, to be a product of Thought, resulting from the synthesis of the Subjects or of the Predicates in several Judgments.

"The common Subject in a Predicate-Concept, or the common Predicate in a Subject-Concept, on which the Concept is formed, is called its **Base**.

"The name, **Concept**, is derived from the Latin word **Conceptum**, meaning **something taken with another.** The corresponding word used to denote the act of forming a Concept is **Conception**, which is also in common discourse often used to denote the product. It is used, in fact, like other words of this kind, in the threefold import of **faculty, act,** and **product.**

"The Law of Identity, or as, in its fuller expression, it may be denominated, the Law of the Same and Different, it will have been seen, presides over this product of Thought, as over the Judgment. No valid Concept can be formed, unless from Judgments which have either identical subjects or identical predicates. The Concept arises from the Synthesis of the different under the same ; of different subjects having the same predicate, or of different predicates having the same subject. In other words, in the Base is to be found the identifying principle governing in the Concept.

"It will have been observed, moreover, from the mode of its formation that a Concept is essentially a **relative cognition**. It is not only the result of a synthesis, not only the aggregate of a plurality of Judgments, and accordingly of relative cognitions, but the cognitions that are brought together in this synthesis sustain a determined and peculiar relation to one another. If the Concepts be formed from the subjects of the Judgments, those Judgments must have a common—the same predicate ; if from the predicates, the Judgments must have the same subject. Concepts are thus from their very nature relative cognitions, and the principle of relation is in the sameness of the term of the Judgment which is not synthesized into the Concept—in its Base.

"Concepts, however, differ from Judgments, as relative cognitions, in this respect : that in the Judgment the relation is explicit, while in the Concept it is only implied. Thus in the Judgment, **Man is a rational animal**, the relation is articulately declared ; but in the Concept,

Man, the relation to the other term of the Judgment from which it is derived, although real, is not expressed, but only implied. The Base of the Concept, although real, is not expressed.

"Still further, a Concept is essentially a one-sided cognition. It is formed from but one side of a Judgment, from the Subject or from the Predicate. It may be regarded, indeed, as an aggregate of Judgments, that is, a synthesized or composite Judgment, with the single term— the Base, and the Copula dropped.

"A Concept, however, always implies the Judgments from which it is derived ; it implies the other term, which has been dropped, but which is the indispensable condition of its being formed, and is, therefore, appropriately denominated the Base of the Concept ; and also implies that this Base has been identified with each of the terms which compose the Concept. . . .
It will occur to the reflecting mind, on this exposition of the mode in which Concepts are formed, that they are mere products of Thought, aggregates of Subjects, or aggregates of Predicates, and do not imply necessarily any exactly corresponding aggregates in the reality of things. How many individual subjects of Judgments shall be combined, or how many predicates, are questions that will be determined by such considerations as those of extent of observation, practicability of aggregation, convenience of use, the needs of occasion, and the like. The extent of the aggregation, therefore, varies indefinitely with the occasions of Thought ; and it is

not to be supposed that the constitution of things around us fluctuates precisely with the fluctuations of Thought. As the mathematical analyst, in the progress of his demonstration, finds it convenient to substitute single letters or symbols to denote a number of quantities in some respect of like character, so Thought, for its own manifold conveniences, often aggregates like elements and signalizes them by single words." (Day, *Elements of Logic*, ed. 1868, pp. 62-66.)

185. " The Third gradation of Thought is the *Reasoning.* Like the Concept, it is derived from the Judgment. It differs from the Concept in its form, as, unlike that, it retains the full forms of the Judgment, and accordingly, also, to a certain extent, it differs from it in the mode of its derivation. It differs from the Judgment proper in this respect, that it is a derivation from a Judgment—a traced movement of Thought, superadded to that which constitutes the Judgment. It is not the derived Judgment, not the mere terminus, the point at the end of the line over which the Thought has moved, but the line itself as traced in the movement of the Thought. When viewed as a resultant product of Thought, therefore, it must be regarded as the track of Thought left marked by the movement, not the mere attained object or goal of the movement, which is nothing more than a Judgment. We are carefully to distinguish, therefore, a Reasoning from the Conclusion—from the Judgment which is attained by the reasoning.

"**A Reasoning**, thus, is a derivation of a Judg-

ment from another Judgment or Judgments.
. . . . '**Reasoning** is a modification from the French **raisonner** (and this is a derivation from the Latin **ratio**), and corresponds to **ratiociatio**, which has indeed been immediately transferred into our language under the form of **ratiocination**. **Ratiocination** denotes properly the process, but improperly, also, the product of reasoning ; **Ratiocinium** marks exclusively the product. The original meaning of **ratio** was **computation**, and from the calculation of numbers it was transferred to the process of mediate comparison in general. **Discourse (discursus,** $\delta\iota\alpha\nu o\iota\alpha$) indicates the operation of comparison, the running backward and forward between the characters or notes of objects (**discurrere inter notas,** $\delta\iota\alpha\nu o\text{-}\varepsilon\tilde{\iota}\sigma\theta\alpha\iota$). The terms **discourse** and discursus, $\delta\iota\acute{\alpha}\nu o\iota\alpha$, are, however, often used for the reasoning process, strictly considered, and **discursive** is even applied to denote mediate, in opposition to intuitive, judgment, as is done by Milton. The compound term, **discourse of reason**, unambiguously marks its employment in this sense. **Argumentation** is derived from **argumentari**, which means **argumentis uti ; argument** again, **argumentum**—what is assumed in order to argue something—is properly the middle notion in a reasoning—that through which the conclusion is established ; and by the Latin Rhetoricians it was defined, ' **probabile inventum ad faciendam-fidem.**' It is often, however, applied as co-extensive with **argumentation. Inference** or **Illation** (from **infero**) indicates the carrying out into the

last proposition what was virtually contained in the antecedent judgments. **To conclude (concludere)**, again, signifies the act of connecting and shutting into the last proposition the two notions which stood apart in the two first. A **conclusion (conclusio)** is usually taken, in its strict or proper signification, to mean the last proposition of a reasoning ; it is, sometimes, however, used to express the product of the whole process. **To syllogize** means to form syllogisms. **Syllogism** (συλλογισμος) seems originally, like **ratio**, to have denoted a **computation**—an **adding up**; and like the greater part of the technical terms of Logic in general, was brorrowed by Aristotle from the mathematicians. Συλλογισμος may, however, be considered as expressing only what the composition of the word denotes—a **collecting together**; for συλλογίζεσθαι comes from συλλέγειν,, which signifies **to collect.** Finally, in Latin, a syllogism is called **collectio**, and to reason, **colligere.** This refers to the act of collecting, in the conclusion, the two notions scattered in the premises.'

" A Reasoning is composed of two parts—the original Judgment or Judgments which are the original **datum** in the process, and the movement of the Thought in the process. As the **datum** is regarded as logically determining and preceding, it is called the **Antecedent,** and the other part, regarded as logically determined, or following, is called the **Consequent.** Its proper sign is **therefore.** These are the parts of a Reasoning regarded as an Integrate Whole.

"The antecedent in a Reasoning may consist of a single Judgment, or of a plurality of Judgments. If it consist of but one Judgment, the Reasoning is called an **Immediate Reasoning**; as, **Man is a rational animal; therefore, Man is rational.** If the antecedent consists of more than one Judgment, the Reasoning is called a **Mediate Reasoning**, or, more technically, a **Syllogism.**" (Day, "*Elements of Logic,*" ed. 1868, pp. 91–94.)

186. "Reason, on the other hand, has no relation to the body, except as the soul's lodging and instrument; it belongs to the soul, purely and abidingly, and may be exercised without giving the slightest external token. Instead of framing bodily organs, . . . it spans the sciences, sails deliciously through the heavenly realms of poetic analogy, penetrates the significance of things, and looks into the very mind of God himself." (Grindon, *Life, p.* 365, third ed., London.)

187. " Thinking, as Plato has observed, is but the conversation of the soul with herself; and the instrument employed is the echo of that which forms the medium of communication with others. To this it may be added that the notion, as represented in language, is but the substitute for the notion embodied in intuition, and derives all the conditions of its validity from the possibility of the latter; for language, though indispensable as an instrument of thought, lends itself with equal facility to every combination, and thus furnishes no criterion by which we can judge between sense and nonsense—between the conceivable and the inconceivable." (Mansel, *Metaphysics*, pp. 1671-68, ed. 1871.)

(B) ON THE NATURE OF SUBJECT-MATTER.

188. In addition to a knowledge of mind and of knowing, the teacher, engaged in the discovery of Methods of Teaching, must diligently investigate the nature of the subject-matter that he is to teach.

189. By *nature* of subject-matter is meant that subtle, original, and permanent property of the subject-matter, at the presence of which the faculties of the mind are intuitively incited to their specific activities.

190. Some of this matter lies in the world that is external to the mind of man, and is called material.

191. Other matter rests exclusively within the ego. The mind creates it both as to its matter and form. In the case of material subject-matter, the mind determines only the form under which it exists as knowledge. In the other case, the immaterial, the matter and form would never exist as knowledge, or as matter for knowledge, were it not for the mind. The investigation of this whole subject is too vast to attempt to do more, at this time, than touch upon two or three subjects, except in the most cursory manner. The inquiry is directed towards the nature of Object Teaching, a familiar expression, and the nature of the subject-matter of mathematics, one branch of which, arithmetic, forms so important an element in the lower schools.

192. Object Teaching is that teaching in which a knowledge of objects, or object-matter, —or where the subject-matters are objects—is the real end and purpose of the instruction. Object Teaching regards a knowledge of objects as an end—it does not consider anything beyond the objects themselves—it is served fully when this knowledge of facts is secured—its province is with the actual, which exists as individual facts —its subject-matter is that which addresses itself exclusively to the perceptive and discriminative faculties of the mind, as matter to be learned for its own sake. The powers of the mind that are mainly instrumental in acquisitions by the learner, who is taught by Object Teaching, are the perceptive, which cognize intuitively and immediately; the discriminative, which outline one object from another; and memory, which retains. Whatever is purely distinctive of Object Teaching is found within the above limitations. It relates to the region of individual facts.

193. Wherever an abundance of facts is wanted as materials for the other faculties of the mind to use subsequently in constructing science, Object Teaching is the way by which the necessities can be met.

194. But Object Teaching is only possible where a knowledge of facts, as such, is to be obtained, and where the materials, the matters, of knowledge, exist as objects of perception and discrimination.

195. All those ways of teaching where objects, as charts, maps, apparatus, pictures, are used, by the teacher and pupil, not as ends of knowledge unto themselves, but as helps, by analogy, to acquiring knowledge of other things as ends—all these ways of teaching are not Objective, they are **Illustrative.**

196. Ideas in the memory are joined together by the nexus of their nature, termed the Laws of Association. When, by any chance, one idea is brought into consciousness from unconsciousness —one modification reproduced—the whole group of ideas, related by sameness of time, space, or circumstances, come flitting as flocks through consciousness. Connected with this association of ideas is the power of imagination, which creates new mental beings, and which seizes upon analogies. These states or modes of the activities make Illustrative Teaching possible.

197. Illustrations are lights set by the wayside in parabolic mirrors, to illuminate obscure passages—they are voices which call out a welcome to him who is bewildered in the midst of a mazy mass of half-obscured and obscuring numbers—they are guides that accompany the student to reveal to him on a sudden the secret labyrinths through which he may arise into the upper levels of light—they are the Aladdin Lamp and Ring, by whose mystic power their possessor may be instantaneously transported into the palaces of the Beautiful and the True. The value of an illustration consists in its brevity, its brilliancy, its pointedness, its unexpected and unforeseen applicability, and its convincing force of plain analogy.

"Illustration is vivid elucidation (= to make **more fully** intelligible) by certain specific and effective means, as similitudes, comparisons, appropriate incidents or anecdotes, and the like, graphic representations, and even artistic drawings." (Smith, *Syn. Discr.*)

"**Analogy** is often used familiarly, as if it meant mere moral resemblance or similarity. Strictly speaking, however, analogy implies a third term, or four terms, as follows:—As A is to B, so is C; or as A is to B, so is C to D. Analogy, therefore, is similarity of relations. When we argue from example, we argue from the likeness of things; when from analogy, we argue from the likeness of their relations. If I argue that, because the seed dies in the earth before it springs up anew, therefore it is probable that the human body will rise again after death; this is, as to the character of the idea, a resemblance, as to the argument, an analogy; the principle being that, as the same God is the author of a natural and a spiritual world, He may be expected to act toward each upon similar and common laws." (*Ibid.*)

"**Analogy and Induction.**—There are two requisites in order to every analogical argument: 1. That the two or several particulars concerned in the argument should be known to agree in some one point ; for otherwise they could not be referable to any one class, and there would consequently be no basis to the subsequent inference drawn in the conclusion. 2. That the conclusion must be modified by a reference to the circumstances of the particular to which we argue. For herein consists **the essential distinction between an analogical and an inductive argument.**" (Fleming, *Vocab Phil.*)

198. " I hate set dissertations ; and, above all things in the world, 'tis one of the silliest things in one of them, to darken your hypothesis by placing a number of tall, opake words, one before another, in a right line, betwixt your own and your reader's conception,—when, in all likelihood, if you had looked about, you might have seen something standing, or hanging up, which would have cleared the point at once ;— ' for what hindrance, hurt, or harm doth the laudable desire of knowledge bring to any man, if even from a sot, a pot, a fool, a stool, a winter-mitten, a truckle for a pulley, the lid of a goldsmith's crucible, an oil-bottle, an old slipper, or a cane-chair ?' I am this moment sitting upon one. Will you give me leave to illustrate this affair of wit and judgment, by the two knobs on the top of the back of it ?—they are fastened on, you see, with two pegs stuck slightly into two gimlet-holes, and will place what I have to say in so clear a light, as to let you see through the drift and meaning of my whole preface, as plainly as if every point and particle of it was made up of sunbeams. I enter now directly upon the point. Here stands **wit**,—and there stands **judgment**, close beside it, just like the two knobs I'm speaking of, upon the back of this self-same chair on which I am sitting. You see, they are the highest and most ornamental parts of its **frame**,—as wit and judgment are of **ours**,—and, like them too, indubitably both made and fitted to go together, in order, as we may say in all such cases of duplicated embellishment, **to answer one another.** Now, for the sake of an experiment, and for the clearer illustrating this matter,—let us for a moment take off one of these two curious ornaments (I care not which) from the point or pinnacle of the chair it now stands on;—nay, don't laugh at it,—but did you ever see, in the whole course of your lives, such a ridiculous business as this has made of it? —Why, 'tis as miserable a sight as a sow with one ear; and there is just as much sense and symmetry in the one as in the other.—Do,—pray, get off your seats, only to take a view of it.—Now, would any man who valued his character a straw, have turned a piece of work out of his hand in such a condition?—Nay, lay your hands upon your hearts, and answer this plain question, Whether this one single knob, which now stands here like a block-head by itself, can serve any purpose upon earth, but to put one in mind of the want of the other?—and let me farther ask, in case the chair was your own, if you would not in **your** consciences think, rather than be as it is, that it would be ten times better without any knobs at all?

"Now these two knobs, or top-ornaments of the mind of man, which crown the whole entablature,—being, as I said, wit and judgment, which, of all others, as I have proved it, are the most needful, —the most prized,—the most calamitous to be without, and consequently the hardest to come at ;—for all these reasons put together, there is not a mortal among us so destitute of a love of good fame or feeding,—or so ignorant of what will do him good therein,—who does not wish and steadfastly resolve in his own mind, to be, or to be thought at least, master of the one or the other, and indeed of both of them, if the thing seems any way feasible, or likely to be brought to pass." (Sterne, *Tristram Shandy*, pp. 88–9, *ed.* 1844, Philadelphia.)

199. Illustrative Teaching is seeking something that bears a resemblance in form, nature, or kind to the point to be learned, or taught, presenting it instead of the point, and thus enabling the powers of comparison possessed by the pupil to act by inference from the analogy. This is a process of extending the meaning of words, called sometimes "the process of **analogous or metaphorical extension** of the meaning of words. This change may be said, no doubt, to consist in generalization, since there must always be a resemblance between the new and old applications of the term. But the resemblance is often one of a most distant and obscure kind, such as we should call analogy rather than identity." (Jevons, *El. Lessons in Logic*, p. 50, *ed.* 1878.)

200. Example would be something akin to analogy, excepting that example may be of the kind of thing itself, as well as an example illustrating the case at issue.

201. Illustrative Teaching is often called, unfortunately in conception, **Objective** Teaching. An object can be used for but two possible purposes in teaching : (1) To be learned, in and for itself ; (2) Or to be an aid in learning something else. The first is Object Teaching, the second is Illustrative Teaching.

202. The distinction between the province of Object Teaching and that of Illustrative Teaching has been indistinctly apprehended by teachers. This misapprehension has led to serious obscurity of conceptions of teaching, for the expression Object Teaching has been applied without discrimination to all kinds of teaching where objects were used, whatever their purpose, whether as objects to be learned, or as objects to use in illustrating other points.

" The science which enlightens, and the physick that cures, are doubtless very useful : but the pretended science that misleads, and the physick that kills, are as certainly destructive. Teach us, therefore, to distinguish between them. . . . It may be replied, as it constantly is, the fault is in the physician, and not in the science of medicine, which is otherwise infallible. Well, well, be it so : take care, however, the physick be never accompanied by the doctor : for, as sure as ever they come together, there will be an hundred times more to fear from the blunders of the artist, than to hope for from the efficacy of the art." (Rousseau, *Emilius*, Vol. I., pp. 45-6.)

203. It has already been remarked that Object Teaching can be resorted to only with those subjects where facts obtained by perception and discrimination are desired. There are branches to be taught where it is impossible, from the nature of the subject-matter, to teach in this way. The subject of mathematics is one that has grown from a basis of definitions. The axioms follow definitions, but they are phases of conclusive reasoning, and assume things which are the creations of definitions. Definitions are the bases of mathematic science in its matter. Axioms are the bases in its logical processes of reasoning. Definitions are things which are products growing out of relations. Relations are objects only as they are products of the activities of the faculty of Thought. Hence all mathematical subjects are, from their nature, incapable of being taught objectively. All lines, mathematical blocks, charts, astronomical apparatus, and calculating machines, are but objects which illustrate mathematical truths, its definitions, and results, as intellectual products—they are not the things which are learned in themselves. What are called **Applied Mathematics** are only hypothetical illustrations of mental creations. It is also true that this science is one " in whose reasonings both matter and form can be furnished by the mind itself," and not one where " the form alone is from the mind, the matter being derived from experience." (Mansel, *Prol. Log.* p. 93, ed. 1860.)

204. " Abstract terms are strongly distinguished from general terms by possessing only one kind of meaning ; for as they denote qualities there is nothing which they cannot in addition imply. The adjective ' red ' is the name of red objects, but it implies the possession by them of the quality **redness**; but this latter term has one single meaning—the quality alone. Thus it arises that abstract terms are incapable of plurality." (Jevons, *Prin. Science*, p. 27, ed. 1877.) . . . "**Numerical Abstraction** consists in abstracting the character of the difference from which plurality arises, retaining merely the fact. When I speak of **three men** I need not at once specify the marks by which each may be known from each. Those marks must exist if they are really three men and not one and the same, and in speaking of them as many I imply the existence of the requisite differences. Abstract number, then, is the **empty form of difference ;** the abstract number **three** asserts the existence of marks without specifying their kind. Numerical abstraction is thus seen to be a different process from logical abstraction, for in the latter process we drop out of notice the very existence of difference and plurality. . . . The origin of the great generality of number is now apparent. Three sounds differ from three colours, or three riders from three horses ; but they agree in respect of the variety of marks by which they can be discriminated. The symbols $1+1+1$ are thus the empty marks asserting the existence of discrimination. But in dropping out of sight the character of the differences we give rise to new agreements on which mathematical reasoning is founded. . . . The common distinction between concrete and abstract number can now be easily stated. In proportion as we specify the logical characters of the things numbered, we render them concrete. In the abstract number **three** there is no statement of the points in which the three objects agree ; but in **three coins, three men,** or **three horses,** not only are the objects numbered, but their nature is restricted. Concrete number thus implies the same consciousness of difference as abstract number, but it is mingled with a groundwork of similarity expressed in the logical terms. There is identity so far as logical terms enter ; difference so far as the terms are merely numerical. The reason of the important Law of Homogeneity will now be apparent. This law asserts that in every arithmetical calculation the logical nature of the things numbered must remain unaltered. The specified logical agreement of the things must not be affected by the unspecified numerical differences. A calculation would be palpably absurd which, after commencing with length, gave a result in hours. It is equally absurd, in a purely arithmetical point of view, to deduce areas from the calculation of lengths, masses from the combination of volume and density, or momenta from mass and velocity. It must remain for subsequent consideration to decide in what sense one may truly say that two linear feet multiplied by two linear feet give four superficial feet ; arithmetically it is absurd, because there is a change of unit. As a general rule we treat in each calculation only objects of one nature. We do not, and cannot properly add, in the same sum yards of cloth and pounds of sugar. We cannot even conceive the result of adding area to velocity, or length to density, or weight to value. The units added must have a basis of homogeneity, or must be reducible to some common denominator. Nevertheless it is possible, and in fact common, to treat in one complex calculation the most heterogeneous quantities, on the condition that each kind of object is kept distinct, and treated numerically only in conjunction with its own kind. Different units, so far as their logical differences are specified, must never be substituted one for the other. (*Ibid.*, pp. 158–60.)

"Abstractly considered, Number is the measure of the relation between quantities or things of the same kind. We can form no conception of the absolute magnitude of any quantity, and can only acquire a relative conception of it, by comparing it with some other quantity of the same kind, assumed as a standard of comparison. The comparison is made by seeking how many times the standard is contained in the quantity measured. The result of this comparison is a **number.**" (Davies and Peck, *Dict. of Math.*)

" Groups of units are what we really treat in arithmetic. The number **five** is really $1+1+1$

$+1+1$, but for the sake of conciseness we substitute the more compact sign 5, or the name **five**. These names being arbitrarily imposed in any one manner, an infinite variety of relations spring up between them which are not in the least arbitrary. If we define **four** as $1+1+1+1$, and **five** as $1+1+1+1+1$, then of course it follows that **five**=**four**$+1$; but it would be equally possible to take this latter equality as a definition, in which case one of the former equalities would become an inference. It is hardly requisite to decide how we define the names of numbers, provided we remember that out of the infinitely numerous relations of one number to others, some one relation expressed in an equality must be a definition of the number in question and the other relations immediately become necessary inferences.

"In the science of number the variety of classes which can be formed is altogether infinite, and statements of perfect generality may be made subject only to difficulty or exception at the lower end of the scale. Every existing number for instance belongs to the class **M**$+7$; that is, every number must be the sum of another number and seven, except of course the first six or seven numbers, negative quantities not being here taken into account. Every number is the half of some other, and so on. The subject of generalization, as exhibited in mathematical truths, is an infinitely wide one. In number we are only at the first step of an extensive series of generalizations. As number is general com-

pared with the particular things numbered, so
we have general symbols for numbers, and general symbols for relations between undetermined
numbers. There is an unlimited hierarchy of
successive generalizations." (Jevons, *Pr. Sc.*,
pp. 167–168.)
" A large proportion of the mathematical
functions which are conceivable have no application to the circumstances of this world. Phy-
sicists certainly do investigate the nature and
consequences of forces which nowhere exist.
Newton's *Principia* is full of such investigations.
In one chapter of his *Mécanique*, Céleste Laplace
indulges in a remarkable speculation as to what
the laws of motion would have been if momen-
tum, instead of varying simply as the velocity,
had been a more complicated function of it.
. . . Thought is not bound down to the limits
of what is materially existent, but is circum-
scribed only by those Fundamental Laws of
Identity, Contradiction, and Duality, which have
already been laid down." (*Ibid.*, pp. 70–45.)

205. " Mathematical Judgments may be divided into two kinds—indemonstrable or axiom-
atic judgments, whose necessity is self-evident;
and demonstrable judgments, whose necessity
depends on some previous assumption. The
necessity of the latter is derived from that of the
former, so that the indemonstrable judgments
alone require a special examination. Under
this class are comprehended the axioms of geometry, properly so-called—viz., the original as-
sumptions concerning magnitudes in space as

such, and the propositions belonging to the fundamental operations of arithmetic—addition and subtraction. (Distinguish between postulates, and some axioms which are logical, not geometrical principles, and depend solely on the laws of thought.) (Though in some things, as in numbers, besides adding and subtracting, men name other operations, as **multiplying** and **dividing**, yet are they the same ; for multiplication is but adding together of things equal ; and division but subtracting of one thing as often as we can. Hobbes, *Leviathan*, p. i., chap. 5.) The necessity of these judgments results from the existence in the mind of the *a priori* forms of intuition—Space and Time. The axioms of geometry are self-evident statements concerning magnitudes in space ; such as that two straight lines cannot enclose a space. Their self-evidence or necessity is to be explained by the circumstance that the presented intuition, as well as the representative thought, is derived from within, not from without. For geometrical propositions are primarily necessary, not as truths relating to objects without the mind, but as thoughts relating to objects within : their necessity, as regards real objects, is only secondary and hypothetical. If there exist anywhere in the world two perfect straight lines, those lines cannot enclose a space ; but if such lines exist nowhere but in my imagination, it is equally true that I cannot think of them as invested with the contrary attributes. This necessity of thought is dependent on a corresponding necessity of intuition. The object of which pure geometry treats is not dependent on sensation, but sensation on it : it is a condition under which alone sensible experience is possible ; and therefore its characteristics must accompany all our thoughts concerning any possible object of such experience ; for, however much we may abstract from the attributes of this or that particular phenomenon of experience, we are clearly incompetent to deprive it of those conditions under which alone, from the constitution of our minds, experience itself is possible. We can perceive only as we are permitted by the laws of our perceptive faculties, as we can think only in accordance with the laws of the understanding. If, then, by a law of my perceptive faculty, I am compelled to regard all objects as existing in space, the attributes which are once presented to me as the properties of a given portion of space, such as the pair of straight lines now present to my sight or imagination, must necessarily be thought as existing in all space and at all times. For to imagine a portion of space in which such properties are not found, would not be to imagine merely a different combination of sensible phenomena, such as continually takes place without any change in the laws of sensibility : it would be to imagine myself as perceiving under other conditions than those to which, by a law of my being, I am subjected. But a condition, though potentially existing in the original constitution of the mind, is actually manifested only in conjunction with that of which it is the condition. Space, therefore, and its laws, are first made known to consciousness on the occasion of an actual phenomenon of sense. Hence the twofold character of geometrical principles: empirical, as suggested in and through an act of experience; necessary, as relating to the conditions under which alone such experience is possible to human faculties.

"Arithmetic is related to Time as Geometry to Space; and the necessity of its propositions may be explained upon similar principles. The two sciences, however, present some important features of distinction. Most of the propositions of geometry are deductive: it contains very few axioms, properly so called, and its processes consist in the demonstration of a multitude of dependent propositions from the combination of these axioms with certain logical principles of thought in general. On the other hand, the fundamental operations of arithmetic —addition and subtraction—present to us a vast number of independent judgments, every one of which is derived immediately from intuition, and cannot, by any reasoning process, be deduced from any of the preceding ones. (Although it is simpler to regard addition and subtraction as independent processes, yet no result of either can be derived from a preceding result of the same operation.) Pure geometry cannot advance a step without demonstration, and its processes are therefore all reducible to the syllogistic form. Pure arithmetic contains no demonstration; and it is only when its calculus is applied to the solution of particular problems that reasoning takes place, and the laws of the syllogism become applicable. It is not reasoning which tells us that two and two make four ; nor, when we have gained this proposition, can we in any way deduce from it that two and four make six. We must have recourse, in each separate case, to the senses or the imagination (memory), and by counting up the individual succession corresponding to each term, intuitively perceive the resulting sum. The intuition thus serves nearly the same purpose as the figure in a geometrical demonstration ; with the exception that, in the latter case, the construction is adopted to furnish premises to a proposed conclusion ; while in the former it gives us a judgment which we have no immediate intention of applying to any further use.

"The intuition in the case of arithmetic is furnished by the consciousness of successive states of our own minds. Setting aside all other characteristics of those states, save that of their succession in time, we have the immediate consciousness of **one, two, three, four,** etc. A purely natural arithmetic would consist in carrying on this series, with no other relation between its members but that of succession, until the memory became unable to continue the process. The artificial methods by which calculation is facilitated and extended, such as that of a scale of notation, in which the series recommences after a certain number of members, vastly increase the utility of the calculus, but do not affect its psychological basis. To construct the science of arithmetic in all its essential features, it is only necessary that we should be conscious of a succession in time, and should be able to give names to the several members of the series; and since in every act of consciousness we are subject to the condition of succession, it is impossible in any form of consciousness to represent to ourselves the facts of arithmetic as other than they are.

"The necessity of propositions in geometry and arithmetic is thus derived from their relation to the universal forms of intuition—Space and Time. We can suppose the possibility of beings existing whose consciousness has no relation to space or time at all. This is no more than to admit the possible existence of intelligent beings otherwise constituted than ourselves, and consequently incomprehensible by us. But to suppose the existence of geometrical figures or arithmetical numbers such as those with which we are now acquainted, is to suppose the existence of space and time as we are now conscious of them, and therefore relatively to beings whose mental constitution is so far similar to our own. Such a supposition necessarily carries with it all the mathematical relations in which space and time, as given to us, are necessarily thought. For mathematical judgments strictly relate only to objects of thought as existing in my mind, not to distinct realities existing in relation to my mind. They therefore imply no other existence than that of a thinking subject, modified in a certain manner. Destroy this subject, or change its modification, and we cannot say, as in other cases, that the object may possibly exist still without the subject, or may exist in a new relation to a new subject ; for the object exists only in and through that particular modification of the subject, and, on any other supposition, is annihilated altogether. Thus it is impossible to suppose that a triangle can, in relation to any intelligence whatever, have its angles greater or less than two right angles, or that two and two should not be equal to four ; though it is quite possible to suppose the existence of intelligent beings destitute of the idea of a triangle or of the number two. This is a **necessary matter** in the strict sense of the term ; a relation which our own minds are incapable of reversing, not merely positively, in our own acts of thought, but also negatively, by supposing others who can do so." (Mansel, *Metaphysics*, pp. 226–31, ed. 1871.)

206. " The main branches of mathematical science were formerly stated to be arithmetic and geometry, springing out of the simple notions of number and space. This is too limited a description. Unquestionably the science of numbers, strictly and demonstratively treated, and that of geometry, or the deduction of the elementary properties of figure from definitions which are entirely exclusive of numerical considerations, must be considered as the elementary foundations, but not as the ultimate divisions, of mathematics. To them we must add the science of operation, or algebra in its widest sense,—the method of deducing from symbols which imply operations on magnitude, and which are to be used in a given manner, the consequences of the fundamental definitions. The leading idea of this science is operation or process, just as number is that of arithmetic, and space and figure of geometry : it is of a more abstract and refined character than the latter two, only because it does not immediately address itself to the notions which are formed in the common routine of life. It is the most exact of the exact sciences, according to the idea of their exactness which frequently entertained, being more nearly based upon definition than either arithmetic or geometry. It is true that the definitions must be such as to present results which admit of application to number, space, force, time, &c., or the science would be useless in mathematics, commonly so called ; but it is not the less true that a system of methods of operation, based upon general definitions, and conducted by strict logic, may be made to apply either to arithmetic or geometry, according to the manner in which the generalities of the definition are afterwards made specific." (*English Cyclopædia, Mathematics.*)

207. " The methods of observation of quantity in general are, Numeration, which is precise by the nature of number ; the Measurement of Space and Time, which are easily made precise ; the Conversion of Space and Time, by which each aids the measurement of the other ; the Method of Repetition ; the Method of Coincidence or Interferences." (Whewell, *Nov. Org. Ren.* p. 145.)

208. The branches known as the Natural Sciences can be taught by Object Teaching in so far as facts are needed and can be observed, for the things shown or observed are the immediate objects to be learned. History cannot, from its nature, be taught objectively, except it happen that the learner can be an eyewitness of the events narrated. Language and Literature can be taught by Object Teaching, they being ends unto themselves, and subjects of inspection. Applied mathematics, being themselves illustrations, can hardly be taught illustratively.

209. As soon as perception and determination have given to the mind knowledge of individual facts, the power of retention holds them for future use—they are reproduced and represented in consciousness where Thought seizes them, and constructs science from them. When knowledge of individual objects is gained, the usefulness of the objects ceases. All beyond is a work of the power of Thought. Hence the stages, for subject matter that will admit of it, are :—(1) Knowledge of facts obtained by Perception and Discrimination, which is the province of Object Teaching ; (2) The activity of Thought upon this knowledge, aided as it may be by Imagination. In this second stage, Objects are rather a hindrance if present than an aid, because they are so much useless material that should be put aside—Perception has done its work, Discrimination has separated, and now the senses may slumber while Thought is rearing science out of similarities and identities—any energy of attention which is diverted, at this time, towards the objects themselves is so much abstracted from Thought, which is thereby weakened, and Science so much endangered, for Science is not possible without Thought.

"A real experiment is a very valuable product of the mind, requiring great knowledge to invent it and great ingenuity to carry it out. . . . It may be said that a boy takes more interest in the matter by seeing for himself, or by performing for himself, that is by working the handle of the air-pump: this we admit, while we continue to doubt the educational value of the transaction. . . . The function of experiment, properly so called, in the investigation of the laws and processes of nature can hardly be unduly exalted; but it may be said of the experimenter, as of the poet, that he is born and not manufactured." (I. Todhunter, *Conflict of Studies*, pp. 16-19.)

210. Ignorance of the province of Object Teaching leads to disaster, in practice, in mental discipline. This teaching addresses the attention of Perception and Discrimination. Then the objects have served their purpose. If the knowledge of facts which the learner has obtained be not wrought up by Thought into Concepts, which are general in their character and form the data for Reasoning, his mind is left far short of discipline. For true intellectual power comes only by constant exercise of Thought, and Thought busies itself only with mental products. Neglect of demanding maximum amounts of work for the powers of Thought of pupils habituates them to superficial scholarship—they may be apt at observing, when objects are placed before them, but they will develop little power of independent research, of vigorous application to thinking, or of the power to generalize. The mere acquisition and memorizing of a number of isolated, heterogeneous, or unrelated facts, is neither learning nor discipline, whether the facts are obtained from personal observation and examination, from oral statements of teachers, or gleaned from books.

(c) ON DISCOVERING METHODS OF TEACHING SPECIAL SUBJECTS.

211. Having outlined the powers of knowing and the nature of subject-matter, it yet remains to investigate the Methods of Teaching, when they are to be applied in the teaching of any given subject. "In every Treatise upon any Science two Points are indispensably required ; the First, that the science which is the subject of it be fully explained ; the second, . . . that plain Directions be given, how and by what method such science may be attained." (Longinus, *On The Sublime*, pp. 1–2, Tr. by Wm. Smith, 1739, London.) It is not the purpose of this discussion to develop a complete Method and Mode in any subject—simply to present the magnitude, importance, and direction in general, of Methods in special studies. To discover a Method to teach any branch is no easy task. The exact psychological faculties to be addressed are often difficult to name—the subject-matter must be maintained in its integrity while it is manipulated into a system to suit the capacities of the mind taught. This latter point is all important, as it sometimes happens that the truths of science are sacrificed to error when they appear in Modes of Teaching. It often happens that systems, in their steps or degrees of advancement, do only scant justice to the mind to be taught, because they are too diffuse, too prolix, too narrow in their steps, or too inelastic. These faults of systems are grave ones, and show the teacher uninformed concerning Methods of Teaching. The subject-matter should be properly divided and subdivided, but never below the present attainments of the learner, for mind grows from reaching out after the unknown and the difficult, provided it be not clouded by discouragement in the pursuit. The subject-matter should be carefully freed from all that is not to be learned in that lesson—the steps to be presented should be those which are vital to the system of the subject taught. Too many words and points, and too much related subject-matter, distract the mind of the learner so that the real and vital points are only dimly apprehended. He is most fortunate in the classroom who sets forth, in sharp outline, just the maximum of subject-matter for his class—inspiring a zeal and determination for an increased power on the morrow's lesson.

212. Suppose that a teacher wishes to discover the Method of Teaching children the process of Adding Numbers. How, in practice, shall he proceed ?

1. Concerning the nature of the subject-matter:

 (*a*) Addition, being purely mathematical in its nature, is incapable of being presented by Object Teaching.

 (*b*) Being capable of a hypothetical application to material objects, it can be taught by Illustrative Teaching.

 (*c*) The numbers to be added together are but so many forms for the aggregate of many smaller parts, having no logical connection.

 (*d*) The subject-matter is represented by certain characters called Figures, which are arbitrary in their form, and have no logical connection with each other.

2. Concerning the faculties of mind that are primarily active in learning addition:

 (*a*) The Perceptive faculties are required to note, intuitively, the individuals that are presented to them.

 (*b*) Discrimination, or Comparison, distinguishes one individual in Consciousness from another.

 (*c*) Memory in general, or, according to Hamilton, Retentiveness (or Memory), Recollection (or Reproduction), and Representation, preserves for future use the knowledge obtained through Perception and Discrimination.

(*d*) The Power of Detecting Identity, or the Power of Comparison, or the Power of Thought, compares or identifies what may come within Consciousness through Perception, with what may come there through Memory.

(*e*) The Power of expressing Thought, or Language.

3. Having discovered these principles, which are the Method of Teaching addition, he proceeds to invent his Mode of Teaching addition. This Mode may be by illustration, by telling, by questioning, and the like.

213. He regards these particular points : 1. To what degree of power are the faculties of these children grown ? 2. Is this System of Addition philosophically constructed ? 3. In what quantity of subject-matter shall the points of the system be set to these faculties ? He may write out the complete lesson, as he proposes to present it. This is his Mode. He may then appear before the class to teach. His individuality, when presenting the subject-matter, exhibits his Manner.

The only guide possible for procedure in the case is the intelligence of the teacher, who now invents the Mode. If there be deficiency here, it will be no matter for surprise if the children are poorly taught.

When a System of subject-matter is arranged in detail in Modes of Teaching it, the arrangement is called **Methodical.** All methodical discussions for teaching must rest upon Methods of Teaching.

214. In the foregoing procedure, the discovering of the Method of Teaching—the process of discovering the faculties, and the nature of the subject-matter that is to be adjusted to them, comprised under (1) and (2)—is the conception of the **Science of Teaching**.

215. The Invention of the Mode of Teaching, together with the Manner of exhibiting it in practice, is the conception of the **Art of Teaching**.

216. The Investigation of the Science and the Art of Teaching constitutes the Conception of the **Profession of Teaching.**

III.

CONCLUDING REFLECTIONS.

217. Whatever qualifications of mind and person the teacher may have, he is still lacking in a most important element of success if he has not a quick apprehension of adopting means to ends. He must possess versatility of powers to discover Methods of Teaching, in order to invent Modes by which he shall incite to activity the pupil's mind with certainty. To do this, he needs a large stock of "That unacquired, unbought, untaught sagacity, which certain men have by nature," called Common Sense or good sense. (McCosh, *Int. of Mind, p.* 93, *ed.* 1870.) "Common Sense is the spontaneous action of right reason." (M. Bautain, *Art of Ext. Speaking, ed.* 1871.) This ability is needed nowhere more than in the school-room, and he who lacks it should diligently apply himself to cultivating his "good sense," if he would attain eminence in the Profession of Teaching.

218. "An open-eyed and open-minded physician keeps adding to his knowledge and altering and widening his theories to the day of his death; there is not less to be learned in the world of mind—in the world of the school-room.

... The kind of teacher who stiffens into the school-master misses his opportunities, or falls a victim to that arrestment of development which has overtaken many school subjects, and which sometimes overtakes the whole of school life." (Meiklejohn, *Inaugural Address, Bell Chair of Education*, p. 11, 1876, Edinburgh.)

219. " Intellectually, as well as morally, he (Arnold) felt that the teacher ought himself to be perpetually learning, and so constantly above the level of his scholars. ' I am sure,' he said, speaking of his pupils at Lalcham, ' that I do not judge of them or expect of them, as I should, if I were not taking pains to improve my own mind.' For this reason he maintained that no schoolmaster ought to remain at his post much more than fourteen or fifteen years, lest, by that time, he should have fallen behind the scholarship of the age ; and by his own reading and literary works he endeavored constantly to act upon this principle himself. . . . ' The dangers ' (of falling behind), he observed, ' were of various kinds. One boy may acquire a contempt for the information itself, which he sees possessed by a man whom he feels nevertheless to be far below him. Another (pupil) will fancy himself as much above nearly all the world as he feels he is above his own tutor, and will become self-sufficient and scornful. A third will believe it to be his duty, as a point of humility, to bring himself down intellectually to a level with one whom he feels bound to reverence ; and thus there have been instances where the veneration of a young man of ability for a teacher of small powers has been like a millstone round the neck of an eagle.'" (Arnold, *Life of*, p. 137, ed. 1870.)

220. "We may say that common sense scarcely claims to provide more than rather indefinite general rules, which no prudent man should neglect without giving himself a reason for doing so. Such reasons may either be drawn from one's knowledge of some peculiarities in one's nature, or from the experience of others whom one has ground for believing to be more like oneself than the average of mankind are. For though, as we saw, there is considerable risk of error in thus appropriating the experience of others—and in fact the expression of it will sometimes appear to be as hesitating and contradictory as the judgments of common sense—we may extract from it counsel sufficiently consistent and authoritative to supplement at least roughly the deficiencies of our own empirical generalizations." (Sidgwick, *Methods of Ethics*, p. 145, ed. 1874.)

221. "But many who allow the use of systematic principles in other things, are accustomed to cry up Common-Sense as the sufficient and only safe guide in Reasoning. Now by Common-Sense is meant, I apprehend, (when the term is used with any distinct meaning,) an exercise of the judgment unaided by any Art or system of rules : such an exercise as we must necessarily employ in numberless cases of daily occurrence ; in which, having no established principles to guide us,—no line of procedure, as it were, distinctly chalked out—we must needs act on the best extemporaneous conjectures we can form. He who is eminently skilful in doing this, is said to possess a superior degree of Common-Sense. But that Common-Sense is only our **second best** guide—that the rules of Art, if judiciously framed are always desirable when they can be had, is an assertion, for the truth of which I may appeal to the testimony of mankind in general; which is so much the more valuable, inasmuch as it may be accounted the testimony of **adversaries.** For the generality have a strong predilection in favor of Common-Sense, except in those points in which they, respectively, possess the knowledge of a system of rules; but in these points they deride any one who trusts to unaided Common-Sense. " A sailor *e.g.* will, perhaps, despise the pretensions of medical men, and prefer treating a disease by Common-Sense: but he would ridicule the proposal of navigating a ship by Common-Sense, without regard to the maxims of nautical art. A physician, again, will perhaps contemn Systems of Political-Economy, of Logic, or Metaphysics, and insist on the superior wisdom of trusting to Common-Sense in such matters; but he would never approve of trusting to Common-Sense in the treatment of diseases.

" Neither, again, would the Architect recommend a reliance on Common-Sense alone, in building, nor a Musician, in music, to the neglect of those systems of rules, which, in their respective arts have been deduced from scientific reasoning aided by experience. And the induction might be extended to every department of practice. Since, therefore, each gives the preference to unassisted Common-Sense only in those cases where he himself has nothing else to trust to, and invariably resorts to the rules of art, wherever he possesses the knowledge of them, it is plain that mankind universally bear their testimony, though unconsciously and often unwillingly, to the preferableness of systematic knowledge to conjectural judgments.

"There is, however, abundant room for the employment of Common-Sense in the **application** of the system. To **bring** arguments out of the form in which they are expressed in conversation and in books, into the regular logical shape, must be of course, the business of Common-Sense, aided by practice, for such arguments are, by supposition, not as yet within the province of science." (Whately, *Elements of Logic*, 1859, pp. xi.-xii. of Preface.)

222. "The one talent which is worth all other talents put together in all human affairs is the talent of judging right upon imperfect materials, the talent if you please of guessing right. It is a talent which no rules will ever teach and which even experience does not always give. It often coexists with a good deal of slowness and dulness and with a very slight power of expression. All that can be said about it is, that to see things as they are, without exaggeration or passion, is essential to it; but how can we see things as they are? Simply by opening our eyes and looking with whatever power we may have." (Stephen, *Liberty, Equality, Fraternity*, p. 352, ed. 1874, London.)

223. "The assumed logical perfection of thought bears about the same relation to the ordinary state of the human mind as the assumption of perfectly rigid levers and perfectly flexible cords bears in the action of those instruments in practice. But, on the other hand, the possibility of making such allowances implies that the difference between practice and theory is one of degree only, and not of kind. The instrument as used may not be identical with the instrument as contemplated, but it must be supposed capable of approximation to it." (Mánsel, *Prol. Log.*, p. 17.)

224. "It is a common notion, or at least it is implied in many common modes of speech, that the thoughts, feelings, and actions of sentient beings are not a subject of science, in the same strict sense in which this is true of the objects of outward nature. This notion seems to involve some confusion of ideas, which it is necessary to begin by clearing up. Any facts are fitted, in themselves, to be a subject of science which follow one another according to constant laws, although those laws may not have been discovered, nor even be discoverable by our existing resources. . . . Scientific inquiry has not yet succeeded in ascertaining the order of antecedence and consequence among phenomena, so as to be able, at least in our regions of the earth, to predict them with certainty, or even with a high degree of probability. . . . But meteorology not only has in itself every natural requisite for being, but actually is, a science ; though the science is extremely imperfect. . . . No one doubts that Tidology (as Dr. Whewell proposes to call it) is really a science. . . But circumstances of a local or casual nature, such as the configuration of the bottom of the ocean, the degree of confinement from shores, the direction of the wind, etc., influence, in many or all places, the height and time of the tide ; and a portion of these circumstances being either not accurately knowable, not precisely measurable, or not capable of being certainly foreseen, the tide in known places commonly varies from the calculated result of general principles by some difference that we are not able to foresee or conjecture. . . . And this is what is or ought to be meant by those who speak of sciences which are not **exact** sciences. Astronomy was once a science, without being an exact science. . . . It has become an exact science. . . . The science of human nature is of this description. It falls far short of the standard of exactness now realized in Astronomy ; but there is no reason that it should not be as much a science as Tidology is, or as Astronomy was when its calculations had only mastered the main phenomena, but not the perturbations.

" The phenomena with which this science of (human) nature is conversant being the thoughts, feelings, and actions of human beings, it would have attained the ideal perfection of a science if it enabled us to foretell how an individual would think, feel, or act throughout life, with the same certainty with which astronomy enables us to predict the places and the occultations of the heavenly bodies. It need scarcely be stated that nothing approaching to this can be done. The actions of individuals could not be predicted with scientific accuracy, were it only because we can not foresee the whole of the circumstances in which those individuals will be placed. But further, even in any given combination of (present) circumstances, no assertion, which is both precise and universally true, can be made respecting the manner in which human beings will think, feel, and act. This is not, however, because every person's modes of thinking, feeling, and acting do not depend on causes; nor can we doubt that if, in the case of any individual, our data could be complete, we even now know enough of the ultimate laws by which mental phenomena are determined, to enable us in many cases to predict, with tolerable certainty, what, in the greater number of supposable combinations of circumstances, his conduct or sentiments would be. But the impressions and actions of human beings are not solely the result of their present circumstances, but the joint result of those circumstances and of the characters of the individuals; and the agencies which determine human character are so numerous and diversified (nothing which has happened to the person throughout life being without its portion of influence), that in the aggregate they are never in any two cases exactly similar. Hence, even if our science of human nature were theoretically perfect, that is, if we could calculate any character as we can calculate the orbit of any planet, **from given data**; still, as the data are never all given, nor ever precisely alike in different cases, we could neither make positive predictions, nor lay down universal propositions.

"Inasmuch, however, as many of those effects which it is of most importance to render amenable to human foresight and control are determined, like the tides, in an incomparably greater degree by general causes, than by all partial causes taken together; depending in the main on those circumstances and qualities which are common to all mankind, or at least to large bodies of them, and only in a small degree on the idiosyncrasies of organization or the peculiar history of individuals; it is evidently possible with regard to all such effects, to make predictions which will **almost** always be verified, and general propositions which are almost always true. And whenever it is sufficient to know how the great majority of the human race, or of some nation or class of persons, will think, feel, and act, these propositions are equivalent to universal ones. For the purpose of political and social science this **is** sufficient. As we formerly remarked, an approximate generalization is, in social inquiries, for most practical purposes equivalent to an **exact** one; that which is only probable when asserted of individual human beings indiscriminately selected, being certain when affirmed of the character and collective conduct of masses.

"It is no disparagement, therefore, to the science of Human Nature, that those of its general propositions which descend sufficiently into detail to serve as a foundation for predicting phenomena in the concrete, are for the most part only approximately true. But in order to give a genuinely scientific character to the study, it is indispensable that these approximate generalizations, which in themselves would amount only to the lowest kind of empirical laws, should be connected deductively with the laws of nature from which they result ; should be resolved into the properties of the causes on which the phenomena depend. In other words, the science of Human Nature may be said to exist in proportion as the approximate truths, which compose a practical knowledge of mankind, can be exhibited as corollaries from the universal laws of human nature on which they rest ; whereby the proper limits of those approximate truths would be shown, and we should be enabled to deduce others for any new state of circumstances, in anticipation of specific experience. . . . The proposition now stated is the text on which are based the ' Laws of Mind,' and ' Ethology, or the science of the Formation of Character.' " (Mill, *System of Logic*, pp. 586–596, 8° ed. 1874.)

APPENDIX OF QUOTATIONS.

SECTION		PAGE
225. Appendix A.—On Method		346
226.	B.—On System	376
227.	C.—On Analysis	380
228.	D.—On Synthesis	383
229.	E.—On Definition	385
230.	F.—On Abstraction	390
231.	G.—On Generalization	392
232.	H.—On Classification	398
233.	I.—On Induction	413
234.	J.—On Interpretation	473
235.	K.—On Deduction	478

APPENDIX A.

225. EXTRACTS SHOWING THE USE OF THE TERM METHOD.

1. From Hedge's *Logick*, ed. 1854, pp. 149–150.

Method, in logick, is a proper classification and arrangement of our thoughts on any subject, either to facilitate the discovery of new truths, or to assist us in communicating to others truths already known; or, lastly, to enable us to preserve for future use the knowledge, which we have acquired. The disposition best adapted to the investigation of truth is the **analytick method;** which is therefore denominated the method of **invention**; and that which is best suited to the communication of knowledge, is the **synthetick method,** which for this reason has been called the method of **instruction**. In both of these methods, ideas are arranged in such order, as to exhibit their mutual connexions and relations.

2. From Coppée's *Elements of Logic*, ed. 1860, pp. 23–25.

Method is the order and arrangement of facts to produce a certain result; to establish new truth, to investigate old, and to explain and teach both. It is derived from the Greek $\mu\varepsilon\theta'o\delta o\nu$;

which denotes the **way through which** we arrive at a certain result.

Whatever steps are taken to make knowledge profitable, to reduce theory to practice, and to give clear and intelligible ideas of science, constitute Method. The extension of the term **Method**, it is evident, will differ according to the subject to which it is applied.

The **methods of investigation** differ slightly for the different kinds of science, but may generally be classified under two heads, **Analysis** and **Synthesis**, of which the former is generally used in the private investigation of truth, and the latter for the purposes of instruction. . . . We speak of the Method of a single science, or a Method which is applied to all—as in that which leads to the Classification of the sciences. In either investigation the division of Method into Analysis and Synthesis, is a just one, as both are used in either process.

3. From Day's *Elements of Logic*, ed. 1868, pp. 132–133.

"*Method* in general is the regulated procedure towards a certain end ; that is, a process governed by rules, which guide us by the shortest way straight towards a certain point, and guard us against devious aberrations. Now the end of Thought is Truth, Knowledge, Science—expressions which may here be considered as convertible. Science, therefore, may be regarded as the perfection of thought, and to the accomplishment of this perfection the Methodology of Logic must be accommodated and be conducive."

But while Science, thus, is the proper end of all Thought, and Logical Method must have reference to Thought as its one end, it is still to be regarded only as the immediate end, which may, itself, be modified and controlled by still higher ends. In fact, Science or Truth may have its end either in itself—in the True, or in the Beautiful, or in the Right and Good ; and the Method of Thought will vary in some respects with this specific remoter end. Still further, the Method of Thought will vary with the more specific ends under each of these higher governing ends. We may deal with Thought for the purpose of acquiring knowledge, or for the purpose of communicating knowledge ; and the Method requisite for the Investigation of Truth will so far vary from the Method requisite for the Communication of Truth.

In like manner the Method of Thought, as governed by the higher end of guiding to the Beautiful, will vary specifically, as the particular end is the Contemplation or the Creation of the Beautiful.

So, too, we have a specific variation in the Method of Thought, where the governing idea is the Right or the Good, according as Subjective or Objective Rectitude or Goodness is the particular end.

It is sufficient to point out here these modifications of Logical Method in respect to these several general ends in thinking. The full, detailed consideration of them belongs either to modified Logic or to Applied or Special Logic.

Pure Logic confines itself to the domain of Truth in itself—Science for its own sake.

4. From Fleming's *Vocabulary of Philosophy*, ed. 1858, pp. 316-319.

Method means the way or path by which we proceed to the attainment of some object or aim. In its widest acceptation, it denotes the means employed to obtain some end. Every art and every handicraft has its **method**.

Scientific or philosophical **method** is the march which the mind follows in ascertaining or communicating truth. It is the putting of our thoughts in a certain order with a view to improve our knowledge or to convey it to others.

Method may be called, in general, **the art of disposing well a series of many thoughts, either for the discovering truth when we are ignorant of it, or for proving it to others when it is already known.** Thus there are two kinds of **method**, one for discovering truth, which is called **analysis**, or the **method of resolution**, and which may also be called the **method of invention**; and the other for explaining it to others when we have found it, which is called **synthesis**, or the **method of composition**, and which may also be called the **method of doctrine**. (*Port Roy. Logic*, Part IV., ch. 2.)

"**Method**, which is usually described as the fourth part of Logic, is rather a complete practical Logic. It is rather a power or spirit of the intellect, pervading all that it does, than its tangible product." (Thomson, *Outline of Laws of Thought*, sect. 119.)

Every department of philosophy has its own proper **method**; but there is a universal **method** or science of **method**. This was called by Plato, dialectic; and represented as leading to the true and real. (*Repub.*, lib. vii.) It has been said that the word μέθοδος, as it occurs in Aristotle's *Ethics*, should be translated 'systems,' rather than 'method.'—(Paul, *Analysis of Aristotle's Ethics*, p. 1.) But the construction of a system implies **method**. And no one was more thoroughly aware of the importance of a right **method** than Aristotle. He has said (*Metaphys.*, lib. ii.), "that we ought to see well what demonstration (or proof) suits each particular subject; for it would be absurd to mix together the research of science and that of **method**; two things, the acquisition of which offers great difficulty." The deductive **method** of philosophy came at once finished from his hand. And the inductive **method** was more extensively and successfully followed out by him than has been generally thought.

James Acontius, or Concio, as he is sometimes called, was born at Trent, and came to England in 1567. He published a work, *De Methodo*. . . . According to him all knowledge deduced from a process of reasoning presupposes some primitive truths, founded in the nature of man, and admitted as soon as announced; and the great aim of **method** should be to bring these primitive truths to light, that by their light we may have more light. Truths obtained by the senses, and by repeated experience, become at length positive and certain knowledge.

Descartes has a discourse on **Method**. He has reduced it to four general rules.

I. To admit nothing as true of which we have not a clear and distinct idea. We have a clear and distinct idea of our own existence. And in proportion as our idea of anything else approaches to, or recedes from, the clearness of this idea, it ought to be received or rejected.

II. To divide every object inquired into as much as possible into its parts. Nothing is more simple than the ego, or self-consciousness. In proportion as the object of inquiry is simplified, the evidence comes to be nearer that of self-consciousness.

III. To ascend from simple ideas or cognitions to those that are more complex. The real is often complex : and to arrive at the knowledge of it as a reality, we must by synthesis reunite the parts which were previously separated.

IV. By careful and repeated enumeration to see that all the parts are reunited. For the synthesis will be deceitful and incomplete if it do not reunite the whole, and thus give the reality.

This **method** begins with provisory doubt, proceeds by analysis and synthesis, and ends by accepting evidence in proportion as it resembles the evidence of self-consciousness.

These rules are useful in all departments of philosophy. But different sciences have different **methods** suited to their objects and to the end in view.

In prosecuting science with the view of extending our knowledge of it, or the limits of it, we are said to follow the **method** of investigation or inquiry, and our procedure will be chiefly in the way of **analysis**. But in communicating what is already known, we follow the **method** of exposition or doctrines, and our procedure will be chiefly in the way of **synthesis**.

In some sciences the principles or laws are given, and the object of the science is to discover the possible application of them. In these sciences the **method** is deductive, as in geometry. In other sciences, the facts or phenomena are given, and the object of the science is to discover the principles or laws. In these sciences the proper **method** is inductive, proceeding by observation or experiment, as in psychology and physics. The **method** opposed to this, and which was long followed, was the constructive **method**; which, instead of discovering causes by induction, imagined or assigned them *à priori*, or *ex hypothesi*, and afterwards tried to verify them. This **method** is seductive and bold but dangerous and insecure, and should be resorted to with great caution.

The use of **method**, both in obtaining and applying knowledge for ourselves, and in conveying and communicating it to others, is great and obvious.

" Marshal thy notions into a handsome **method**. One will carry twice as much weight, trussed and packed up in bundles, than when it lies untoward, flapping, and hanging about his shoulders." (*Pleasures of Literature*, 12mo, Lond., 1851, p. 104.)

5. From *Preface of* "*A Brief English Grammar on a Logical Method*," by Alexander Bain,

The chief peculiarity in the plan of the present work lies in anticipating the unavoidable difficulties of the subject by a previous handling of certain elementary notions (belonging to all science), without which no one can hope to understand the scope or method of grammar. . . . After such preliminary explanations, I make no scruple to introduce a strict mode of defining the Parts of Speech. I also exemplify the leading subdivisions or classes of each. Moreover, I bring forward at once the equivalent phrases, which, in the case of the Adverb in particular, are used more frequently than single words. On this method, the Grammatical parsing of a sentence directs attention forcibly to the meaning. . . . It (the Key) also includes a large selection of additional examples, which are commented on with a view to set forth still farther the methods of parsing, and to illustrate the constructions and idioms of the language.

6. From Whewell's *Novum Organon Renovatum*, ed. 1858, pp. 141–144.

The name *Organon* was applied to the works of Aristotle which treated of Logic, *i.e.*, of the method of establishing and proving knowledge, and of refuting errour, by means of Syllogisms. Francis Bacon, holding that this method was insufficient for the augmentation of real knowledge, published his *Novum Organon* in which he proposed for that purpose methods from which he promised a better success. (p. 3.)

The Methods by which the construction of Science is promoted are, Methods of Observation, Methods of obtaining clear Ideas, **and** Methods of Induction.

Aphorism xxvii. . . . I shall, therefore, attempt to resolve the Process of Discovery into its parts, and to give an account as distinct as may be of Rules and Methods which belong to each portion of the process.

In Book II. we considered the three main parts of the process by which science is constructed: namely, the Decomposition and Observation of Complex Facts; the Explication of our Ideal Conceptions; and the Colligation of Elementary Facts by means of those conceptions. The first and last of these three steps are capable of receiving additional accuracy by peculiar processes. They may further the advance of science in a more effectual manner, when directed by special technical **Methods,** of which in the present book we must give a brief view. In this more technical form, the observation of facts involves the **Measurement of Phenomena;** and the Colligation of Facts includes all arts and rules by which the process of Induction can be assisted. Hence we shall have here to consider **Methods of Observation,** and **Methods of Induction,** using these phrases in the widest sense. The second of the three steps above mentioned, the Explication of our Conceptions, does not admit of being much assisted by methods, although something may be done by Education and Discussion.

The Methods of Induction, of which we have to speak, apply only to the first step in our ascent from phenomena to laws of Nature ;—the discovery of **Laws of Phenomena**. A higher and ulterior step remains behind, and follow in natural order the discovery of Laws of Phenomena ; namely, the **Discovery of Causes**; and this must be stated as a distinct and essential process in a complete view of the course of science. Again, when we have thus ascended to the causes of phenomena and of their laws, we can often reason downwards from the cause so discovered ; and we are thus led to suggestions of new phenomena, or to new explanations of phenomena already known. Such proceedings may be termed **Applications** of our discoveries ; including in the phrase, **Verifications** of our Doctrines by such an application of them to observed facts.

Hence we have the following series of processes concerned in the formation of science.

(1.) Decomposition of Facts ;
(2.) Measurement of Phenomena ;
(3.) Explication of Conceptions ;
(4.) Induction of Laws of Phenomena ;
(5.) Induction of Causes ;
(6.) Application of Inductive Discoveries.

Of these six processes, the methods by which the second and fourth may be assisted are here our peculiar object of attention. The treatment of these subjects in the present work must necessarily be scanty and imperfect, although we may perhaps be able to add something to what has hitherto been systematically taught on these heads. Methods of Observation and of Induction might of themselves form an abundant subject for a treatise, and hereafter probably will do so, in the hands of future writers. A few remarks, offered as contributions on this subject, may serve to show how extensive it is, and how much more ready it now is than it ever before was, for a systematic discussion.

Of the above steps of the formation of science, the first, the Decomposition of Facts, has already been sufficiently explained in the last Book : for if we pursue it into further detail and exactitude, we find that we gradually trench upon some of the succeeding parts. I, therefore, proceed to treat of the second step, the Measurement of Phenomena ;—of **Methods** by which this work, in its widest sense, is executed, and these I shall term Methods of Observation.

7. From Bowen's *Logic*, ed. 1874, pp. 30-38.

Logic is the Science of the Necessary Laws of Pure Thought, . . . that is, it treats of Language so far only as this is the vehicle of Thought. Just the reverse is true of the science of Grammar, which treats primarily of Language, and only secondarily of Thought. Logic might be called the Grammar of Thought. .
Pure, or, as it is sometimes termed, Formal Thought, is **the mere process of thinking, irrespective of what we are thinking about.** It has already been said that the Acquisitive or Perceptive Faculty furnishes " the Matter," while

the Understanding supplies "the Form," of our knowledge. This distinction between Matter and Form is one of considerable importance in the history of philosophy. The former is the crude material or the stuff of which anything consists, or out of which it is made; while the latter is the peculiar shape or modification given to it by the artist, whereby it has become this particular thing which it is, and not something else which might have been fashioned out of the same substance. Thus, **wood** is the Matter of the desk on which I am writing, whilst the Form is that which entitles it to be called a desk, rather than a table or a chair. Vocal sound is the Matter of speech, and articulation is its Form. It is evident that these are two correlative notions, each of which implies the other: Matter cannot exist except under some Form, and there cannot be any Form except of some given Matter. But though the two cannot actually be separated, the mind can consider each separately through that process, called **abstraction**, whereby the attention is wholly given to the one to the exclusion of the other. We may think separately of the attributes which are common to a whole class of Forms, disregarding altogether, for the moment, the Matter of which each of them really consists. Borrowing algebraic symbols, the Matter in each case may be designated by a letter of the alphabet, the peculiar significance of which is, that it stands for any Matter whatever, and not for any one in particular. Thus, **A is B**, is the Form of an affirmative judgment, wherein A and B stand for any two Concepts whatever. Hence, whatever is true of the general formula, **A is B**, will be true also of any such particular instances, as **Iron is malleable**, **Trees are plants**, etc., wherein the Form is associated with some particular Matter. In saying, then, that Logic is concerned only with the Forms of Thought, or Pure Thought, or Thought in the abstract,—for all these expressions signify the same thing,—we mean only, that what is Material in Thought is extralogical, and, as logicians, we have nothing to do with it; just as the geometer has nothing to do with the particular diagram on the paper before him, except so far as it is a symbol, or universal Form, of all possible figures of the same general character. . . .

Again, the definition of Logic assumes that the process of Thinking, like every other operation in nature, does not take place at random, but according to certain fixed Laws or invariable modes of procedure. There could be no communication of Thought from one mind to another, if the process of Thinking in all minds were not subject to the same general rules. We follow these laws for the most part unconsciously, as a distinct recognition of them is not by any means necessary for correct thinking; just so, many persons speak and write correctly without any knowledge of the grammarian's rules. . . .

Properly speaking, Pure Logic terminates with the consideration of the three classes of products—namely, Concepts, Judgments, and

Reasonings—which are the elements into which all Thought is resolved. But Thought itself is subsidiary to the attainment of knowledge,—that is, to Science. The question remains, then, after we have fully treated of Concepts, Judgments, and Reasonings, taken separately or considered in themselves alone, what use is to be made of them, taken together, in the construction of Science. A full answer to this question, as it would involve a study of the **objects** of Science,—that is, of the matter of the special sciences,—evidently falls outside of the province of Logic. But a partial answer to it, regarding Science in its relation, not to the objects known, but to the knowing mind, may be considered as a natural appendage to Logic, as it embraces the conditions not merely of possible, but of perfect, Thought. Such an answer is usually called the Doctrine of Method, or Logical Methodology. Pure Logic considers only the Necessary Laws to which all Thought **must** conform ; the Doctrine of Method regards those rules and principles to which all Thought **ought** to conform in order to obtain its end, which is the advancement of Science. Pure Logic treats merely of the elements of Thought, while Logical Methodology regards the proper arrangement of these elements into an harmonious whole. All Method is a well-defined progress towards some end ; and the end in this case is the attainment of truth. Practically speaking, the Doctrine of Method is a body of rules or precepts looking to the proper regulation of the Thinking Faculty in the pursuit of knowledge ; and, as such, it necessarily lacks the precision and the demonstrative certainty which are characteristic of the principles of Pure Logic. The laws of Pure Thought are absolute ; the merits of Perfect Thought are various, and attainable in different degrees, according to circumstances.

Another distinction has been taken, in this science, between Pure and Applied Logic, or as Sir William Hamilton prefers to call the latter, Modified Logic. The former, as we have seen, considers the Thinking Faculty alone, as if it constituted the whole of the human mind, and therefore as if its Laws and Products were unaffected by any collateral and disturbing influences, but were manifested in precisely the same manner by different persons. It takes no account of the defects and hinderances which obstruct the normal action of the understanding. Modified Logic, on the other hand, considers Thought as it is, and not merely as it ought to be. It regards " the Causes of Error and the Impediments to Truth by which man is beset in the employment of his Faculties, and what are the means of their removal." And yet it is a **universal** science,—as much so as Pure Logic ;—for it does not consider the Matter of Thought. . . . . . But Modified Logic is not properly called Logic, as it is a branch of Psychology, which treats of the phenomena of mind in general, and not merely of the normal action and necessary laws of one special faculty, the Understanding. As Modified Logic, however, is nearly allied in purpose with the Doctrine of Method, both looking to the same general end,—the attainment of truth through the proper regulation of the Thinking Faculty,—the two may well be considered together, under the general name of **Applied Logic**, as a kind of supplement to the science properly so called.

8. From *Outlines of Ontological Science, by H. N. Day*, ed. 1878, pp. 123 and following.

The very conception of method involves, together with something that changes, a source or origin from which the change begins; an end or goal in which it rests or to which it tends; and a way by which the end is reached from the beginning.

A rational method, moreover, implies a unity of nature and imposes a unity on each of the fundamental elements of true method. It prescribes the right movement from some single source, to some single end, by some single way. Its function is discharged when it indicates this movement and directs it as to such single source, end, and way.

We have found in all knowledge a twofold, a subjective and an objective element—a knowing and a known. A rational method respects the change in both aspects. At every stage of progress, in all true and right knowledge the correspondence between these two constituents is maintained perfect and exact. The subjective constituent increases by the growth effected through exercise in a living agent; and the objective constituent increases in exact correspondence;—

the capacity of knowing is enlarged and intensified as the matter known is broadened and deepened. The view of method, however, will be modified according as the one or the other of these constituents is prominently regarded. We conveniently distinguish, accordingly, a **subjective** and an **objective** method in knowledge. . . .

The subjective method in knowledge respects the knowing subject. The source or origin here is ever the knowing power or function itself at each of the ever advancing stages of its progress.

The end or goal is primarily the perfection of the knowing faculty, and through that the perfection, according to its nature, of the whole organism of which this faculty is a part;—a goal ever aimed at, but never reached as a final knowing, yet in each specific act of knowing attained in its own proper degree and measure.

The way is by a continuous endeavor in accordance with the laws of thinking or knowing, in which each new measure of thinking energy attained is made the occasion and means of a still more vigorous life of thought. This is prescribed by the principle of adjacence; continuousness is but progress from next to next in order of proximity or adjacence. . . .

The objective method in knowledge respects the matter known.

The beginning in knowledge here is the **datum** presented to thought. This **datum** must be of the nature of that which can be known;—must be of the nature of truth. Every fresh attainment of truth adds so much to the volume of attainment which, with what is given on each successive occasion of thought, constitutes the **datum** for the succeeding stage.

The objective end in knowledge is truth acquired in its complete fulness and comprehensiveness—the universe of truth ;—an end never fully reached, yet in its measure attained in every new acquisition.

The way in objective knowledge is in undeviating course through the adjacent fields of truth, from boundary through to boundary, avoiding, as far as may be, under the conditions of human life, skips and divisions and devious windings.

9. From Comte's *Philosophy of the Sciences*, G. H. Lewes, London, 1853.

Atheists may therefore be regarded as the most illogical of theologians, since they attempt the theological problems while rejecting the only suitable method. (p. 25.)

That the positive Method is the only Method adapted to human capacity, the only one on which truth can be found, is easily proved : on it alone can **prevision** of phenomena depend. (p. 39.)

The present condition of science, therefore, exhibits three Methods instead of one : hence the anarchy.

To remedy the evil, all differences must cease : one Method must preside. (p. 38.)

In passing from one science to another, we discover the several modifications which method (essentially the same in all) undergoes.

A proper knowledge of the positive method can only be acquired in this way. (p. 49.)

I propose to call the relations of co-existence

and succession, usually named Laws, by the name of Methods.

Etymologically, Method is **a path** leading onwards, a way of transit. The Methods of Nature would therefore express the paths along which the activities of Nature travelled to results (phenomena). (p. 55.)

What we call Laws are nothing but the paths, or Methods, along which the Forces (of Nature) move. (p. 57.)

Astronomy is more truly scientific and has attained the highest degree of philosophical perfection that any science can ever pretend to, as respects Method,—the exact reduction of all phenomena, both in kind and in degree, to one general law (solar astronomy). (p. 83.)

A law of Nature can only be discovered by Induction or Deduction. Often, however, neither method is of itself sufficient. (p. 105.)

The Methods in which these masses (suns, planets, etc.) move, science attempts to ascertain ; but in Astronomy we speak of Motion, in Chemistry of Combination ; both are Methods of the unknown unknowable Force. (p. 113.)

The methods by which the construction of science is promoted are, Methods of Observation, Methods of obtaining clear Ideas, and Methods of Instruction. (p. 141.) (Whewell.)

The methods of observation of quantity in general are, Numeration, which is precise by the nature of number : the Measurement of Space and Time, by which aids the Measurement of the other ; the Method of Repetition ; the Method of Coincidences or Interferences. (p. 145.) (Whewell.)

QUOTATIONS ON SYSTEM.

APPENDIX B.

226. From Fleming—*Vocabulary of Philosophy*, ed. 1867.

SYSTEM is a full and connected view of all the truths of some department of knowledge. An organized body of truth, or truths arrange under one and the same idea, which idea is as the life or soul which assimilates all those truths. No truth is altogether isolated. Every truth has relation to some other. And we should try to unite the facts of our knowledge so as to see them in their several bearings. This we do when we frame them into a **system**. To do so legitimately we must begin by analysis and end with synthesis. But **system** applies not only to our knowledge, but to the objects of our knowledge. Thus we speak of the planetary **system**, the muscular **system**, the nervous **system**. We believe that the order to which we would reduce our ideas has a foundation in the nature of things. And it is this belief that encourages us to reduce our knowledge of things into a systematic order. The doing so is attended with many advantages. At the same time a spirit of systematizing may be carried too far. It is only in so far as it is in accordance with the order of nature that it can be useful or sound. Condillac has a **Traite des Systemes,** in which he traces their causes and their dangerous consequences.

SYSTEM, ECONOMY, OR CONSTITUTION. — "A **System, Economy, or Constitution**, is a one or a whole, made up of several parts, but yet that the several parts even considered as a whole do not complete the idea, unless in the notion of the whole you include the relations and respects which these parts have to each other. Every work, both of nature and of art, is a **system**; and as every particular thing, both natural and artificial, is for some use or purpose out of and beyond itself, one may add to what has been already brought into the idea of a **system**, its conduciveness to this one or more ends. Let us instance in a watch—suppose the several parts of it taken to pieces, and placed apart from each other; let a man have ever so exact a notion of these several parts, unless he considers the respects and relations which they have to each other, he will not have anything like the idea of a watch. Suppose these several parts brought together and anyhow united: neither will he yet, be the union ever so close, have an idea which will bear any resemblance to that of a watch. But let him view these several parts put together, or consider them as to be put together in the manner of a watch; let him form a notion of the relations which these several parts have to each other—all conducive in their respective ways to this purpose, showing the hour of the day; and then he has the idea of a watch. Thus it is with regard to the inward frame of man. Appetites, passions, affections, and the principle of reflection, considered merely as the several parts of our inward nature, do not give us an idea of the system or constitution of this nature ; because the constitution is formed by somewhat not yet taken into consideration, namely, by the relations which these several parts have to each other, the chief of which is the authority of reflection or conscience. It is from considering the relations which the several appetites and passions in the inward frame have to each other, and, above all, the supremacy of reflection or conscience, that we get the idea of the **system** or constitution of human nature. And from the idea itself it will as fully appear, that this our nature, *i.e.*, constitution, is adapted to virtue, as from the idea of a watch it appears that its nature, *i.e.*, constitution or **system**, is adapted to measure time."

QUOTATIONS ON ANALYSIS.

APPENDIX C.

227. From Fleming's *Vocabulary of Philosophy*, ed. 1867.

ANALYSIS and SYNTHESIS, or decomposition and recomposition. Objects of sense and of thought are presented to us in a complex state, but we can only, or at least best, understand what is simple. Among the varied objects of a landscape, I behold a tree, I separate it from the other objects, I examine separately its different parts—trunk, branches, leaves, etc., and then reuniting them into one whole I form a notion of the tree. The first part of this process is **analysis**, the second is **synthesis.** If this must be done with an individual, it is more necessary with the infinitude of objects which surround us, to evolve the one out of many, to recall the multitude to unity. We compare objects with one another to see wherein they agree ; we next, by a synthetical process, infer a general law, or generalize the coincident qualities, and perform an act of induction which is purely a synthetical process, though commonly called analytical. Thus, from our experience that bodies attract within certain limits, we infer that all bodies gravitate towards each other. The antecedent here only says that certain bodies gravitate, the consequent says all bodies gravitate. They are brought together by the mental insertion of a third proposition, which is, "that nature is uniform." This is not the product of induction, but antecedent to all induction. The statement fully expressed is, this and that body, which we know, gravitate, but nature is uniform; this and that body represent all bodies—all bodies gravitate. It is the mind which connects these things, and the process is synthetical. This is the one universal **method** in all philosophy, and different schools have differed only in the way of employing it. **Method** is the following of one thing **through** another. **Order** is the following of one thing **after** another. **Analysis** is **real**, as when a chemist separates two substances. **Logical,** as when we consider the properties of the sides and angles of a triangle separately, though we cannot think of a triangle without sides and angles.

The instruments of **analysis** are **observation** and **experiment**; of **synthesis, definition** and **classification.**

Take down a watch, **analysis**; put it up, **synthesis.**

Analysis is decomposing what is compound to detect its elements. Objects may be compound, as consisting of several distinct parts united, or of several properties equally distinct. In the former view, **analysis** will divide the object into its parts, and present them to us successively, and then the relations by which they are united. In the second case, **analysis** will separate the distinct properties, and show the relations of every kind which may be between them.

Analysis is the resolving into its constituent elements of a compound heterogeneous substance. Thus, water can be analyzed into oxygen and hydrogen, atmospheric air into these and azote.

Abstraction is **analysis,** since it is decomposition, but what distinguishes it is that it is exercised upon qualities which by themselves have no real existence. **Classification** is **synthesis. Induction** rests upon **analysis. Deduction** is a **synthetical process. Demonstration** includes both.

QUOTATIONS ON SYNTHESIS.

APPENDIX D.

228. From Fleming's *Vocabulary of Philosophy*, ed. 1867.

SYNTHESIS "consists in assuming the causes discovered and established as principles, and by them explaining the phenomena proceeding from them and proving the explanation."

" Every **synthesis** which has not started with a complete **analysis** ends at a result which, in Greek, is called **hypothesis**; instead of which, if **synthesis** has been preceded by a sufficient **analysis**, the **synthesis** founded upon that **analysis** leads to a result which in Greek is called **system**. The legitimacy of every **synthesis** is directly owing to the exactness of **analysis**; every system which is merely an hypothesis is a vain system ; every **synthesis** which has not been preceded by analysis is a pure imagination : but at the same time every analysis which does not aspire to a **synthesis** which may be equal to it, is an analysis which halts on the way. On the one hand, **synthesis** without analysis gives a false science ; on the other hand, analysis without **synthesis** gives an incomplete science. An incomplete science is a hundred times more valuable than a false science ; but neither a false science nor an incomplete science is the ideal of science. The ideal of science, the ideal of philosophy, can be realized only by a method which combines the two processes of **analysis** and **synthesis.**"

QUOTATIONS ON DEFINITION.

APPENDIX E.

229. From Fleming's *Vocabulary of Philosophy*, ed. 1867.

DEFINITION (**definio**, to mark out limits).

"The simplest and most correct notion of a **definition** is, a proposition declaratory of the meaning of a word."

Definition signifies "laying down a boundary;" and is used in Logic to signify "an expression which explains any term so as to **separate** it from everything else, as a boundary separates fields. Logicians distinguish **definitions** into **Nominal** and **Real.**

"Definitions are called **nominal,** which explain merely the **meaning of the term**; and **real,** which explain the nature of the thing signified by that term. Logic is concerned with **nominal** definitions alone."

"By a **real,** in contrast to a **verbal** or **nominal definition,** the logicians do not intend 'the giving an adequate conception of the nature and essence of a thing;' that is, of a thing considered in itself, and apart from the conceptions of it already possessed. By **verbal** definition is meant the more accurate determination of the signification of a **word**; by **real** the more accurate determination of the contents of a **notion**. The one clears up the relation of **words to notions**; the other of **notions to things**. The substitution of **notional** for **real** would, perhaps, remove the ambiguity. But if we retain the term **real**, the aim of a **verbal** definition being to specify the **thought denoted by the word,** such definition ought to be called **notional,** on the principle on which the definition of a notion is called **real**; for this definition is the exposition of what things are comprehended in a thought."

" In the sense in which **nominal** and **real** definitions were distinguished by the scholastic logicians, logic is concerned with **real,** *i.e.*, **notional** definitions only ; to explain the meaning of words belongs to dictionaries or grammars."

" There is a real distinction between definitions of names and what are erroneously called definitions of things ; but it is that the latter, along with the meaning of a name, covertly asserts a matter of fact. This covert assertion is not a **definition,** but a postulate. The **definition** is a mere identical proposition, which gives information only about the use of language, and from which no conclusions respecting matters of fact can possibly be drawn. The accompanying postulate, on the other hand, affirms a fact which may lead to consequences of every degree of importance. It affirms the real existence of things, possessing the combination of attributes set forth in the definition, and this, if true, may be foundation sufficient to build a whole fabric of scientific truth."

Real definitions are divided into **essential** and **accidental.** An **essential** definition states what are regarded as the constituent parts of the essence of that which is to be defined ; and an accidental **definition** (or description) lays down what are regarded as circumstances belonging to it, viz., properties or accidents, such as causes, effects, &c.

"**Essential definition** is divided into **physical** (natural) and **logical** (metaphysical) ; the **physical definition** being made by an enumeration of such parts as are **actually** separable ; such as are the hull, masts, &c., of a ' ship ' ; the root, trunk, branches, bark, &c., of a ' tree.' The **logical definition** consists of the genus and difference, which are called by some the **metaphysical** (ideal) parts ; as being not two real parts into which an **individual** object can (as in the former case), be actually divided, but only different views taken (notions formed) of a **class** of objects, by one mind. Thus a magnet would be defined **logically,** ' an iron ore having attraction for iron.' "

Accidental or descriptive definition may be— 1. **Causal;** as when man is defined as made after the image of God, and for his glory. 2. **Accidental ;** as when he is defined to be **animal, bipes implume.** 3. **Genetic ;** as when the means by which it is made are indicated ; as, if a straight line fixed at one end be drawn round by the other end so as to return to itself, a circle will be described. Or, 4. **Per oppositum**; as, when virtue is said to be flying from vice.

The rules of a good definition are :—1. That it be adequate. If it be too narrow, you explain **a part** instead of **a whole**; if too extensive, **a whole** instead of **a part**. 2. That it be clearer (*i.e.*, consist of ideas less complex) than the thing defined. 3. That it be in just a sufficient number of proper words. Metaphorical words are excluded because they are indefinite.

2. From Mill's *System of Logic*, pp. 105–106, 8° edition.

The simplest and most correct notion of a Definition is, a proposition declaratory of the meaning of a word ; namely, either the meaning which it bears in common acceptation, or that which the speaker or writer, for the particular purposes of his discourse, intends to annex to it.
. . . . This form of definition is the most precise and least equivocal of any ; but it is not brief enough, and is besides too technical for common discourse. The more usual mode of declaring the connotation of a name, is to predicate of it another name or names of known signification, which connote the same aggregation of attributes. . . . . . The definition of a name, according to this view of it, is the sum total of all the **essential** propositions which can be framed with that name for their subject. All propositions the truth of which is implied in the name, all those which we are made aware of by merely hearing the name, are included in the definition, if complete, and may be evolved from it without

the aid of any other premises ; whether the definition expresses them in two or three words, or in a larger number. It is, therefore, not without reason that Condillac and other writers have affirmed a definition to be an **analysis**. To resolve any complex whole into the elements of which it is compounded, is the meaning of analysis : and this we do when we replace one word which connotes a set of attributes collectively, by two or more which connote the same attributes singly, or in smaller groups.

QUOTATIONS ON ABSTRACTION.

APPENDIX F.

230. From Fleming's *Vocabulary of Philosophy*.

ABSTRACT, ABSTRACTION (**abstractio**, from **abs traho**, to draw away from. It is also called **separatio** and **resolutio**). Dobrisch observes that the term **abstraction** is used sometimes in a psychological, sometimes in a logical sense. In the former we are said to abstract the attention from certain distinctive features of objects presented. In the latter, we are said to abstract certain portions of a given concept from the remainder. (Mansel.)

"ABSTRACTION (Psychological)," says Mr. Stewart, "is the power of considering certain qualities or attributes of an object apart from the rest ; or, as I would rather choose to define it, the power which the understanding has of separating the combinations which are presented to it." Perhaps it may be more correctly regarded as a **process** rather than a **power**—as a **function** rather than a **faculty**. Dr. Reid has called it " an **operation** of the understanding." . . . The chemist separates into their elements those bodies which are submitted to his analysis. The psychologist does the same thing mentally. . . . In contemplating mind, he may think of its capacity of feeling without thinking of its power of activity, or the faculty of memory apart from any or all of the other faculties with which it is allied.

ABSTRACTION (LOGICAL), " As we have described it," says Mr. Thomson (*Outline of the Laws of Thought* p. 107), " would include three separate acts ; first, an act of **comparison**, which brings several intuitions together ; next, one of **reflection**, which seeks for some marks which they all possess, and by which they may be combined into one group ; and last, one of **generalization**, which forms the new general notion or conception. Kant, however, confines the name of **abstraction** to the last of the three ; others apply it to the second. It is not of much consequence whether we enlarge or narrow the meaning of the word, so long as we see the various steps in the process. The word means a drawing away of the common marks from all the distinctive marks which the single objects have." . .

Mr. J. S. Mill uses the term **abstract** as opposed to **concrete**. By an abstract name he means the name of an attribute—by a concrete name the name of an object.

QUOTATIONS ON GENERALIZATION.

APPENDIX G.

231. 1. From Fleming's *Vocabulary of Philosophy*, ed. 1867.

Generalization " is the act of comprehending, under a common name, several objects agreeing in some point which we abstract from each of them, and which that common name serves to indicate."

" When we are contemplating several individuals which **resemble** each other in some **part** of their nature, we can (by attending to **that part alone,** and not to those points wherein they differ) assign them **one common name,** which will express or stand for them merely as far as they all **agree;** and which, of course, will be applicable to all or any of them (which process is called generalization) ; and each of these names is called a **common** term, from its belonging to them **all alike;** or a **predicable,** because it may be predicated affirmatively of them or any of them."

Generalization is of two kinds—**classification** and **generalization** properly so called.

When we observe facts accompanied by diverse circumstances, and reduce these circumstances to such as are essential and common, we obtain a law.

When we observe individual objects and arrange them according to their common characters, we obtain a class. When the characters selected are such as belong essentially to the nature of the objects, the class corresponds with the law. When the character selected is not natural the **classification** is artificial. If we were to class animals into white and red, we would have a **classification** which had no reference to the laws of their nature. But if we classify them as vertebrate or invertebrate, we have a **classification** founded on their organization. Artificial **classification** is of no value in science, it is a mere aid to the memory. Natural **classification** is the foundation of all science. This is sometimes called **generalization**. It is more properly **classification**.

The law of gravitation is exemplified in the fall of a single stone to the ground. But many stones and other heavy bodies must have been observed to fall before the fact was generalized, and the law stated. And in this process of **generalizing** there is involved a principle which experience does not furnish. Experience, how extensive soever it may be, can only give the particular, yet from the particular we rise to the general, and affirm not only that all heavy bodies which have been observed, but that all heavy bodies whether they have been observed or not, gravitate. In this is implied a belief that there is order in nature, that under the same circumstances the same substances will present the same phenomena. This is a principle furnished by reason, the process founded on it embodies elements furnished by experience.

The results of **generalization** are general notions expressed by general terms. Objects are classed according to certain properties which they have in common, into genera and species. Hence arose the question which caused centuries of acrimonious discussion. Have genera and species a real, independent existence, or are they only to be found in the mind?

The principle of **generalization** is, that beings howsoever different agree or are homogeneous in some respect.

2. From Jevon's *Principles of Science*, pp. 597–599, ed. 1877.

The term generalization, as commonly used, includes two processes which are of different character, but are often closely associated together. In the first place, we generalize when we recognize even in two objects a common nature. We cannot detect the slightest similarity without opening the way to inference from one case to the other. If we compare a cubical crystal with a regular octahedron, there is little apparent similarity; but, as soon as we perceive that either can be produced by the symmetrical modification of the other, we discover a groundwork of similarity in the crystals, which enable us to infer many things of one, because they are true of the other. Our knowledge of ozone took its rise from the time when the similarity of smell, attending electric sparks, strokes of lightning, and the slow combustion of phosphorus, was noticed by Schönbein. There was a time when the rainbow was an inexplicable phenomenon—a portent, like a comet, and a cause of superstitious hopes and fears. But we find the true spirit of science in Roger Bacon, who desires us to consider the objects which present the same colours as the rainbow; he mentions hexagonal crystals from Ireland and India, but he bids us not suppose that the hexagonal form is essential, for similar colours may be detected in many transparent stones. Drops of water scattered by the oar in the sun, the spray from a water-wheel, the dewdrops lying on the grass in the summer morning, all display a similar phenomenon. No sooner have we grouped together these apparently diverse instances, than we have begun to generalise, and have acquired a power of applying to one instance what we can detect of others. Even when we do not apply the knowledge gained to new objects, our comprehension of those already observed is greatly strengthened and deepened by learning to view them as particular cases of a more general property.

A second process, to which the name of generalization is often given, consists in passing from a fact or partial law to a multitude of unexamined cases, which we believe to be subject to the same conditions. Instead of merely recognising similarity as it is brought before us, we predict its existence before our senses can detect it, so that generalisation of this kind endows us with a prophetic power of more or less probability. Having observed that many substances assume, like water and mercury, the three states of solid, liquid, and gas, and having assured ourselves by frequent trial that the greater the means we possess of heating and cooling, the more substances we can vaporise and freeze, we pass confidently in advance of fact, and assume that all substances are capable of these three forms. Such a generalisation was accepted by Lavoisier and Laplace before many of the corroborative facts now in our possession were known. The reduction of a single comet beneath the sway of gravity was considered sufficient indication that all comets obey the same power. Few persons doubted that the law of gravity extended over the whole heavens ; certainly the fact that a few stars out of many millions manifest the action of gravity, is now held to be sufficient evidence of its general extension over the visible universe

QUOTATIONS ON CLASSIFICATION.

APPENDIX H.

232. 1. From Fleming's *Vocabulary of Philosophy*, ed. 1858, pp. 91-92.

"Montesquieu observed very justly, that in their **classification** of the citizens, the great legislators of antiquity made the greatest display of their powers, and even soared above themselves." Burke, *On the French Revolution.*

"A **class** consists of several things coming under a common description." Whately, *Log.*, b. i., § 3.

"The sorting of a multitude of things into parcels, for the sake of knowing them better, and remembering them more easily, is **classification.** When we attempt to classify a multitude of things, we first observe some respects in which they differ from each other; for we could not classify things that are entirely alike; as, for instance, a bushel of peas; we then separate things that are not alike, and bring together things that are similar." Taylor, *Elements of Thought.*

"In every act of **classification**, two steps must be taken; certain marks are to be selected, the possession of which is to be the title to admission into the class, and then all the objects that possess them are to be ascertained. When the marks selected are really important and connected closely with the nature and functions of the thing, the **classification** is said to be **natural**; where they are such as do not affect the nature of the objects materially, and belong in common to things the most different in their main properties, it is **artificial**." Thomson, *Outline of Laws of Thought*, 2d edit., p. 377.

The condition common to both modes of **classification**, is to comprehend everything and to suppose nothing. But the rules for a natural **classification** are more strict than for an artificial or arbitrary one. We may classify objects arbitrarily in any point of view in which we are pleased to regard them. But a natural **classification** can only proceed according to the real nature and qualities of the objects. The advantages of **classification** are to give a convenient form to our acquirements, and to enlarge our knowledge of the relations in which different objects stand to one another. A good **classification** should—1st, Rest on one principle or analogous principles. 2d, The principle or principles should be of a constant and permanent character. 3d, It should be natural, that is, even when artificial, it should not be violent or forced. 4th, It should clearly and easily apply to all the objects classified.

The principles on which **classification** rests are these :—1st, of **Generalization**; 2d, of **Specification**; and 3d, of **Continuity**.

Classification proceeds upon observed resemblances. **Generalization** rests upon the principle, that the same or similar causes will produce similar effects.—Mill, *Log.*, b. i., chap. 7, § 4; McCosh, *Typical Forms*, b. iii., chap. 1.

2. From Jevons' *Elementary Lessons in Logic*, ed. 1878, pp. 276-286.

It may be said that the subject we are treating is coextensive with the science of logic. All thought, all reasoning, so far as it deals with general names or general notions, may be said to consist in classification. Every common name or general name is the name of a class, and every name of a class is a common name. "Metal" is the name of one class of substantives so often used in our syllogistic examples; "Element" of another class, of which the former class is part. Reasoning has been plausibly represented to consist in affirming of the parts of a class whatever may be affirmed of the whole. Every law of nature which we arrive at enables us to classify together a number of facts, and it would hardly be too much to define logic as the **theory of classification.** . . . **Classification** may perhaps be best defined as **the arrangement of things, or our notions of them, according to their resemblances, or identities.**

Every class should so be constituted as to contain objects exactly resembling each other in certain definite qualities, which are stated in the definition of the class. The more numerous and extensive the resemblances which are thus indicated by any system of classes, the more perfect and useful must that system be considered.

Mr. Mill thus describes his view of the meaning—"Classification is a contrivance for the best possible ordering of the ideas of objects in our minds ; for causing the ideas to accompany or succeed one another in such a way as shall give us the greatest command over our knowledge already acquired, and lead most directly to the acquisition of more. The general problem of classification, in reference to these purposes may be stated as follows : To provide that things shall be thought of in such groups, and those groups in such an order, as will best conduce to the remembrance, and to the ascertainment of their laws."

A collection of objects may be classified in an indefinite number of ways. Any quality which is possessed by some and not by others may be taken as the first **difference**, and the groups thus distinguished may be subdivided in succession by any other qualities taken at will. Thus a library of books might be arranged, (1) according to size, (2) according to the language in which they are written, (3) according to the alphabetic order of their authors' names, (4) according to their subjects ; and in various other ways. In large libraries and in catalogues such modes of arrangement are adopted and variously combined. . . . The population of a kingdom, again, may be classified in an almost endless number of ways with regard to different purposes or sciences. The population of the United Kingdom may be divided according to their place of birth, as English, Welsh, Scotch, Irish, Colonial-born and aliens. The ethnographer would divide them into Anglo-Saxons, Cymri, Gaels, Picts, &c. The statist arranges them according to age; to condition, as married, unmarried, widowed, etc.; to state of body, as able, incapacitated, blind, imbecile. . . .

In the natural world, again, we may make various classifications. Plants may be arranged according to the country from which they are derived; the kind of place or habitat in which they flourish; the time they live, as annual, biennial, perennial; their size, as herbs, shrubs, trees; their properties, as esculents, drugs, or poisons: all these are distinct from the classifications which the botanist devises to represent the natural affinities or relationships of plants. It is thus evident that in making a classification we have no one fixed method which can be ascertained by rule, but that an indefinite number of choices or alternatives are usually open to us. Logic cannot in such cases do much; and it is really the work of the special sciences to investigate the character of the classification required. All that logic can do is to point out certain general requirements and principles.

The first requisite of a good classification is, that it should be **appropriate to the purpose in hand**; that is to say, the points of resemblance selected to form the leading classes shall be those of importance to the practical use of the classification. All those things must be arranged together which require to be treated alike, and those things must be separated which require to be treated separately. . . .

Another and, in a scientific point of view, the most important requisite of a good classification, is that **it shall enable the greatest possible number of general assertions to be made.** This is the criterion, as stated by Dr. Whewell, which distinguishes a natural from an artificial system of classification, and we must carefully dwell upon its meaning. It will be apparent that a good classification is more than a mere orderly arrangement; it involves a process of induction which will bring to light all the more general relations which exist between the things classified. An arrangement of books will generally be artificial; the octavo volumes will not have any common character except being of an octavo size. An alphabetical arrangement of names again is exceedingly appropriate and convenient to many purposes, but is artificial because it allows of few or no general assertions. We cannot make any general assertions whatever about persons because their names happen to begin with an A or a B, a P or a W. . . .

In a classification of plants again we meet with most deep and natural distinctions between the great classes called Exogens, Endogens, and Acrogens. . . . These are the very widest classes in what is called **the natural system of botanical arrangement;** but similar principles are observed in all its minor classes.

The continual efforts of botanists are directed

to bringing the great multitudes of plants together in species, genera, orders, classes, and in various intermediate groups, so that the members of each group shall have the greatest number of points of mutual resemblance and the fewest points of resemblance to members of other groups. Thus is best fulfilled the great purpose of classification, which reduces multiplicity to unity, and enables us **to infer of all the other members of a class what we know of any one member**, provided we distinguish properly between those qualities which are likely or are known to belong to the class, and those which are peculiar to the individual. It is a necessary condition of correct classification, as remarked by Prof. Huxley, that the definition of a group shall hold exactly true of all the members of a group, and not of the members of any other group. . . .

Natural classifications give us the deepest resemblances and relations, and may lead us ultimately to a knowledge of the way in which the varieties of things are produced. They are, therefore, essential to a true science, and may almost be said to constitute the framework of the science. . . .

Closely connected with the process of Classification is that of **abstraction.** To abstract is to separate the qualities common to all individuals of a group from the peculiarities of each individual. The notion " triangle" is the result of abstraction in so far as we can reason concerning triangles, without any regard to the particular size or shape of any one triangle. **All classification implies abstraction,** for in framing and defining the class I must separate the common qualities from the peculiarities. When I abstract, too, I form a general conception, or one, which, generally speaking, embraces many objects. If, indeed, the quality abstracted is a peculiar property of the class, or one which belongs to the whole and not to any other objects, I may not increase the extent of the notion, so that Mr. Herbert Spencer is, perhaps, right in holding that **we can abstract without generalizing.** We often use this word **generalization,** and the process may be defined as inferring of a whole class what we know only of a part. Whenever we regard the qualities of a thing as not confined to that thing only but as extended to other objects; when, in fact, we consider a thing only as a member of a class, we are said to generalize. . . . Dr. Whewell added to the superabundance of terms to express the same processes when he introduced the expression **Colligation of facts.**

Whenever two things are found to have similar properties so as to be placed in the same class they may be said to be **connected together.**

We connect together the places of a planet as it moves round the sun, when we conceive them as points upon a common ellipse. Whenever we thus join together previously disconnected facts, by a suitable general notion or hypothesis, we are said to colligate them. Dr. Whewell adds that the general conceptions employed must be (1) clear, and (2) appropriate ; but it may well be questioned whether there is anything really different in these processes from the general process of natural classification which we have considered.

QUOTATIONS ON INDUCTION.

APPENDIX I.

233. 1. From Smith—*Synonyms Discriminated*—"Inference"—ed. 1878.

Inference (Lat. **in**, and **ferre**, to bring) is the broadest of these terms (see below), denoting any process by which from one truth or fact laid down or known we draw another. Inference may be either by induction or deduction, and hence may be probable or certain. Inference by induction is more or less probable, except where all cases of the kind have been collated, when it ceases, strictly speaking, to be inference, and is only the assigning of a common name, or stating an universal proposition. From having seen twenty swans all white, one might infer that all swans are so. This would be only a probability in itself, and, as a fact, not true. In induction we observe a sufficient number of individual facts or cases, and extending by analogy what is true of them to others of the same class, establish a general principle or law. This is the method of physical science. The process of deduction is the converse of this. We lay down a general truth, and connect a particular case with it by means of a middle term. When inference is conducted by the syllogistic process, it is **Deduction** (Lat. **deducere,** to draw from), which, if rightly conducted, must be logically sound, though not necessarily true in fact. In a chain of reasoning the minor, subordinate, or less fully-expressed conclusions are called inferences, as distinguished from the great common inference or **Conclusion,** which terminates and establishes, or, as it were, shuts up (**Concludere,** to shut) the argument. A conclusion is a proposition viewed relatively to others from which it has been deduced. A **Consequence** (Lat. **consequi,** to follow) is a conclusion regarded as admitting of degrees of closeness or directness. Between the first stage of any argument and any particular consequence several links of reasoning may intervene. Hence the common phrase, " remote consequences," as meaning results which will follow sooner or later from what has been stated or conceded.

2. From Day's *Elements of Logic,* ed. 1868, p. 226.

The accepted characteristics of Induction are :

(*a*) It is a process of Thought that is identical in essential character in all those movements of Intelligence which induce, which infer mediately otherwise than by deduction. There is but one Induction, as there is but one Deduction in all Thought.

(*b*) It is a reasoning, being a derivative Judgment, not a Concept ; an inference from a **datum,** implying a new proper Judgment-Cognition, not a mere synthesis of subjects or of predicates—that is, not a Concept.

(c) It is a mediate reasoning, being derived not from a single Judgment, but from a plurality of Judgments, related to each other under the relationship of part to complementary part in two of their terms which are alike related to the third or middle term as parts to a whole.

3. From Fleming's *Vocabulary of Philosophy*, ed. 1858, pp. 252–254.

Method or Process of Induction.—"It has been said that Aristotle attributed the **discovery** of **induction** to Socrates, deriving the word from the Socratic accumulation of instances, serving as antecedents to establish the requisite conclusion."—Devey, *Log.*, p. 151, note.

Induction is a kind of argument which infers, respecting a whole class, what has been ascertained respecting one or more individuals of that class.—Whately, *Log.*, book ii., chap. 5, § 5.

"**Induction** is that operation of mind by which we infer that what we know to be true in a particular case or cases, will be true in all cases which resemble the former in certain assignable respects. In other words, **induction** is the process by which we conclude that what is true of certain individuals of a class, is true of the whole class, or that what is true at certain times will be true under similar circumstances at all times."—Mill, *Log.*, b. iii., ch. 2, § 1.

"**Induction** is usually defined to be the process of drawing a general rule from a sufficient number of particular cases ; **deduction** is the converse process of proving that some property belongs to the particular case from the consideration that it belongs to the whole class in which the case is found. That all bodies tend to fall towards the earth is a truth which we have obtained from examining a number of bodies coming under our notice, by **induction**; if from this general principle we argue that the stone we throw from our hand will show the same tendency, we adopt the **deductive** method. . . . More exactly, we may define the **inductive** method as the process of discovering laws and rules from facts, and causes from effects; and the **deductive**, as the method of deriving facts from laws and effects from their causes."— (Thomson, *Outline of the Laws of Thought*, 2d edit., *pp.* 321, 323.)

According to Sir William Hamilton (*Discussions*, p. 156), "**Induction** has been employed to designate three very different operations—1. The objective process of investigating particular facts, as preparatory to **induction**, which is not a process of reasoning of any kind. 2. A material illation of the universal from the singular, as warranted either by the general analogy of nature, or the special presumptions afforded by the object-matter of any real science. 3. A formal illation of the universal from the individual, as legitimated solely by the laws of thought, and abstract from the conditions of this or that 'particular matter.' The second of these is the **inductive** method of Bacon, which proceeds by way of rejections and conclusions, so as to arrive at those axioms or general laws from which we infer by way of synthesis other particulars unknown to us, and perhaps placed beyond reach of direct examination. Aristotle's definition coincides with the third, and '**induction** is an inference drawn from all the particulars' (*Prior Analyt.*, ii., c. 23). The second and third have been confounded. But the second is not a logical process at all, since the conclusion is not necessarily inferrible from the premiss, for the **some** of the antecedent does not necessarily legitimate the **all** of the conclusion, notwithstanding that the procedure may be warranted by the material problem of the science or the fundamental principles of the human understanding. The third alone is properly an **induction** of Logic; for Logic does not consider things, but the general forms of thought under which the mind conceives them; and the logical inference is not determined by any relation of casuality between the premiss and the conclusion, but by the subjective relation of reason and consequence as involved in the thought."

" The Baconian or Material **Induction** proceeds on the assumption of general laws in the relations of physical phenomena, and endeavours, by select observations and experiments, to detect the law in any particular case. This, whatever be its value as a general method of physical investigation, has no place in Formal Logic. The Aristotelian or Formal **Induction** proceeds on the assumption of general laws of thought, and inquires into the instances in which, by such laws, we are necessitated to reason from an accumulation of particular instances to an universal rule."—Mansel, *Prolegom. Log.*, p. 209.

Principle of Induction.—By the principle of **induction** is meant the ground or warrant on which we conclude that what has happened in certain cases, which have been observed, will also happen in other cases, which have not been observed. This principle is involved in the words of the wise man, Eccles. i. 9, " The thing that hath been, it is that which shall be : and that which is done is that which shall be done." In nature there is nothing insulated. All things exist in consequence of a sufficient reason, all events occur according to the efficacy of proper causes. In the language of Newton, **Effectuum naturalium ejusdem generis eædem sunt causæ.** The same causes produce the same effects. The principle of **induction** is an application of the principle of casuality. Phenomena have their proper causes, and these causes operate according to a fixed law. This law has been expressed by saying, substance is persistent. Our belief in the established order of nature is a primitive judgment, according to Dr. Reid and others, and the ground of all the knowledge we derive from experience. According to others this belief is a result or inference derived from experience.

4. From Whewell's *Novum Organon Renovatum*, 3d edition, 1858, p. 139 :—

The **Pure** Mathematical Sciences can hardly be called **Inductive** Sciences. Their principles are not obtained by Induction from Facts, but are necessarily assumed in reasoning upon the subject-matter which those sciences involve.

5. From *English Cyclopædia*, edition 1867.

Induction ($\dot{\epsilon}\pi\alpha\gamma\omega\gamma\dot{\eta}$), as defined by Archbishop Whately, is "a kind of argument which infers respecting a whole class what has been ascertained respecting one or more individuals of that class." According to Sir William Hamilton the word has been employed to designate three very different operations :—1. The objective process of investigating particular facts, as preparatory to Induction, which he observes is manifestly not a process of reasoning of any kind ; 2. A material illation of a universal from a singular, as warranted either by the general analogy of nature or the special presumptions afforded by the object matter of any real science ; 3. A formal illation of a universal from the individual, as legitimated solely by the laws of thought and abstracted from the conditions of any particular matter. The second of these operations is the inductive method of Bacon, which proceeds by means of rejections and conclusions, so as to arrive at those axioms or general laws from which we may infer by way of synthesis other particulars unknown to us, and perhaps placed beyond reach of direct examination. ('*Nov. Org.*,' '*Aph.*,' c. iii., c. v.) Aristotle's definition coincides with the third, and induction " is an inference drawn from all particulars." ('*Prior Analy.*,' ii., c. xxiii.) The second and third processes are improperly confounded by most writers on logic, and treated as one simple and purely logical operation. But the second is not a logical process at all; since the conclusion is not necessarily inferrible from the premise, for the **some** of the antecedent does not necessarily legitimate the **all** of the conclusion, notwithstanding that the procedure may be warranted by the material problem of the science, or the fundamental principles of the human understanding. The third alone is properly an induction of logic; for logic does not consider things, but the general forms of thought under which the mind conceives them; and the logical inference is not determined by any relation of causality between the premise and conclusion, but by the subjective relation of reason and consequence as involved in the thought. The inductive process is exactly the reverse of the deductive; for while the latter proceeds from the whole to the part, the former ascends from the part to the whole: since it is only under the character of a constituted or containing whole, or as a constituent and contained part, that anything can become the term of logical argumentation. Of these two processes, Sir William Hamilton gives the following figures:—

Induction.	Deduction.
X Y Z are **A**.	**B** is **A**.
X Y Z are whole **B**.	**X Y Z** are under **B**.
∴ whole **B** is **A**.	∴ **X Y Z** are **A**.
or,	or,
A contains **X Y Z**.	**A** contains **B**.
X Y Z contains **B**.	**B** contains **X Y Z**.
∴ **A** contains **B**.	∴ **A** contains **X Y Z**.

This confusion of material and logical induction led Gillies and others to insist on the sameness of the Baconian and Aristotelian induction; while Campbell and Dugald Stewart, who totally mistook the value of all logical inference, yet rightly maintained their difference.

By Aristotle, induction and deduction are viewed as in certain respects similar in form; but in others as diametrically opposed, the latter being an analysis of the whole into its parts, by descending from the more general to the more particular; but the former descends by a synthetical process from the parts to the whole. The logicians, who misapprehended the nature of induction, reduced it to a deductive syllogism of the third form, and thereby overthrew the validity of all deduction itself, since the latter is only possible by means of the former, which legitimates the proposition from which its reasoning proceeds.

Again, the Aristotelian induction was drawn from all the particulars, whereas the confusion which Sir W. Hamilton has pointed out gave rise to a division of the inductive process into perfect and imperfect, according as the enumeration of particulars is complete or incomplete. The latter gives only a probable result, whereas the necessity of the conclusion is essential to all logical inference, as its demonstrative stringency depends upon the form of the illation, and not upon the truth of the premises. It is proper to add, that no one ever knew the distinction between the imperfect and perfect forms of the conclusion better than Aristotle himself.

Induction (Mathematics). The method of induction, in the sense in which the word is used in natural philosophy, is not known in pure mathematics. There certainly are instances in which a general proposition is proved by a collection of the demonstrations of different cases, which may remind the investigator of the inductive process, or the collection of the general from the particular. Such instances however must not be taken as permanent, for it usually happens that a general demonstration is discovered as soon as attention is turned to the subject.

There is however one particular method of proceeding which is extremely common in mathematical reasoning, and to which we propose to give the name of **successive induction.** It has the character of induction as defined by the logicians, because it is really the collection of a general truth from a demonstration which implies the examination of every particular case; but it adds to the necessary character of induction that each case depends upon one or more of those which precede. ·Substituting demonstration for observation, the mathematical process is truly inductive. A couple of instances of the method will enable the mathematical reader to recognize a mode of investigation with which he is already familiar.

Example 1.—The sum of any number of successive odd numbers, beginning from unity, is a square number, namely, the square of half the even number which follows the last odd number.

Let this proposition be true in any one single instance; that is, n being some whole number, let $1, 3, 5 \ldots$ up to $2n+1$ put together give $(n+1)^2$. Then the next odd number being $2n+3$, the sum of all the odd numbers up to $2n+3$ will be $(n+1)^2 + 2n + 3$, or $n^2 + 4n + 4$, or $(n+2)^2$. But $n+2$ is the half of the even number next following $2n+3$: consequently, if the proposition be true of any one set of odd numbers, it is true of one more. But it is true of the first odd number 1, for this is the square of half the even number next following. Consequently, being true of 1, it is true of $1+3$; being true of $1+3$, it is true of $1+3+5$; being true of $1+3+5$, it is true of $1+3+5+7$, and so on **ad infinitum**.

Example 2.—The formula $x^n - a^n$, n being a whole number, is always algebraically divisible by $x-a$.

$$x^n - a^n = x^n - a^{n-1}x + a^{n-1}x - a^n$$
$$= x(x^{n-1} - a^{n-1}) + a^{n-1}(x-a)$$

In this last expression the second term $a^{n-1}(x-a)$ is obviously divisible by $x-a$: if then any one of the succession

$$x-a, \; x^2-a^2, \; x^3-a^3, \; x^4-a^4, \; \&c.$$

be divisible by $x-a$, so is the next. But this is obviously true of the first, therefore it is true of the second; being true of the second, it is true of the third; and so on, **ad infinitum**.

There are cases in which the successive induction only brings any term within the general rule, when two, three, or more of the terms immediately preceding are brought within it. Thus in the application of this method to the deduction of the well known consequence of

$$x + \frac{1}{x} = 2\cos\theta,$$

namely,

$$x^n + \frac{1}{x^n} = 2\cos n\theta,$$

it can only be shown that any one case of this theorem is true, by showing that the preceding two cases are true; thus its truth, when n = 5 and n = 6, makes it necessarily follow when n = 7. In this case the two first instances must be established (when n=1 by hypothesis, and when n=2 by independent demonstration), which two establish the third, the second and third establish the fourth, and so on.

An instance of mathematical induction occurs in many equations of differences, in every recurring series, etc.

6. From Jevons' *Elementary Lessons in Logic*, pp. 208-28, ed. 1878.

To express the difference between knowledge derived deductively and that obtained inductively the Latin phrases *à priori* and *à posteriori* are often used. By **A priori** reasoning we mean argument based on truths previously known; **A posteriori** reasoning, on the contrary, proceeds to infer from the consequences of a general truth what that general truth is. Many philosophers consider that the mind is naturally in possession of certain laws or truths which it must recognise in every act of thought ; all such, if they exist, would be *à priori* truths. It cannot be doubted, for instance, that we must always recognise in thought the three Primary Laws of Thought considered in Lesson xiv. We have there an *à priori* knowledge that "matter cannot both have weight and be without weight," or that "every thing must be either self-luminous or not self-luminous." But there is no law of thought which can oblige us to think that matter has weight, and luminous ether has not weight ; that Jupiter and Venus are not self-luminous, but that comets are to some extent self-luminous. These are facts which are no doubt necessary consequences of the laws of nature and the general constitution of the world ; but as we are not naturally acquainted with all the secrets of creation, we have to learn them by observation, or by the *à posteriori* method.

It is not however usual at the present time to restrict the name *à priori* to truths obtained altogether without recourse to observation. Knowledge may originally be of an *à posteriori* origin, and yet having been long in possession, and having acquired the greatest certainty, it may be the ground of deductions, and may then be said to give *à priori* knowledge. Thus it is now believed by all scientific men that force cannot be created or destroyed by any of the processes of nature. If this be true the force which disappears when a bullet strikes a target must be converted into something else, and on à priori grounds we may assert that heat will be the result. It is true that we might easily learn the same truth à posteriori, by picking up portions of a bullet which has just struck a target and observing that they are warm. But there is a great advantage in à priori knowledge; we can often apply it in cases where experiment or observation would be difficult. If I lift a stone and then drop it, the most delicate instruments could hardly show that the stone was heated by striking the earth; yet on à priori grounds I know that it must have been so, and can easily calculate the amount of heat produced. Similarly we know, without the trouble of observation, that the Falls of Niagara and all other waterfalls produce heat. This is fairly an instance of à priori knowledge because no one that I have heard of has tried the fact or proved it à posteriori; nevertheless the knowledge is originally founded on the experiments of Mr. Joule, who observed in certain well-chosen cases how much force is equivalent to a certain amount of heat. The reader, however, should take care not to confuse the meaning of à priori thus explained with that given to the words by the philosophers who hold the mind to be in the possession of knowledge independently of all observation.

It is not difficult to see that the à priori method is equivalent to the synthetic method considered in intension, the à posteriori method of course being equivalent to the analytic method. But the same difference is really expressed in the words deductive and inductive; and we shall frequently need to consider it in the following lessons.

PERFECT INDUCTION AND THE INDUCTIVE SYLLOGISM.

WE have in previous lessons considered deductive reasoning, which consists in combining two or more general propositions synthetically, and thus arriving at a conclusion which is a proposition or truth of less generality than the premises, that is to say, it applies to fewer individual instances than the separate premises from which it was inferred. When I combine the general truth that " metals are good conductors of heat," with the truth that " aluminium is a metal," I am enabled by a syllogism in the mood Barbara to infer that " aluminium is a good conductor of heat." As this is a proposition concerning one metal only, it is evidently less general than the premise, which referred to all metals whatsoever. In induction, on the contrary, we proceed from less general, or even from individual facts, to more general propositions, truths, or, as we shall often call them, Laws of Nature. When it is known that Mercury moves in an elliptic orbit round the Sun, as also Venus, the Earth, Mars, Jupiter, &c., we are able to arrive at the simple and general truth that " all the planets move in elliptic orbits round the sun." This is an example of an inductive process of reasoning.

It is true that we may reason without rendering our conclusion either more or less general than the premises, as in the following :—

Snowdon is the highest mountain in England or Wales.

Snowdon is not so high as Ben Nevis.

Therefore the highest mountain in England or Wales is not so high as Ben Nevis.

Again :

Lithium is the lightest metal known.

Lithium is the metal indicated by one bright red line in the spectrum.*

Therefore the lightest metal known is the metal indicated by a spectrum of one bright red line.

In these examples all the propositions are singular propositions, and merely assert the identity of singular terms, so that there is no alteration of generality. Each conclusion applies to just such an object as each of the premises applies to. To this kind of reasoning the apt name of **Traduction** has been given.

Induction is a much more difficult and more important kind of reasoning process than Traduction or even Deduction ; for it is engaged in detecting the general laws or uniformities, the relations of cause and effect, or in short all the general truths that may be asserted concerning the numberless and very diverse events that take place in the natural world around us. The greater part, if not, as some philosophers think, the whole of our knowledge, is ultimately due to inductive reasoning. The mind, it is plausibly

* Roscoe's *Lessons in Elementary Chemistry*, p. 199.

said, is not furnished with knowledge in the form of general propositions ready made and stamped upon it, but is endowed with powers of observation, comparison, and reasoning, which are adequate, when well educated and exercised, to procure knowledge of the world without us and the world within the human mind. Even when we argue synthetically and deductively from simple ideas and truths which seem to be ready in the mind, as in the case of the science of geometry, it may be that we have gathered those simple ideas and truths from previous observation or induction of an almost unconscious kind. This is a debated point upon which I will not here speak positively; but if the truth be as stated, **Induction** will be the mode by which all the materials of knowledge are brought to the mind and analysed. **Deduction** will then be the almost equally important process by which the knowledge thus acquired is utilised, and by which new Inductions of a more complicated character, as we shall see, are rendered possible.

An Induction, that is an act of Inductive reasoning, is called **Perfect** when all the possible cases or instances to which the conclusion can refer, have been examined and enumerated in the premises. If, as usually happens, it is impossible to examine all cases, since they may occur at future times or in distant parts of the earth or other regions of the universe, the Induction is called **Imperfect.** The assertion that all the months of the year are of less length than thirty-two days is derived from Perfect Induction, and is a certain conclusion because the calendar is a human institution, so that we know beyond doubt how many months there are, and can readily ascertain that each of them is less than thirty-two days in length. But the assertion that all the planets move in one direction round the sun, from West to East, is derived from Imperfect Induction; for it is possible that there exist planets more distant than the most distant-known planet, Neptune, and to such a planet of course the assertion would apply.

Hence it is obvious that there is a great difference between Perfect and Imperfect Induction. The latter includes some process by which we are enabled to make assertions concerning things that we have never seen or examined or even known to exist. But it must be carefully remembered also that no Imperfect Induction can give a certain conclusion. It may be highly probable or nearly certain that the cases unexamined will resemble those which have been examined, but it can never be certain. It is quite possible, for instance, that a new planet might go round the sun in an opposite direction to the other planets. In the case of the satellites belonging to the planets more than one exception of this kind has been discovered, and mistakes have constantly occurred in science from expecting that all new cases would exactly resemble old ones. Imperfect Induction thus gives only a certain degree of probability or likelihood that all instances will agree with those examined. Perfect Induction, on the other hand, gives a necessary and certain conclusion, but it asserts nothing beyond what was asserted in the premises.

Mr. Mill, indeed, differs from almost all other logicians in holding that Perfect Induction is improperly called Induction, because it does not lead to any new knowledge. He defines **Induction** as *inference from the known to the unknown*, and considers the unexamined cases which are apparently brought into our knowledge as the only gain from the process of reasoning. Hence Perfect Induction seems to him to be of no scientific value whatever, because the conclusion is a mere reassertion in a briefer form, a mere summing up of the premises. I may point out, however, that if Perfect Induction were no more than a process of abbreviation it is yet of great importance, and requires to be continually used in science and common life. Without it we could never make a comprehensive statement, but should be obliged to enumerate every particular. After examining the books in a library and finding them to be all English books we should be unable to sum up our results in the one proposition, "all the books in this library are English books;" but should be required to go over the list of books every time we desired to make any one acquainted with the contents of the library. The fact is, that the power of expressing a great number of particular facts in a very brief space is essential to the progress of science. Just as the whole science of arithmetic consists in nothing but a series of processes for abbreviating addition and subtraction, and enabling us to deal with a great number of units in a very short time, so Perfect Induction is absolutely necessary to enable us to deal with a great number of particular facts in a very brief space.

It is usual to represent Perfect Induction in the form of an **Inductive Syllogism**, as in the following instance :—

Mercury, Venus, the Earth, &c., all move round the sun from West to East.

Mercury, Venus, the Earth, &c., are all the known Planets.

Therefore all the known planets move round the sun from West to East.

This argument is a true Perfect Induction because the conclusion only makes an assertion of all *known* planets, which excludes all reference to possible future discoveries ; and we may suppose that all the known planets have been enumerated in the premises. . . .

As another example of a Perfect Induction we may take—

January, February,..........December, each contain less than 32 days.

January...........December are all the months of the year.

Therefore all the months of the year contain less than 32 days.

Although Sir W. Hamilton has entirely rejected the notion, it seems worthy of inquiry whether the Inductive Syllogism be not really of the Disjunctive form of Syllogism. Thus I should be inclined to represent the last example in the form :

A month of the year is either January, or February, or March............or December ; but January has less than 32 days ; and February has less than 32 days ; and so on until we come to December, which has less than 32 days.

It follows clearly that a month must in any case have less than 32 days ; for there are only 12 possible cases, and in each case this is affirmed. The fact is that the major premise of the syllogism on the last page is a compound sentence with twelve subjects, and is therefore equivalent to twelve distinct logical propositions. The minor premise is either a disjunctive proposition, as I have represented it, or something quite different from anything we have elsewhere had.

From Perfect Induction we shall have to pass to **Imperfect Induction**; but the opinions of Logicians are not in agreement as to the grounds upon which we are warranted in taking a part of the instances only, and concluding that what is true of those is true of all. Thus if we adopt the example found in many books and say—

This, that, and the other magnet attract iron ;
This, that, and the other magnet are all magnets ;
Therefore all magnets attract iron,

we evidently employ a false minor premise, because this, that, and the other magnet which we have examined, cannot possibly be all existing magnets. In whatever form we put it there must be an assumption that the magnets which we have examined are a fair specimen of all magnets, so that what we find in some we may expect in all. Archbishop Whately considers that this assumption should be expressed in one of the premises, and he represents Induction as a Syllogism as follows :—

That which belongs to this, that, and the other magnet, belongs to all ;
Attracting iron belongs to this, that, and the other ;
Therefore it belongs to all.

But though this is doubtless a correct expression of the assumption made in an Imperfect Induction, it does not in the least explain the grounds on which we are allowed to make the assumption, and under what circumstances such an assumption would be likely to prove true. Some writers have asserted that there is a Principle called the **Uniformity of Nature**, which enables us to affirm that what has often been found to be true of anything will continue to be found true of the same sort of thing. It must be observed, however, that if there be such a principle it is liable to exceptions ; for many facts which have held true up to a certain point have afterwards been found not to be always true. Thus there was a wide and unbroken induction tending to show that all the Satellites in the planetary system went in one uniform direction round their planets. Nevertheless the Satellites of Uranus when discovered were found to move in a *retrograde* direction, or in an opposite direction to all Satellites previously known, and the same peculiarity attaches to the Satellite of Neptune more lately discovered.

We may defer to the next lesson the question of the varying degree of certainty which belongs to induction in the several branches of knowledge.

The advanced student may consult the following with advantage :—Mansel's Aldrich, Appendix, Notes G and H. Hamilton's *Lectures on Logic*, Lecture XVII., and Appendix VII., *On Induction and Example*, Vol. II., p. 358. J. S. Mill's *System of Logic*, Book III. Chap. 2, *Of Inductions improperly so-called*.

GEOMETRICAL AND MATHEMATICAL INDUCTION, ANALOGY AND EXAMPLE.

It is now indispensable that we should consider with great care upon what grounds Imperfect Induction is founded. No difficulty is encountered in Perfect Induction because all possible cases which can come under the general conclusion are enumerated in the premises, so that in fact there is no information in the conclusion which was not given in the premises. In this respect the Inductive Syllogism perfectly agrees with the general principles of deductive reasoning, which require that the information contained in the conclusion should be shown only from the data, and that we should merely unfold, or transform into an explicit statement what is contained in the premises implicitly.

In **Imperfect Induction** the process seems to

be of a wholly different character, since the instances concerning which we acquire knowledge may be infinitely more numerous than those from which we acquire the knowledge. Let us consider in the first place the process of **Geometrical Reasoning** which has a close resemblance to inductive reasoning. When in the fifth proposition of the first book of Euclid we prove that the angles at the base of an isosceles triangle are equal to each other, it is done by taking one particular triangle as an example. A figure is given which the reader is requested to regard as having two equal sides, and it is conclusively proved that if the sides be really equal then the angles opposite to those sides must be equal also. But Euclid says nothing about other isosceles triangles; he treats one single triangle as a sufficient specimen of all isosceles triangles, and we are asked to believe that what is true of that is true of any other, whether its sides be so small as to be only visible in a microscope, or so large as to reach to the furthest fixed star. There may evidently be an infinite number of isosceles triangles as regards the length of the equal sides, and each of these may be infinitely varied by increasing or diminishing the contained angle, so that the number of possible isosceles triangles is infinitely infinite; and yet we are asked to believe of this incomprehensible number of objects what we have proved only of one single specimen. This might seem to be the most extremely Imperfect Induction possible, and yet every one allows that it gives us really certain knowledge.

We do know with as much certainty as knowledge can possess, that if lines be conceived as drawn from the earth to two stars equally distant, they will make equal angles with the line joining those stars; and yet we can never have tried the experiment.

The generality of this geometrical reasoning evidently depends upon the certainty with which we know that all isosceles triangles exactly resemble each other. The proposition proved does not in fact apply to a triangle unless it agrees with our specimen in all the qualities essential to the proof. The absolute length of any of the sides or the absolute magnitude of the angle contained between any of them were not points upon which the proof depended—they were purely accidental circumstances; hence we are at perfect liberty to apply to all new cases of an isosceles triangle what we learn of one case. Upon a similar ground rests all the vast body of certain knowledge contained in the mathematical sciences—not only all the geometrical truths, but all general algebraical truth. It was shown, for instance, in p. 58, that if a and b be two quantities, and we multiply together their sum and difference, we get the difference of the squares of a and b. However often we try this it will be found true; thus if $a=10$ and $b=7$, the product of the sum and difference is $17 \times 3 = 51$; the squares of the quantities are 10×10 or 100 and 7×7 or 49, the difference of which is also 51. But however often we tried the rule no certainty would be added to it; because when proved algebraically there was no condition which restricted the result to any particular numbers, and *a* and *b* might consequently be any numbers whatever. This generality of algebraical reasoning by which a property is proved of infinite varieties of numbers at once, is one of the chief advantages of algebra over arithmetic. There is also in algebra a process called **Mathematical Induction** or **Demonstrative Induction**, which shows the powers of reasoning in a very conspicuous way. A good example is found in the following problem:—If we take the first *two* consecutive odd numbers, 1 and 3, and add them together the sum is 4, or exactly *twice two;* if we take *three* such numbers $1+3+5$, the sum is 9 or exactly *three times three;* if we take *four*, namely $1+3+5+7$ the sum is 16, or exactly *four times four;* or generally, if we take any given number of the series, $1+3+5+7+...$ the sum is equal to the number of the terms multiplied by itself. Anyone who knows a very little algebra can prove that this remarkable law is universally true, as follows—Let n be the number of terms, and assume for a moment that this law is true up to n terms, thus—

$$1 + 3 + 5 + 7 + \ldots + (2n-1) = n^2.$$

Now add $2n + 1$ to each side of the equation. It follows that—

$$1+3+5+7+\ldots+(2n-1)+(2n+1)$$
$$= n^2 + 2n + 1.$$

But the last quantity $n^2 + 2n + 1$ is just

equal to $(n+1)^2$; so that if the law is true for n terms it is true also for $n+1$ terms. We are enabled to argue from each single case of the law to the next case; but we have already shown that it is true of the first few cases, therefore it must be true of all. By no conceivable labor could a person ascertain by trial what is the sum of the first billion odd numbers, and yet symbolically or by general reasoning we know with certainty that they would amount to a billion billion, and neither more nor less even by a unit. This process of Mathematical Induction is not exactly the same as Geometrical Induction, because each case depends upon the last, but the proof rests upon an equally narrow basis of experience, and creates knowledge of equal certainty and generality.

Such mathematical truths depend upon observation of a few cases, but they acquire certainty from the perception we have of the exact similarity of one case to another, so that we undoubtingly believe what is true of one case to be true of another. It is very instructive to contrast with these cases certain other ones where there is a like ground of observation, but not the same tie of similarity. It was at one time believed that if any integral number were multipled by itself, added to itself and then added to 41, the result would be a prime number, that is a number which could not be divided by any other integral number except unity; in symbols,

$$x^2 + x + 41 = \text{prime number.}$$

This was believed solely on the ground of trial and experience, and it certainly holds for a great many values of x. Thus when x is successively made equal to the numbers in the first line below, the expression x^2+x+41 gives the values in the second line, and they are all prime numbers:

0	1	2	3	4	5	6	7	8	9	10
41	43	47	53	61	71	83	97	113	131	151

No reason however could be given why it should always be true, and accordingly it was found that the rule does not always hold true, but fails when $x=40$. Then we have $40\times40+40+41=1681$, but this is clearly equal to $41\times40+41$ or 41×41, and is not a prime number.

In that branch of mathematics which treats of the peculiar properties and kinds of numbers, other propositions depending solely upon observation have been asserted to be always true. Thus Fermat believed that $2^{2^x}+1$ always represents a prime number, but could not give any reason for the assertion. It holds true in fact until the product reaches the large number 4294967297, which was found to be divisible by 641, so that the generality of the statement was disproved.

We find then that in some cases a single instance proves a general and certain rule, while in others a very great number of instances are insufficient to give any certainty at all; all depends upon the perception we have of similarity or identity between one case and another. We can perceive no similarity between all prime numbers which assures us that because one is represented by a certain formula, also another is; but we do find such similarity between the sums of odd numbers, or between isosceles triangles.

Exactly similar considerations apply to inductions in physical science. When a chemist analyses a few grains of water and finds that they contain exactly 8 parts of oxygen and 1 of hydrogen for 9 parts of water, he feels warranted in asserting that the same is true of all pure water whatever be its origin, and whatever be the part of the world from which it comes. But if he analyse a piece of granite, or a sample of sea-water from one part of the world, he does not feel any confidence that it will resemble exactly a piece of granite, or a sample of sea-water from another part of the earth; hence he does not venture to assert of all granite or sea-water, what he finds true of a single sample. Extended experience shows that granite is very variable in composition, but that sea-water is rendered pretty uniform by constant mixture of currents. Nothing but experience in these cases could inform us how far we may assert safely of one sample what we have ascertained of another. But we have reason to believe that chemical compounds are naturally fixed and invariable in composition, according to Dalton's laws of combining proportions. No *à priori* reasoning from the principles of thought could have told us this, and we only learn it by extended experiment. But having once shown it to be true with certain substances we do not need to repeat the trial with all other substances, because we have every reason to believe that it is a natural law in which all chemical substances resemble each other. It is only necessary then for a single accurate analysis of a given fixed compound to be made in order to inform us of the composition of all other portions of the same substance.

It must be carefully observed however that **all inductions in physical science are only probable,** or that if certain, it is only hypothetical certainty they possess. Can I be absolutely certain that all water contains one part of hydrogen in nine ? I am certain only on two conditions :—

1. That this was certainly the composition of the sample tried.
2. That any other substance I call water exactly resembles that sample.

But even if the first condition be undoubtedly true, I cannot be certain of the second. For how do I know what is water except by the fact of its being a transparent liquid, freezing into a solid and evaporating into steam, possessing a high specific heat, and a number of other distinct properties ? But can I be absolutely certain that every liquid possessing all these properties is water ? Practically I can be certain, but theoretically I cannot.

7. From Mill's *System of Logic*, pp. 125, 126 : 210–228, 8vo edition.

Reasoning, in the extended sense in which I use the term, and in which it is synonymous with Inference, is popularly said to be of two kinds : reasoning from particulars to generals, and reasoning from generals to particulars ; the former being called Induction, the latter Ratiocination or Syllogism. It will presently be shown that there is a third species of reasoning, which falls under neither of these descriptions, and which, nevertheless, is not only valid, but is the foundation of both the others. . . . Of Induction, therefore, we shall say no more at present, than that it at least is, without doubt, a process of real inference. The conclusion in an induction embraces more than is contained in the premises. The principle or law collected from particular instances, the general proposition in which we embody the result of our experience, covers a much larger extent of ground than the individual experiments which form its basis. A principle ascertained by experience, is more than a mere summing up of what has been specifically observed in the individual cases which have been examined ; it is a generalization grounded on those cases, and expressive of our belief, that what we there found true is true in an indefinite number of cases which we have not examined, and are never likely to examine. The nature and grounds of this inference, and the conditions necessary to make it legitimate, will be the subject of discussion in the Third Book : but that such inference really takes place is not susceptible of question. In every induction we proceed from truths which we knew, to truths which we did not know; from facts certified by observation, to facts which we have not observed, and even to facts not capable of being now observed; future facts, for example; but which we do not hesitate to believe on the sole evidence of the induction itself. Induction, then, is a real process of Reasoning or Inference.

OF INDUCTIONS IMPROPERLY SO CALLED.

§ 1. Induction, then, is that operation of the mind, by which we infer that what we know to be true in a particular case or cases, will be true in all cases which resemble the former in certain assignable respects. In other words, Induction is the process by which we conclude that what is true of certain individuals of a class is true of the whole class, or that what is true at certain times will be true in similar circumstances at all times.

This definition excludes from the meaning of the term Induction, various logical operations, to which it is not unusual to apply that name.

Induction, as above defined, is a process of inference·; it proceeds from the known to the unknown ; and any operation involving no inference, any process in which what seems the conclusion is no wider than the premises from which it is drawn, does not fall within the meaning of the term. Yet in the common books of Logic we find this laid down as the most perfect, indeed the only quite perfect, form of induction. In those books, every process which sets out from a less general and terminates in a more general expression—which admits of being stated in the form, " This and that A are B, therefore every A is B "—is called an induction, whether any thing be really concluded or not : and the induction is asserted not to be perfect, unless every single individual of the class A is included in the antecedent, or premise : that is, unless what we affirm of the class has already been ascertained to be true of every individual in it, so that the nominal conclusion is not really a conclusion, but a mere re-assertion of the premises. If we were to say, All the planets shine by the sun's light, from observation of each separate planet, or All the Apostles were Jews, because this is true of Peter, Paul, John, and every other apostle—these, and such as these, would, in the phraseology in question, be called perfect, and the only perfect, Inductions. This, however, is a totally different kind of induction from ours ; it is not an inference from facts known to facts unknown, but a mere short-hand registration of facts known. The two simulated arguments which we have quoted, are not generalizations ; the propositions purporting to be conclusions from them, are not really general propositions. A general proposition is one in which the predicate is affirmed or denied of an unlimited number of individuals ; namely, all, whether few or many, existing or capable of existing, which possess the properties connoted by the subject of the proposition. "All men are mortal" does not mean all now living, but all men past, present, and to come. When the signification of the term is limited so as to render it a name not for any and every individual falling under a certain general description, but only for each of a number of individuals, designated as such, and as it were, counted off individually, the proposition, though it may be general in its language, is no general proposition, but merely that number of singular propositions, written in an abridged character. The operation may be very useful, as most forms of abridged notation are; but it is no part of the investigation of truth, though often bearing an important part in the preparation of the materials for that investigation.

As we may sum up a definite number of singular propositions in one proposition, which will be apparently, but not really, general, so we may sum up a definite number of general propositions in one proposition, which will be apparently, but not really, more general. If by a separate induction applied to every distinct species of animals, it has been established that each possesses a nervous system, and we affirm thereupon that all animals have a nervous system; this looks like a generalization, though as the conclusion merely affirms of all what has already been affirmed of each, it seems to tell us nothing but what we knew before. A distinction, however, must be made. If in concluding that all animals have a nervous system, we mean the same thing and no more as if we had said "all known animals," the proposition is not general, and the process by which it is arrived at is not induction. But if our meaning is that the observations made of the various species of animals have discovered to us a law of animal nature, and that we are in a condition to say that a nervous system will be found even in animals yet undiscovered, this indeed is an induction; but in this case the general proposition contains more than the sum of the special propositions from which it is inferred. The distinction is still more forcibly brought out when we consider, that if this real generalization be legitimate at all, its legitimacy probably does not require that we should have examined without exception every known species. It is the number and nature of the instances, and not their being the whole of those which happen to be known, that makes them sufficient evidence to prove a general law : while the more limited assertion, which stops at all known animals, cannot be made unless we have rigorously verified it in every species. In like manner (to return to a former example) we might have inferred, not that all *the* planets, but that all *planets*, shine by reflected light : the former is no induction ; the latter is an induction, and a bad one, being disproved by the case of double stars—self-luminous bodies which are properly planets, since they revolve round a centre.

§ 2. There are several processes used in mathematics which require to be distinguished from Induction, being not unfrequently called by that name, and being so far similar to Induction properly so called, that the propositions they lead to are really general propositions. For example, when we have proved with respect to the circle, that a straight line can not meet it in more than two points, and when the same thing has been successively proved of the ellipse, the parabola, and the hyperbola, it may be laid down as a universal property of the sections of the cone. The distinction drawn in the two previous examples can have no place here, there being no difference between all *known* sections of the cone and *all* sections, since a cone demonstrably can not be intersected by a plane except in one of these four lines. It would be difficult, therefore, to refuse to the proposition arrived at, the name of a generalization, since there is no room for any generalization beyond it. But there is no induction, because there is no inference: the conclusion is a mere summing up of what was asserted in the various propositions from which it is drawn. A case somewhat, though not altogether, similar, is the proof of a geometrical theorem by means of a diagram. Whether the diagram be on paper or only in the imagination, the demonstration (as formerly observed) does not prove directly the general theorem; it proves only that the conclusion, which the theorem asserts generally, is true of the particular triangle or circle exhibited in the diagram; but since we perceive that in the same way in which we have proved it of that circle, it might also be proved of any other circle, we gather up into one general expression all the singular propositions susceptible of being thus proved, and embody them in a universal proposition. Having shown that the three angles of the triangle ABC are together equal to two right angles, we conclude that this is true of every other triangle, not because it is true of ABC, but for the same reason which proved it to be true of ABC. If this were to be called Induction, an appropriate name for it would be, induction by parity of reasoning. But the term can not properly belong to it ; the characteristic quality of Induction is wanting, since the truth obtained, though really general, is not believed on the evidence of particular instances. We do not conclude that all triangles have the property because some triangles have, but from the ulterior demonstrative evidence which was the ground of our conviction in the particular instances.

There are nevertheless, in mathematics, some examples of so-called Induction, in which the conclusion does bear the appearance of a generalization grounded on some of the particular cases included in it. A mathematician, when he has calculated a sufficient number of the terms of an algebraical or arithmetical series to have ascertained what is called the *law* of the series, does not hesitate to fill up any number of the succeeding terms without repeating the calculations. But I apprehend he only does so when it is apparent from *a priori* considerations (which might be exhibited in the form of demonstration) that the mode of formation of the subsequent terms, each from that which preceded it, must be similar to the formation of the terms which have been already calculated. And when the attempt has been hazarded without the sanction of such general considerations, there are instances on record in which it has led to false results.

It is said that Newton discovered the binomial theorem by induction; by raising a binomial successively to a certain number of powers, and comparing those powers with one another until he detected the relation in which the algebraic formula of each power stands to the exponent of that power, and to the two terms of the binomial. The fact is not improbable: but a mathematician like Newton, who seemed to arrive *per saltum* at principles and conclusions that ordinary mathematicians only reached by a succession of steps, certainly could not have performed the comparison in question without being led by it to the *a priori* ground of the law; since any one who understands sufficiently the nature of multiplication to venture upon multiplying several lines of symbols at one operation, can not but perceive that in raising a binomial to a power, the co-efficients must depend on the laws of permutation and combination: and as soon as this is recognized, the theorem is demonstrated. Indeed, when once it was seen that the law prevailed in a few of the lower powers, its identity with the law of permutation would at once suggest the considerations which prove it to obtain universally. Even, therefore, such cases as these, are but examples of what I have called Induction by parity of reasoning, that is, not really Induction, because not involving inference of a general proposition from particular instances.

§ 3. There remains a third improper use of the term Induction, which it is of real importance to clear up, because the theory of Induction has been, in no ordinary degree, confused by it, and because the confusion is exemplified in the most recent and elaborate treatise on the inductive philosophy which exists in our language. The error in question is that of confounding a mere description, by general terms, of a set of observed phenomena, with an induction from them.

Suppose that a phenomenon consists of parts, and that these parts are only capable of being observed separately, and as it were piecemeal. When the observations have been made, there is a convenience (amounting for many purposes to a necessity) in obtaining a representation of the phenomenon as a whole, by combining, or as we may say, piecing these detached fragments together. A navigator sailing in the midst of the ocean discovers land : he can not at first, or by any one observation, determine whether it is a continent or an island ; but he coasts along it, and after a few days finds himself to have sailed completely round it : he then pronounces it an island. Now there was no particular time or place of observation at which he could perceive that this land was entirely surrounded by water : he ascertained the fact by a succession of partial observations, and then selected a general expression which summed up in two or three words the whole of what he so observed. But is there any thing of the nature of an induction in this process? Did he infer any thing that had not been observed, from something else which had? Certainly not. He had observed the whole of what the proposition asserts. That the land in question is an island, is not an inference from the partial facts which the navigator saw in the course of his circumnavigation; it is the facts themselves; it is a summary of those facts; the description of a complex fact, to which those simpler ones are as the parts of a whole.

Now there is, I conceive, no difference in kind between this simple operation, and that by which Kepler ascertained the nature of the planetary orbits: and Kepler's operation, all at least that was characteristic in it, was not more an inductive act than that of our supposed navigator.

The object of Kepler was to determine the real path described by each of the planets, or let us say by the planet Mars (since it was of that body that he first established the two of his three laws which did not require a comparison of planets). To do this there was no other mode than that of direct observation: and all which observation could do was to ascertain a great number of the successive places of the planet; or rather, of its apparent places. That the planet occupied successively all these positions, or at all events, positions which produced the same impressions on the eye, and that it passed from one of these to another insensibly, and without any apparent breach of continuity; thus much the senses, with the aid of the proper instruments, could ascertain. What Kepler did more than this, was to find what sort of a curve these different points would make, supposing them to be all joined together. He expressed the whole series of the observed places of Mars by what Dr. Whewell calls the general conception of an ellipse. This operation was far from being as easy as that of the navigator who expressed the series of his observations on successive points of the coast by the general conception of an island. But it is the very same sort of operation; and if the one is not an induction but a description, this must also be true of the other.

The only real induction concerned in the case, consisted in inferring that because the observed places of Mars were correctly represented by points in an imaginary ellipse, therefore Mars would continue to revolve in that same ellipse; and in concluding (before the gap had been filled up by further observations) that the positions of the planet during the time which intervened between two observations, must have coincided with the intermediate points of the curve. For these were facts which had not been directly observed. They were inferences from the observations; facts inferred, as distinguished from facts seen. But these inferences were so far from being a part of Kepler's philosophical operation, that they had been drawn long before he was born. Astronomers had long known that the planets periodically returned to the same places.

When this had been ascertained, there was no induction left for Kepler to make, nor did he make any further induction. He merely applied his new conception to the facts inferred, as he did to the facts observed. Knowing already that the planets continued to move in the same paths; when he found that an ellipse correctly represented the past path, he knew that it would represent the future path. In finding a compendious expression for the one set of facts, he found one for the other: but he found the expression only, not the inference; nor did he (which is the true test of a general truth) add any thing to the power of prediction already possessed.

§ 4. The descriptive operation which enables a number of details to be summed up in a single proposition, Dr. Whewell, by an aptly chosen expression, has termed the Colligation of Facts. In most of his observations concerning that mental process I fully agree, and would gladly transfer all that portion of his book into my own pages. I only think him mistaken in setting up this kind of operation, which according to the old and received meaning of the term, is not induction at all, as the type of induction generally; and laying down, throughout his work, as principles of induction, the principles of mere colligation.

Dr. Whewell maintains that the general proposition which binds together the particular facts, and makes them, as it were, one fact, is not the mere sum of those facts, but something more, since there is introduced a conception of the mind, which did not exist in the facts themselves. "The particular facts," says he,* "are not merely brought together, but there is a new element added to the combination by the very act of thought by which they are combined. . . . When the Greeks, after long observing the motions of the planets, saw that these motions might be rightly considered as produced by the motion of one wheel revolving in the inside of another wheel, these wheels were creations of their minds, added to the facts which they perceived by sense. And even if the wheels were no longer supposed to be material, but were reduced to mere geometrical spheres or circles, they were not the less products of the mind alone—something additional to the facts observed. The same is the case in all other discoveries. The facts are known, but they are insulated and unconnected, till the discoverer supplies from his own store a principle of connection. The pearls are there, but they will not hang together till some one provides the string."

Let me first remark that Dr. Whewell, in this passage, blends together, indiscriminately, examples of both the processes which I am endeavoring to distinguish from one another. When the Greeks abandoned the supposition that the planetary motions were produced by the revolution of material wheels, and fell back upon the idea of "mere geometrical spheres or circles,"

---

* *Novum Organum Renovatum*, pp. 72, 73.

there was more in this change of opinion than the mere substitution of an ideal curve for a physical one. There was the abandonment of a theory, and the replacement of it by a mere description. No one would think of calling the doctrine of material wheels a mere description. That doctrine was an attempt to point out the force by which the planets were acted upon, and compelled to move in their orbits. But when, by a great step in philosophy, the materiality of the wheels was discarded, and the geometrical forms alone retained, the attempt to account for the motions was given up, and what was left of the theory was a mere description of the orbits. The assertion that the planets were carried round by wheels revolving in the inside of other wheels, gave place to the proposition, that they moved in the same lines which would be traced by bodies so carried : which was a mere mode of representing the sum of the observed facts ; as Kepler's was another and a better mode of representing the same observations.

It is true that for these simply descriptive operations, as well as for the erroneous inductive one, a conception of the mind was required. The conception of an ellipse must have presented itself to Kepler's mind, before he could identify the planetary orbits with it. According to Dr. Whewell, the conception was something added to the facts. He expresses himself as if Kepler had put something into the facts by his mode of conceiving them. But Kepler did no such thing. The ellipse was in the facts before Kepler recognized it; just as the island was an island before it had been sailed round. Kepler did not *put* what he had conceived into the facts, but *saw* it in them. A conception implies, and corresponds to, something conceived: and though the conception itself is not in the facts, but in our mind, yet if it is to convey any knowledge relating to them, it must be a conception *of* something which really is in the facts, some property which they actually possess, and which they would manifest to our senses, if our senses were able to take cognizance of it. If, for instance, the planet left behind it in space a visible track, and if the observer were in a fixed position at such a distance from the plane of the orbit as would enable him to see the whole of it at once, he would see it to be an ellipse; and if gifted with appropriate instruments and powers of locomotion, he could prove it to be such by measuring its different dimensions. Nay, further: if the track were visible, and he were so placed that he could see all parts of it in succession, but not all of them at once, he might be able, by piecing together his successive observations, to discover both that it was an ellipse and that the planet moved in it. The case would then exactly resemble that of the navigator who discovers the land to be an island by sailing round it. If the path was visible, no one I think would dispute that to identify it with an ellipse is to describe it: and I can not see why any difference should be made by its not being directly an object of sense, when every point in it is as exactly ascertained as if it were so.

Subject to the indispensable condition which has just been stated, I do not conceive that the part which conceptions have in the operation of studying facts, has ever been overlooked or undervalued. No one ever disputed that in order to reason about any thing we must have a conception of it; or that when we include a multitude of things under a general expression, there is implied in the expression a conception of something common to those things. But it by no means follows that the conception is necessarily pre-existent, or constructed by the mind out of its own materials. If the facts are rightly classed under the conception, it is because there is in the facts themselves something of which the conception is itself a copy; and which if we can not directly perceive, it is because of the limited power of our organs, and not because the thing itself is not there. The conception itself is often obtained by abstraction from the very facts which, in Dr. Whewell's language, it is afterward called in to connect. This he himself admits, when he observes (which he does on several occasions), how great a service would be rendered to the science of physiology by the philosopher " who should establish a precise, tenable, and consistent conception of life." * Such a conception can only be abstracted from the phenomena of life itself; from the very facts which it is put in requisition

---

* *Novum Organum Renovatum*, p. 32.

to connect. In other cases, no doubt, instead of collecting the conception from the very phenomena which we are attempting to colligate, we select it from among those which have been previously collected by abstraction from other facts. In the instance of Kepler's laws, the latter was the case. The facts being out of the reach of being observed, in any such manner as would have enabled the senses to identify directly the path of the planet, the conception requisite for framing a general description of that path could not be collected by abstraction from the observations themselves; the mind had to supply hypothetically, from among the conceptions it had obtained from other portions of its experience, some one which would correctly represent the series of the observed facts. It had to frame a supposition respecting the general course of the phenomenon, and ask itself, If this be the general description, what will the details be? and then compare these with the details actually observed. If they agreed, the hypothesis would serve for a description of the phenomenon: if not, it was necessarily abandoned, and another tried. It is such a case as this which gives rise to the doctrine that the mind, in framing the descriptions, adds something of its own which it does not find in the facts.

Yet it is a fact surely, that the planet does describe an ellipse; and a fact which we could see, if we had adequate visual organs and a suitable position. Not having these advantages, but possessing the conception of an ellipse, or (to express the meaning in less technical language) knowing what an ellipse was, Kepler tried whether the observed places of the planet were consistent with such a path. He found they were so; and he, consequently, asserted as a fact that the planet moved in an ellipse. But this fact, which Kepler did not add to, but found in, the motions of the planet, namely, that it occupied in succession the various points in the circumference of a given ellipse, was the very fact, the separate parts of which had been separately observed; it was the sum of the different observations.

Having stated this fundamental difference between my opinion and that of Dr. Whewell, I must add, that his account of the manner in which a conception is selected, suitable to express the facts, appears to me perfectly just. The experience of all thinkers will, I believe, testify that the process is tentative; that it consists of a succession of guesses; many being rejected, until one at last occurs fit to be chosen. We know from Kepler himself that before hitting upon the "conception" of an ellipse, he tried nineteen other imaginary paths, which, finding them inconsistent with the observations, he was obliged to reject. But, as Dr. Whewell truly says, the successful hypothesis, though a guess, ought generally to be called, not a lucky, but a skillful guess. The guesses which serve to give mental unity and wholeness to a chaos of scattered particulars, are accidents which rarely occur to any minds but those abounding in knowledge and disciplined in intellectual combinations.

How far this tentative method, so indispensable as a means to the colligation of facts for purposes of description, admits of application to Induction itself, and what functions belong to it in that department, will be considered in the chapter of the present Book which relates to Hypotheses. On the present occasion we have chiefly to distinguish this process of Colligation from Induction properly so called ; and that the distinction may be made clearer, it is well to advert to a curious and interesting remark, which is as strikingly true of the former operation, as it appears to me unequivocally false of the latter.

In different stages of the progress of knowledge, philosophers have employed, for the colligation of the same order of facts, different conceptions. The early rude observations of the heavenly bodies, in which minute precision was neither attained nor sought, presented nothing inconsistent with the representation of the path of a planet as an exact circle, having the earth for its centre. As observations increased in accuracy, facts were disclosed which were not reconcilable with this simple supposition : for the colligation of those additional facts, the supposition was varied ; and varied again and again as facts became more numerous and precise. The earth was removed from the centre to some other point within the circle ; the planet was supposed to revolve in a smaller circle called an epicycle, round an imaginary point which revolved in a circle round the earth : in proportion as observation elicited fresh facts contradictory to these representations, other epicycles and other eccentrics were added, producing additional complication ; until at last Kepler swept all these circles away, and substituted the conception of an exact ellipse. Even this is found not to represent with complete correctness the accurate observations of the present day, which disclose many slight deviations from an orbit exactly elliptical. Now Dr. Whewell has remarked that these successive general expressions, though apparently so conflicting, were all correct :. they all answered the purpose of colligation ; they all enabled the mind to represent to itself with facility, and by a simultaneous glance, the whole body of facts at the time ascertained : each in its turn served as a correct description of the phenomena, so far as the senses had up to that time taken cognizance of them. If a necessity afterward arose for discarding one of these general descriptions of the planet's orbit, and framing a different imaginary line, by which to express the series of observed positions, it was because a number of new facts had now been added, which it was necessary to combine with the old facts into one general description. But this did not affect the correctness of the former expression, considered as a general statement of the only facts which it was intended to represent. And so true is this, that, as is well remarked by M. Comte, these ancient generalizations, even the rudest and most imperfect of them, that of uniform movement in a circle, are so far from being entirely false, that they are even now habitually employed by astronomers when only a rough approximation to correctness is required. "L'astronomie moderne, en détruisant sans retour les hypothèses primitives, envisagées comme lois réelles du monde, a soigneusement maintenu leur valeur positive et permanente, la propriété de représenter commodément les phénomènes quand il s'agit d'une première ébauche. Nos ressources à cet égard sont même bien plus étendues, précisément à cause que nous ne nous faisons aucune illusion sur la réalité des hypothèses; ce qui nous permet d'employer sans scrupule, en chaque cas, celle que nous jugeons la plus avantageuse."*

Dr. Whewell's remark, therefore, is philosophically correct. Successive expressions for the colligation of observed facts, or, in other words, successive descriptions of a phenomenon as a whole, which has been observed only in parts, may, though conflicting, be all correct as far as they go. But it would surely be absurd to assert this of conflicting inductions.

The scientific study of facts may be undertaken for three different purposes: the simple description of the facts; their explanation; or their prediction: meaning by prediction, the determination of the conditions under which similar facts may be expected again to occur. To the first of these three operations the name of Induction does not properly belong: to the

---

* *Cours de Philosophie Positive*, vol. ii., p. 202.

other two it does. Now, Dr. Whewell's observation is true of the first alone. Considered as a mere description, the circular theory of the heavenly motions represents perfectly well their general features: and by adding epicycles without limit, those motions, even as now known to us, might be expressed with any degree of accuracy that might be required. The elliptical theory, as a mere description, would have a great advantage in point of simplicity, and in the consequent facility of conceiving it and reasoning about it; but it would not really be more true than the other. Different descriptions, therefore, may be all true: but not, surely, different explanations. The doctrine that the heavenly bodies moved by a virtue inherent in their celestial nature; the doctrine that they were moved by impact (which led to the hypothesis of vortices as the only impelling force capable of whirling bodies in circles), and the Newtonian doctrine, that they are moved by the composition of a centripetal with an original projectile force; all these are explanations, collected by real induction from supposed parallel cases; and they were all successively received by philosophers, as scientific truths on the subject of the heavenly bodies. Can it be said of these, as was said of the different descriptions, that they are all true as far as they go? Is it not clear that only one can be true in any degree, and the other two must be altogether false? So much for explanations: let us now compare different predictions: the first, that eclipses will occur when one planet or satellite is so situated as to cast its shadow upon another ; the second, that they will occur when some great calamity is impending over mankind. Do these two doctrines only differ in the degree of their truth, as expressing real facts with unequal degrees of accuracy ? Assuredly the one is true, and the other absolutely false.*

---

* Dr. Whewell, in his reply, contests the distinction here drawn, and maintains, that not only different descriptions, but different explanations of a phenomenon, may all be true. Of the three theories respecting the motions of the heavenly bodies, he says (*Philosophy of Discovery*, p. 231) : " Undoubtedly, all these explanations may be true and consistent with each other, and would be so if each had been followed out so as to show in what manner it could be made consistent with the facts. And this was, in reality, in a great measure done. The doctrine that the heavenly bodies were moved by vortices was successfully modified, so that it came to coincide in its results with the doctrine of an inverse-quadratic centripetal force. . . . When this point was reached, the vortex was merely a machinery, well or ill devised, for producing such a centripetal force, and therefore did not contradict the doctrine of a centripetal force. Newton himself does not appear to have been averse to explaining gravity by impulse. So little is it true that if one theory be true the other must be false. The attempt to explain gravity by the impulse of streams of particles flowing through the universe in all directions, which I have mentioned in the *Philosophy*, is so far from being consistent with the Newtonian theory, that it is founded entirely upon it. And even with regard to the doctrine, that the heavenly bodies move by an inherent virtue ; if this doctrine had been maintained in any such way that it was brought to agree

In every way, therefore, it is evident that to explain induction as the colligation of facts by

with the facts, the inherent virtue must have had its laws determined; and then it would have been found that the virtue had a reference to the central body; and so, the 'inherent virtue' must have coincided in its effect with the Newtonian force; and then, the two explanations would agree, except so far as the word 'inherent' was concerned. And if such a part of an earlier theory as this word *inherent* indicates, is found to be untenable, it is of course rejected in the transition to later and more exact theories, in Inductions of this kind, as well as in what Mr. Mill calls Descriptions. There is, therefore, still no validity discoverable in the distinction which Mr. Mill attempts to draw between descriptions like Kepler's law of elliptical orbits, and other examples of induction."

If the doctrine of vortices had meant, not that vortices, existed but only that the planets moved *in the same manner* as if they had been whirled by vortices; if the hypothesis had been merely a mode of representing the facts, not an attempt to account for them; if, in short, it had been only a Description; it would, no doubt, have been reconcilable with the Newtonian theory. The vortices, however, were not a mere aid to conceiving the motions of the planets, but a supposed physical agent, actively impelling them; a material fact, which might be true or not true, but could not be both true and not true. According to Descartes's theory it was true, according to Newton's it was not true. Dr. Whewell probably means that since the phrases, centripetal and projectile force, do not declare the nature but only the direction of the forces, the Newtonian theory does not absolutely contradict any hypothesis which may be framed respecting the mode of their production. The Newtonian theory, regarded as a mere *description* of the planetary motions, does not; but the Newtonian theory as an *explanation* of them does. For in what means of appropriate conceptions, that is, conceptions which will really express them, is to

does the explanation consist? In ascribing those motions to a general law which obtains between all particles of matter, and in identifying this with the law by which bodies fall to the ground. If the planets are kept in their orbits by a force which draws the particles composing them toward every other particle of matter in the solar system, they are not kept in those orbits by the impulsive force of certain streams of matter which whirl them round. The one explanation absolutely excludes the other. Either the planets are not moved by vortices, or they do not move by a law common to all matter. It is impossible that both opinions can be true. As well might it be said that there is no contradiction between the assertions, that a man died because somebody killed him, and that he died a natural death.

So, again, the theory that the planets move by a virtue inherent in their celestial nature, is incompatible with either of the two others: either that of their being moved by vortices, or that which regards them as moving by a property which they have in common with the earth and all terrestrial bodies. Dr. Whewell says that the theory of an inherent virtue agrees with Newton's when the word inherent is left out, which of course it would be (he says) if "found to be untenable." But leave that out, and where is the theory? The word inherent *is* the theory. When that is omitted, there remains nothing except that the heavenly bodies move "by a virtue," *i.e.*, by a power of some sort; or by virtue of their celestial nature, which directly contradicts the doctrine that terrestrial bodies fall by the same law.

If Dr. Whewell is not yet satisfied, any other subject will serve equally well to test his doctrine. He will hardly say that there is no contradiction between the emission theory and the undulatory theory of light; or that there can be both one and two electric-

confound mere description of the observed facts with inference from those facts, and ascribe to

ities ; or that the hypothesis of the production of the higher organic forms by development from the lower, and the supposition of separate and successive acts of creation, are quite reconcilable ; or that the theory that volcanoes are fed from a central fire, and the doctrines which ascribe them to chemical action at a comparatively small depth below the earth's surface, are consistent with one another, and all true as far as they go.

If different explanations of the same fact can not both be true, still less, surely, can different predictions. Dr. Whewell quarrels (on what ground it is not necessary here to consider) with the example I had chosen on this point, and thinks an objection to an illustration a sufficient answer to a theory. Examples not liable to his objection are easily found, if the proposition that conflicting predictions can not both be true, can be made clearer by any examples. Suppose the phenomenon to be a newly-discovered comet, and that one astronomer predicts its return once in every 300 years—another once in every 400 : can they both be right ? When Columbus predicted that by sailing constantly westward he should in time return to the point from which he set out, while others asserted that he could never do so except by turning back, were both he and his opponents true prophets ? Were the predictions which foretold the wonders of railways and steamships, and those which averred that the Atlantic could never be crossed by steam navigation, nor a railway train propelled ten miles an hour, both (in Dr. Whewell's words) " true, and consistent with one another ?"

Dr. Whewell sees no distinction between holding contradictory opinions on a question of fact, and merely employing different analogies to facilitate the conception of the same fact. The case of different Inductions belongs to the former class, that of different Descriptions to the latter.

the latter what is a characteristic property of the former.

There is, however, between Colligation and Induction, a real correlation, which it is important to conceive correctly. Colligation is not always induction ; but induction is always colligation. The assertion that the planets move in ellipses, was but a mode of representing observed facts ; it was but a colligation ; while the assertion that they are drawn, or tend, toward the sun, was the statement of a new fact, inferred by induction. But the induction, once made, accomplishes the purposes of colligation likewise. It brings the same facts, which Kepler had connected by his conception of an ellipse, under the additional conception of bodies acted upon by a central force, and serves, therefore, as a new bond of connection for those facts ; a new principle for their classification.

Further, the descriptions which are improperly confounded with induction, are nevertheless a necessary preparation for induction ; no less necessary than correct observation of the facts themselves. Without the previous colligation of detached observations by means of one general conception, we could never have obtained any basis for an induction, except in the case of phenomena of very limited compass. We should not be able to affirm any predicates at all, of a subject incapable of being observed otherwise than piecemeal : much less could we extend those predicates by induction to other similar subjects. Induction, therefore, always presupposes, not only that the necessary observations are made with the necessary accuracy, but also that the results of these observations are, so far as practicable, connected together by general descriptions, enabling the mind to represent to itself as wholes whatever phenomena are capable of being so represented.

§ 5. Dr. Whewell has replied at some length to the preceding observations, restating his opinions, but without (as far as I can perceive) adding any thing material to his former arguments. Since, however, mine have not had the good fortune to make any impression upon him, I will subjoin a few remarks, tending to show more clearly in what our difference of opinion consists, as well as, in some measure, to account for it.

Nearly all the definitions of induction, by writers of authority, make it consist in drawing inferences from known cases to unknown; affirming of a class, a predicate which has been found true of some cases belonging to the class; concluding because some things have a certain property, that other things which resemble them have the same property—or because a thing has manifested a property at a certain time, that it has and will have that property at other times.

It will scarcely be contended that Kepler's operation was an Induction in this sense of the term. The statement, that Mars moves in an elliptical orbit, was no generalization from individual cases to a class of cases. Neither was it an extension to all time, of what had been found true at some particular time. The whole amount of generalization which the case admitted of, was already completed, or might have been so. Long before the elliptic theory was thought of, it had been ascertained that the planets returned periodically to the same apparent places; the series of these places was, or might have been, completely determined, and the apparent course of each planet marked out on the celestial globe in an uninterrupted line. Kepler did not extend an observed truth to other cases than those in which it had been observed: he did not widen the *subject* of the proposition which expressed the observed facts. The alteration he made was in the predicate. Instead of saying, the successive places of Mars are so and so, he summed them up in the statement, that the successive places of Mars are points in an ellipse. It is true, this statement, as Dr. Whewell says, was not the sum of the observations *merely;* it was the sum of the observations *seen under a new point of view.** But it was not the sum of *more* than the observations, as a real induction is. It took in no cases but those which had been actually observed, or which could have been inferred from the observations before the new point of view presented itself. There was not that transition from known cases to unknown, which constitutes Induction in the original and acknowledged meaning of the term.

Old definitions, it is true, can not prevail against new knowledge: and if the Keplerian

---

* *Phil. of Discov.*, p. 256.

operation, as a logical process, be really identical with what takes place in acknowledged induction, the definition of induction ought to be so widened as to take it in ; since scientific language ought to adapt itself to the true relations which subsist between the things it is employed to designate. Here then it is that I am at issue with Dr. Whewell. He does think the operations identical. He allows of no logical process in any case of induction, other than what there was in Kepler's case, namely, guessing until a guess is found which tallies with the facts ; and accordingly, as we shall see hereafter, he rejects all canons of induction, because it is not by means of them that we guess. Dr. Whewell's theory of the logic of science would be very perfect if it did not pass over altogether the question of Proof. But in my apprehension there is such a thing as proof, and inductions differ altogether from descriptions in their relation to that element. Induction is proof ; it is inferring something unobserved from something observed : it requires, therefore, an appropriate test of proof ; and to provide that test, is the special purpose of inductive logic. When, on the contrary, we merely collate known observations, and, in Dr. Whewell's phraseology, connect them by means of a new conception ; if the conception does serve to connect the observations, we have all we want. As the proposition in which it is embodied pretends to no other truth than what it may share with many other modes of representing the same facts, to be consistent with the facts is all it requires : it neither needs nor admits of proof ; though it may serve to prove other things, inasmuch as, by placing the facts in mental connection with other facts, not previously seen to resemble them, it assimilates the case to another class of phenomena, concerning which real Inductions have already been made. Thus Kepler's so-called law brought the orbit of Mars into the class ellipse, and by doing so, proved all the properties of an ellipse to be true of the orbit : but in this proof Kepler's law supplied the minor premise, and not (as is the case with real Inductions) the major.

Dr. Whewell calls nothing Induction where there is not a new mental conception introduced, and every thing induction where there is. But this is to confound two very different things, Invention and Proof. The introduction of a new conception belongs to Invention : and invention may be required in any operation, but is the essence of none. A new conception may be introduced for descriptive purposes, and so it may for inductive purposes. But it is so far from constituting induction, that induction does not necessarily stand in need of it. Most inductions require no conception but what was present in every one of the particular instances on which the induction is grounded. That all men are mortal is surely an inductive conclusion ; yet no new conception is introduced by it. Whoever knows that any man has died, has all the conceptions involved in the inductive generalization. But Dr. Whewell considers the process of invention which consists in framing a new conception consistent with the facts, to be not merely a necessary part of all induction, but the whole of it.

The mental operation which extracts from a number of detached observations certain general characters in which the observed phenomena resemble one another, or resemble other known facts, is what Bacon, Locke, and most subsequent metaphysicians, have understood by the word Abstraction. A general expression obtained by abstraction, connecting known facts by means of common characters, but without concluding from them to unknown, may, I think, with strict logical correctness, be termed a Description ; nor do I know in what other way things can ever be described. My position, however, does not depend on the employment of that particular word ; I am quite content to use Dr. Whewell's term Colligation, or the more general phrases, ' mode of representing, or of expressing, phenomena : ' provided it be clearly seen that the process is not Induction, but something radically different.

What more may usefully be said on the subject of Colligation, or of the correlative expression invented by Dr. Whewell, the Explication of Conceptions, and generally on the subject of ideas and mental representations as connected with the study of facts, will find a more appropriate place in the Fourth Book, on the Operations Subsidiary to Induction : to which I must refer the reader for the removal of any difficulty which the present discussion may have left.

OF THE GROUND OF INDUCTION.

§ 1. INDUCTION properly so called, as distinguished from those mental operations, sometimes, though improperly, designated by the name, which I have attempted in the preceding chapter to characterize, may, then, be summarily defined as Generalization from Experience. It consists in inferring from some individual instances in which a phenomenon is observed to occur, that it occurs in all instances of a certain class; namely, in all which *resemble* the former, in what are regarded as the material circumstances.

In what way the material circumstances are to be distinguished from those which are immaterial, or why some of the circumstances are material and others not so, we are not yet ready to point out. We must first observe, that there is a principle implied in the very statement of what Induction is; an assumption with regard to the course of nature and the order of the universe; namely, that there are such things in nature as parallel cases; that what happens once, will, under a sufficient degree of similarity of circumstances, happen again, and not only again, but as often as the same circumstances recur. This, I say, is an assumption, involved in every case of induction. And, if we consult the actual course of nature, we find that the assumption is warranted. The universe, so far as known to us, is so constituted, that whatever is true in any one case, is true in all cases of a certain description ; the only difficulty is, to find what description.

This universal fact, which is our warrant for all inferences from experience, has been described by different philosophers in different forms of language : that the course of nature is uniform ; that the universe is governed by general laws ; and the like. One of the most usual of these modes of expression, but also one of the most inadequate, is that which has been brought into familiar use by the metaphysicians of the school of Reid and Stewart. The disposition of the human mind to generalize from experience—a propensity considered by these philosophers as an instinct of our nature—they usually describe under some such name as "our intuitive conviction that the future will resemble the past." Now it has been well pointed out by Mr. Bailey,* that (whether the tendency be or not an original and ultimate element of our nature), Time, in its modifications of past, present, and future, has no concern either with the belief itself, or with the grounds of it. We believe that fire will burn to-morrow, because it burned to-day and yesterday ; but we believe, on precisely the same grounds, that it burned before we were born, and that it burns this very day in Cochin-China. It is not from the past to the future, as past and future, that we infer, but from the known to the unknown ; from facts observed to facts unobserved ; from what we have per-

---

* *Essays on the Pursuit of Truth.*

ceived, or been directly conscious of, to what has not come within our experience. In this last predicament is the whole region of the future; but also the vastly greater portion of the present and of the past.

Whatever be the most proper mode of expressing it, the proposition that the course of nature is uniform, is the fundamental principle, or general axiom, of Induction. It would yet be a great error to offer this large generalization as any explanation of the inductive process. On the contrary, I hold it to be itself an instance of induction, and induction by no means of the most obvious kind. Far from being the first induction we make, it is one of the last, or at all events one of those which are latest in attaining strict philosophical accuracy. As a general maxim, indeed, it has scarcely entered into the minds of any but philosophers; nor even by them, as we shall have many opportunities of remarking, have its extent and limits been always very justly conceived. The truth is, that this great generalization is itself founded on prior generalizations. The obscurer laws of nature were discovered by means of it, but the more obvious ones must have been understood and assented to as general truths before it was ever heard of. We should never have thought of affirming that all phenomena take place according to general laws, if we had not first arrived, in the case of a great multitude of phenomena, at some knowledge of the laws themselves; which could be done no otherwise than by induction. In what sense, then, can a principle, which is so far from being our earliest induction, be regarded as our warrant for all the others ? In the only sense, in which (as we have already seen) the general propositions which we place at the head of our reasonings when we throw them into syllogisms, ever really contribute to their validity. As Archbishop Whately remarks, every induction is a syllogism with the major premise suppressed ; or (as I prefer expressing it) every induction may be thrown into the form of a syllogism, by supplying a major premise. If this be actually done, the principle which we are now considering, that of the uniformity of the course of nature, will appear as the ultimate major premise of all inductions, and will, therefore, stand to all inductions in the relation in which, as has been shown at so much length, the major proposition of a syllogism always stands to the conclusion ; not contributing at all to prove it, but being a necessary condition of its being proved ; since no conclusion is proved, for which there can not be found a true major premise.*

---

* In the first edition a note was appended at this place, containing some criticism on Archbishop's Whately's mode of conceiving the relation between Syllogism and Induction. In a subsequent issue of his *Logic*, the Archbishop made a reply to the criticism, which induced me to cancel part of the note, incorporating the remainder in the text. In a still later edition, the Archbishop observes in a tone of something like disapprobation, that the objections, "doubtless from their being fully answered and found untenable, were silently suppressed," and that hence he might appear to some of his readers to be

The statement, that the uniformity of the course of nature is the ultimate major premise in all cases

combating a shadow. On this latter point, the Archbishop need give himself no uneasiness. His readers, I make bold to say, will fully credit his mere affirmation that the objections have actually been made.

But as he seems to think that what he terms the suppression of the objections ought not to have been made "silently," I now break that silence, and state exactly what it is that I suppressed, and why. I suppressed that alone which might be regarded as personal criticism on the Archbishop. I had imputed to him the having omitted to ask himself a particular question. I found that he had asked himself the question, and could give it an answer consistent with his own theory. I had also, within the compass of a parenthesis, hazarded some remarks on certain general characteristics of Archbishop Whately as a philosopher. These remarks, though their tone, I hope, was neither disrespectful nor arrogant, I felt, on reconsideration, that I was hardly entitled to make; least of all, when the instance which I had regarded as an illustration of them, failed, as I now saw, to bear them out. The real matter at the bottom of the whole dispute, the different view we take of the function of the major premise, remains exactly where it was; and so far was I from thinking that my opinion had been fully "answered" and was "untenable," that in the same edition in which I cancelled the note, I not only enforced the opinion by further arguments, but answered (though without naming him) those of the Archbishop.

For not having made this statement before, I do not think it needful to apologize. It would be attaching very great importance to one's smallest sayings, to think a formal retractation requisite every time that one falls into an error. Nor is Archbishop Whately's well-earned fame of so tender a quality as

of induction, may be thought to require some explanation. The immediate major premise in every inductive argument, it certainly is not. Of that, Archbishop Whately's must be held to be the correct account. The induction, "John, Peter, etc., are mortal, therefore all mankind are mortal," may, as he justly says, be thrown into a syllogism by prefixing as a major premise (what is at any rate a necessary condition of the validity of the argument), namely, that what is true of John Peter, etc., is true of all mankind. But how came we by this major premise? It is not self-evident; nay, in all cases of unwarranted generalization, it is not true. How, then, is it arrived at? Necessarily either by induction or ratiocination; and if by induction, the process, like all other inductive arguments, may be thrown into the form of a syllogism. This previous syllogism it is, therefore, necessary to construct. There is, in the long run, only one possible construction. The real proof that what is true of John, Peter, etc., is true of all mankind, can only be, that a different supposition would be inconsistent with the uniformity which we know to exist in the course of nature. Whether there would be this inconsistency or not, may be a matter of long and delicate inquiry; but unless there would, we have no sufficient ground for the major of the inductive syllogism. It hence appears, that if we throw the whole course of any inductive argument into

---

to require that in withdrawing a slight criticism on him I should have been bound to offer a public *amende* for having made it.

a series of syllogisms, we shall arrive by more or fewer steps at an ultimate syllogism, which will have for its major premise the principle, or axiom, of the uniformity of the course of nature.*

It was not to be expected that in the case of this axiom, any more than of other axioms, there should be unanimity among thinkers with respect to the grounds on which it is to be received as true. I have already stated that I regard it as

---

* But though it is a condition of the validity of every induction that there be uniformity in the course of nature, it is not a necessary condition that the uniformity should pervade all nature. It is enough that it pervades the particular class of phenomena to which the induction relates. An induction concerning the motions of the planets, or the properties of the magnet, would not be vitiated though we were to suppose that wind and weather are the sport of chance, provided it be assumed that astronomical and magnetic phenomena are under the dominion of general laws. Otherwise the early experience of mankind would have rested on a very weak foundation; for in the infancy of science it could not be known that *all* phenomena are regular in their course.

Neither would it be correct to say that every induction by which we infer any truth, implies the general fact of uniformity *as foreknown*, even in reference to the kind of phenomena concerned. It implies, *either* that this general fact is already known, *or* that we may now know it: as the conclusion, the Duke of Wellington is mortal, drawn from the instances A, B, and C, implies either that we have already concluded all men to be mortal, or that we are now entitled to do so from the same evidence. A vast amount of confusion and paralogism respecting the grounds of Induction would be dispelled by keeping in view these simple considerations.

itself a generalization from experience. Others hold it to be a principle which, antecedently to any verification by experience, we are compelled by the constitution of our thinking faculty to assume as true. Having so recently, and at so much length, combated a similar doctrine as applied to the axioms of mathematics, by arguments which are in a great measure applicable to the present case, I shall defer the more particular discussion of this controverted point in regard to the fundamental axiom of induction, until a more advanced period of our inquiry. At present it is of more importance to understand thoroughly the import of the axiom itself. For the proposition, that the course of nature is uniform, possesses rather the brevity suitable to popular, than the precision requisite in philosophical language : its terms require to be explained, and a stricter than their ordinary signification given to them, before the truth of the assertion can be admitted.

§ 2. Every person's consciousness assures him that he does not always expect uniformity in the course of events ; he does not always believe that the unknown will be similar to the known, that the future will resemble the past. Nobody believes that the succession of rain and fine weather will be the same in every future year as in the present. Nobody expects to have the same dreams repeated every night. On the contrary, every body mentions it as something extraordinary, if the course of nature is constant, and resembles itself, in these particulars. To look for constancy where constancy is not to be expected, as for instance that a day which has once brought good fortune will always be a fortunate day, is justly accounted superstition.

The course of nature, in truth, is not only uniform, it is also infinitely various. Some phenomena are always seen to recur in the very same combinations in which we met with them at first; others seem altogether capricious ; while some, which we have been accustomed to regard as bound down exclusively to a particular set of combinations, we unexpectedly find detached from some of the elements with which we had hitherto found them conjoined, and united to others of quite a contrary description. To an inhabitant of Central Africa, fifty years ago, no fact probably appeared to rest on more uniform experience than this, that all human beings are black. To Europeans, not many years ago, the proposition, All swans are white, appeared an equally unequivocal instance of uniformity in the course of nature. Further experience has proved to both that they were mistaken ; but they had to wait fifty centuries for this experience. During that long time, mankind believed in a uniformity of the course of nature where no such uniformity really existed.

According to the notion which the ancients entertained of induction, the foregoing were cases of as legitimate inference as any inductions whatever. In these two instances, in which, the conclusion being false, the ground of inference must have been insufficient, there was, nevertheless, as much ground for it as this conception of induction admitted of. The induction of the ancients has been well described by Bacon, under the name of " Inductio per enumerationem simplicem, ubi non reperitur instantia contradictoria." It consists in ascribing the character of general truths to all propositions which are true in every instance that we happen to know of. This is the kind of induction which is natural to the mind when unaccustomed to scientific methods. The tendency, which some call an instinct, and which others account for by association, to infer the future from the past, the known from the unknown, is simply a habit of expecting that what has been found true once or several times, and never yet found false, will be found true again. Whether the instances are few or many, conclusive or inconclusive, does not much affect the matter: these are considerations which occur only on reflection; the unprompted tendency of the mind is to generalize its experience, provided this points all in one direction; provided no other experience of a conflicting character comes unsought. The notion of seeking it, of experimenting for it, of *interrogating* nature (to use Bacon's expression) is of much later growth. The observation of nature, by uncultivated intellects, is purely passive: they accept the facts which present themselves, without taking the trouble of searching for more: it is a superior mind only which asks itself what facts are needed to enable it to come to a safe conclusion, and then looks out for these.

But though we have always a propensity to generalize from unvarying experience, we are not always warranted in doing so. Before we can be at liberty to conclude that something is universally true because we have never known an instance to the contrary, we must have reason to believe that if there were in nature any instances to the contrary, we should have known of them. This assurance, in the great majority of cases, we can not have, or can have only in a very moderate degree. The possibility of having it, is the foundation on which we shall see hereafter that induction by simple enumeration may in some remarkable cases amount practically to proof. No such assurance, however, can be had, on any of the ordinary subjects of scientific inquiry. Popular notions are usually founded on induction by simple enumeration ; in science it carries us but a little way. We are forced to begin with it ; we must often rely on it provisionally, in the absence of means of more searching investigation. But, for the accurate study of nature, we require a surer and a more potent instrument.

It was, above all, by pointing out the insufficiency of this rude and loose conception of Induction, that Bacon merited the title so generally awarded to him, of Founder of the Inductive Philosophy. The value of his own contributions to a more philosophical theory of the subject has certainly been exaggerated. Although (along with some fundamental errors) his writings contain, more or less fully developed, several of the most important principles of the Inductive Method, physical investigation has now far outgrown the Baconian conception of Induction. Moral and political inquiry, indeed, are as yet far behind that conception. The current and approved modes of reasoning on these subjects are still of the same vicious description against which Bacon protested ; the method almost exclusively employed by those professing to treat such matters inductively, is the very *inductio per enumerationem simplicem* which he condemns ; and the experience which we hear so confidently appealed to by all sects, parties, and interests, is still, in his own emphatic words, *mera palpatio*.

§ 3. In order to a better understanding of the problem which the logician must solve if he would establish a scientific theory of Induction, let us compare a few cases of incorrect inductions with others which are acknowledged to be legitimate. Some, we know, which were believed for centuries to be correct, were nevertheless incorrect. That all swans are white, can not have been a good induction, since the conclusion has turned out erroneous. The experience, however, on which the conclusion rested, was genuine. From the earliest records, the testimony of the inhabitants of the known world was unanimous on the point. The uniform experience, therefore, of the inhabitants of the known world, agreeing in a common result, without one known instance of deviation from that result, is not always sufficient to establish a general conclusion.

But let us now turn to an instance apparently not very dissimilar to this. Mankind were wrong, it seems, in concluding that all swans were white : are we also wrong, when we conclude that all men's heads grow above their shoulders, and never below, in spite of the conflicting testimony of the naturalist Pliny? As there were black swans, though civilized people had existed for three thousand years on the earth without meeting with them, may there not also be "men whose heads do grow beneath their shoulders," notwithstanding a rather less perfect unanimity of negative testimony from observers? Most persons would answer No; it was more credible that a bird should vary in its color, than that men should vary in the relative position of their principal organs. And there is no doubt that in so saying they would be right: but to say why they are right, would be impossible, without entering more deeply than is usually done into the true theory of Induction.

Again, there are cases in which we reckon with the most unfailing confidence upon uniformity, and other cases in which we do not count upon it at all. In some we feel complete assurance that the future will resemble the past, the unknown be precisely similar to the known. In others, however invariable may be the result obtained from the instances which have been observed, we draw from them no more than a very feeble presumption that the like result will hold in all other cases. That a straight line is the shortest distance between two points, we do not doubt to be true even in the region of the fixed stars.* When

---

* In strictness, wherever the present constitution of space exists; which we have ample reason to believe that it does in the reign of the fixed stars.

a chemist announces the existence and properties of a newly-discovered substance, if we confide in his accuracy, we feel assured that the conclusions he has arrived at will hold universally, though the induction be founded but on a single instance. We do not withhold our assent, waiting for a repetition of the experiment ; or if we do, it is from a doubt whether the one experiment was properly made, not whether if properly made it would be conclusive. Here, then, is a general law of nature, inferred without hesitation from a single instance ; a universal proposition from a singular one. Now mark another case, and contrast it with this. Not all the instances which have been observed since the beginning of the world, in support of the general proposition that all crows are black, would be deemed a sufficient presumption of the truth of the proposition, to outweigh the testimony of one unexceptionable witness who should affirm that in some region of the earth not fully explored, he had caught and examined a crow, and had found it to be gray.

Why is a single instance, in some cases, sufficient for a complete induction, while in others, myriads of concurring instances, without a single exception known or presumed, go such a very little way toward establishing a universal proposition ? Whoever can answer this question knows more of the philosophy of logic than the wisest of the ancients, and has solved the problem of induction.

(pp. 431–432). What renders arithmetic the type of a deductive science, is the fortunate applicability to it of a law so comprehensive as

" The sums of equals are equals": or (to express the same principle in less familiar but more characteristic language), whatever is made up of parts, is made up of the parts of those parts. This truth, obvious to the senses in all cases which can be fairly referred to their decision, and so general as to be co-extensive with nature itself, being true of all sorts of phenomena (for all admit of being numbered), must be considered an inductive truth, or law of nature, of the highest order. And every arithmetical operation is an application of this law, or of other laws capable of being deduced from it. This is our warrant for all calculations. We believe that five and two are equal to seven, on the evidence of this inductive law, combined with the definitions of those numbers. We arrive at that conclusion (as all know who remember how they first learned it) by adding a single unit at a time : $5+1=6$, therefore $5+1+1=6+1=7$; and again $2=1+1$, therefore $5+2=5+1+1=7$.

QUOTATIONS ON INTERPRETATION.

APPENDIX J.

234. 1. From Davies and Peck, *Dictionary of Mathematics.*

Interpretation. [L. **interpretatio**, explanation]. The process of explaining results arrived at by the application of mathematical rules. When, for example, an algebraic definition is laid down, there is frequently some restriction implied in making the definition, so that the result to which it leads presents more cases than can be explained by it, or even than was contemplated by it. Thus the abbreviation of a a, a a a, into a^2, a^3, and the rules which spring from it, lead to results of the form.

$$a^{-2},\ a^0,\ a^{\frac{1}{2}},\ a^{-\frac{1}{2}},\ \text{etc.}$$

These results, until interpreted, are without any intelligent algebraic meaning.

When such results arise, the province of interpretation begins; their meaning and force are investigated and explained, and the definitions heretofore too narrow, are extended so as to cover these and other results.

The rule to be adopted in interpreting new expressions obtained by applying known processes, is to attribute to them such a meaning as to make the whole of the process true by which they were obtained. For example : the formula

$$a^m \times a^n = a^{m+n}$$

is perfectly intelligible so long as m and n are whole numbers. Suppose it were required to interpret the symbol a^0, that is, to give to it such a meaning, that the above formula shall be true in that case. Making $m=0$, the formula becomes

$$a^0 \times a^n = a^{0+n} = a^n ;$$

hence, $a^0 = 1$. Again, suppose it were required to interpret the symbol $a^{\frac{1}{2}}$. Make $m = \frac{1}{2}$ and $n = \frac{1}{2}$, and the formula becomes

$$a^{\frac{1}{2}} \times a^{\frac{1}{2}} = a^{\frac{1}{2}+\frac{1}{2}} = a,$$

hence, $a^{\frac{1}{2}} = \sqrt{a}$, for $\sqrt{a} \times \sqrt{a} = a$, by definition.

Besides the application of the principles of interpretation to the explanation of new symbols, another very important application consists in making suppositions upon certain arbitrary quantities which enter formulas, and then comparing the results with known facts, thus deducing new truths. As an example of this method of interpretation let us take the equation of the ellipse

$$a^2 y^2 + b^2 x^2 = a^2 b^2,$$

and suppose $x > a$, finding the value of y in terms of x, we have

$$y = \pm \frac{b}{a} \sqrt{a^2 - x^2},$$

from which we see that for all values of x greater than a, y is **imaginary**. Now an imaginary result indicates an impossibility in the assumption. Hence, we interpret the result as indicating that no point of the ellipse can lie at a greater distance from its conjugate axis than the extremity of the transverse axis.

In integrating the differential of a transcendental function by an algebraic rule, a result ∞ is reached, which is manifestly absurd, since no function can be ∞. We interpret this as indicating that the rule fails in the case considered.

2. From Smith's *Synonyms Discriminated*.

Expound (Lat. **expono**) denotes sustained explanation; while a mere word or phrase may be explained, a whole work or parts of it may be expounded. Exposition is continuous critical explanation. **Interpret** (Lat. **interpres**, an interpreter), beyond the mere sense of verbal translation from one language to another, conveys the idea of private or personal explanation of what is capable of more than one view. Hence interpretation is more arbitrary than exposition, and more theoretical than explanation. Expound relates only to words in series, interpretation is applicable also to anything of a symbolical character, as to interpret a dream or a prophecy. It is also, in common with explain, an application to anything which may be viewed in different lights, as the actions of men. In this way, to explain conduct would rather be to account for it; to interpret it would be to assign motives or significance to it. Explanation deals with facts, interpretation with causes also.

QUOTATIONS ON DEDUCTION.

APPENDIX K.

235. 1. From Fleming's *Vocabulary of Philosophy*, Ed. 1858, pp. 126–7.

Deduction (from **deduco,** to draw from, to cause to come out of,) is the mental operation which consists in drawing a particular truth from a general principle antecedently known. It is opposed to **induction,** which consists in rising from particular truths to the determination of a general principle. Let it be proposed to prove that Peter is mortal; I know that Peter is a man, and this enables me to say that all men are mortal, from which affirmation I **deduce** that Peter is mortal.

The syllogism is the form of **deduction.** Aristotle (*Prior. Analyt.*, lib. 1, cap. 1) has defined it to be "an enunciation in which certain assertions being made, by their being true, it follows necessarily, that another assertion different from the first is true also."

Before we can **deduce** a particular truth, we must be in possession of the general truth. This may be acquired **intuitively,** as every change implies a cause; or **inductively,** as the volume of gas is in the inverse ratio of the pressure.

Deduction, when it uses the former kind of

truths, is demonstration or science. Truths drawn from the latter kind are contingent and relative, and admit of correction by increasing knowledge. The principle of **deduction** is, that things that agree with the same things agree with one another. The principle of **induction** is, that in the same circumstances, and in the same substances, from the same causes the same effects will follow.

The mathematical and metaphysical sciences are founded on **deduction**, the physical sciences rest on **induction.**

2. From Day's *Elements of Logic*, Ed. 1868, p. 105.

A **Deductive Syllogism** is a Mediate Reasoning in which the movement of Thought is from a Whole to a Part, mediated through a middle term, which is, respectively, a part of that whole and a whole of that part; as, Man is mortal; Caius is a man; therefore, Caius is mortal.

As the **Deductive Syllogism** is a Mediate Reasoning, its **datum** must consist of two Judgments, which, as given to Thought, are not of course at all validated by the Reasoning.

They must be regarded consequently as only assumed for the Reasoning, or must rest on evidence foreign to it. But the movement of Thought in itself may be valid, although the given Judgments are false; just as an arithmetical process may be correct, although applied to unreal objects.

3. From Bowen's *Logic*, Ed. 1874, pp. 261, 262.

Reasoning, however, proceeds not only in different wholes, but in different aspects of the same whole. We may, it is evident, regard any whole, considered as the complement of its parts, in either of two ways ; for we may, on the one hand, look from the whole to the parts, and reason accordingly downwards ; or, on the other hand, look from the parts to the whole they constitute, and reason accordingly upwards. The former of these reasonings is called **Deductive**, the latter **Inductive**. **Deductive** reasoning is founded on the maxim, ' What belongs to the containing whole belongs also to the contained parts ;' **Induction**, on the contrary maxim, ' What belongs to the constituent parts belongs also to the constituted whole.' Thus, in Deductive reasoning, the whole is stated first, and what is affirmed of it is affirmed of the parts it contains ; in other words, a general law is laid down, and predicated of the particular instances to which it applies.

In Inductive reasoning, the parts are first stated, and what is predicated of them is also predicated of the whole they constitute ; in other words, the particular instances are first 'stated as facts, and then the law they constitute is evolved.

4. From Hedge's *Elements of Logick*, Ed. 1854, pp. 118, 119.

Syllogism (=Deduction) and induction proceed in opposite directions. Induction . . begins with individual objects, as they exist in nature, and ascends by successive steps to the most general truths. Syllogism (=Deduction) begins where inductions terminates. It commences with some universal proposition, and follows back the footsteps of the former process, transferring at each stage the predicate of the more general to the less general rank of beings ; or, in other words, predicating the genus of the species, and the species of the individual.

. . . Syllogism (=Deduction) is employed with advantage in communicating to others, in an exact and perspicuous manner, the general principles of science. It may also be used with success in exposing the weakness of arguments, stated in loose or figurative language. But it is of no service in helping us to the discovery of new truths. "We must know a thing first," Mr. Locke observes, " and then we can prove it syllogistically "

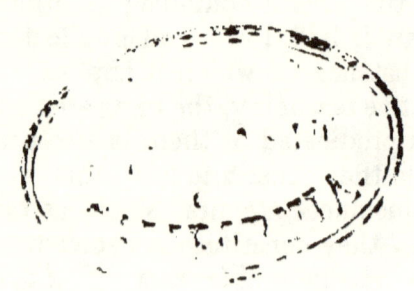

—— *THE SCHOOL BULLETIN PUBLICATIONS.* ——

Books for Young Teachers.

1. *Common School Law for Common School Teachers.* A digest of the provisions of statute and common law as to the relations of the Teacher to the Pupil, the Parent, and the District. With 500 references to legal decisions in 28 different States. 14th edition, wholly re-written, with references to the Code of 1888. By C. W. BARDEEN. 16mo, cloth, pp. 120. Price 75 cts.

The reason why the teacher should make this his first purchase is that without a knowledge of his duties and his rights under the law he may fail either in securing a school, in managing it, or in drawing the pay for his services. The statute provisions are remarkably simple and uniform. The decisions of the Courts, except upon two points, here fully discussed, follow certain defined precedents. An hour to each of the eleven chapters of this little book will make the teacher master of any legal difficulties that may arise, while ignorance of it puts him at the mercy of a rebellious pupil, an exacting parent, or a dishonest trustee.

2. *Hand-Book for Young Teachers.* By H. B. BUCKHAM, late principal of the State Normal School at Buffalo. Cloth, 16mo, pp. 152. Price 75 cts.

It anticipates all the difficulties likely to be encountered, and gives the beginner the counsel of an older friend.

3. *The School Room Guide,* embodying the instruction given by the author at Teachers' Institutes in New York and other States, and especially intended to assist Public School Teachers in the Practical Work of the School-Room. By E. V. DEGRAFF. *Thirteenth edition,* with many additions and corrections. 16mo, cloth, pp. 398. Price $1.50.

As distinguished from others of the modern standards, this is a book of *Methods* instead of theories. It tells the teacher just what to do and how to do it; and it has proved more practically helpful in the school-room than any other book ever issued.

4. *A Quiz-Book on the Theory and Practice of Teaching.* By A. P. SOUTHWICK, author of the "Dime Question Books." 12mo, pp. 220. Price $1.00.

This is one of the six books recommended by the State Department for study in preparation for State Certificates. The others are Hoose's *Methods* ($1.00), Hughes's *Mistakes* (50 cts.), Fitch's *Lectures* ($1.00), Page's *Theory and Practice* ($1.25), and Swett's *Methods* ($1.25). We will send the six post-paid for $5.00.

5. *Mistakes in Teaching.* By JAMES L. HUGHES. American edition, with contents and index. Cloth, 16mo, pp. 135. Price 50 cts.

More than 15,000 have been used in the county institutes of Iowa, and elsewhere superintendents often choose this book for their less thoughtful teachers, assured that its pungent style and chatty treatment will arrest attention and produce good results.

6 *How to Secure and Retain Attention.* By JAMES L. HUGHES. 16mo, cloth, pp. 97. Price 50 cts.

This touches attractively and helpfully upon the first serious difficulty the teacher encounters. No young teacher should neglect these hints.

7. *Primary Helps.* A Kindergarten Manual for Public School Teachers. By W. N. HAILMANN. 8vo, boards, pp. 58, with 15 full-page plates. Price 75 cts.

In these days, no primary teacher can afford to be ignorant of "The New Education," and this is perhaps the only volume that makes kindergarten principles practically available in public schools.

8. *Dime Question Book,* No. 4, *Theory and Practice of Teaching.* 16mo, paper, pp. 40. Price 10 cts. By A. P. SOUTHWICK.

A capital preparation for examination.

C. W. BARDEEN, Publisher, Syracuse, N. Y.

The Five Great English Books.

The recognition of Teaching as a Science was much earlier in England than in this country, and the five books which are there recognized as standards, have probably no equals in soundness and scope. Hence they are usually the first books adopted by Reading Circles, and are indispensable to the library of an intelligent teacher. These are:

1. *Essays on Educational Reformers.* By ROBERT HENRY QUICK. Cloth, 16mo, pp. 330. Price $1.50; or special edition, thinner covers, price $1.00.

This is altogether the best *History* of Education. "With the suggestion that *study should be made interesting*," writes Principal Morgan, of the Rhode Island State Normal School, "we most heartily agree. How this may be done, the attentive reader will be helped in learning by the study of this admirable book."

2. *Lectures on Teaching.* By J. G. FITCH. New Edition with a Preface by an American Normal Teacher. Cloth, 16mo, pp. 393. Price $1.25.

This forms the proper *Basis* for pedagogical knowledge, beginning with the teacher, the school, and the school-room, and giving the *why* as well as the *what*. We publish in our "School Room Classics" the "Art of Questioning," and the "Art of Securing Attention," by the same author, at 15 cents each.

3. *Lectures on the Science and Art of Education.* By JOSEPH PAYNE. Cloth, 16mo, pp. 384. Price $1.00.

The student is now ready to take up the *Science* of Education, which is nowhere else so brilliantly and effectively presented. The lectures are singularly fascinating, and the full analysis and indexes in this edition make it easy to collate and compare all that the author has uttered upon any topic suggested.

4. *The Philosophy of Education, or the Principles and Practice of Teaching.* By THOMAS TATE. Cloth, 16mo, pp. 440. Price $1.50.

This gives the application of the Science to the *Art* of Teaching, and is without a rival in its clear presentation and abundant illustrations. The author is not content with giving directions. He shows by specimens of class-work just what should be done and may be done.

5. *Introductory Text-Book to School Education, Method and School Management.* By JOHN GILL. Cloth, 16mo, pp. 276. Price $1.00.

This supplements the work of all the rest by practical directions as to *School Management*. Of the five this has had a sale equal to that of all the rest combined. The teacher's greatest difficulty, his surest discomfiture if he fails, is in the discipline and management of his school. That this manual has proved of inestimable help is proved from the fact that the present English edition is the 44th thousand printed.

C. W. BARDEEN, Publisher, Syracuse, N. Y.

——— *THE SCHOOL BULLETIN PUBLICATIONS.* ———

The School Room Classics.

Under the above title we have published a series of Monographs upon Education, as follows, all 16mo, in paper, at 15 cts. each.

1. Unconscious Tuition. By Bishop HUNTINGTON. Pp. 45.
"There is probably nothing finer in the whole range of educational literature."—*Ohio Educational Monthly.*
"It cannot be read without a wholesome self-weighing, and a yearning which develops true character."—*The Schoolmaster*, Chicago.

2. The Art of Questioning. By J. G. FITCH. Pp. 36.
"Mr. Fitch is happily *inside* his subject, and as clear as a bell."—*Christian Register.*

3. The Philosophy of School Discipline. By JOHN KENNEDY. Pp. 23.
"Clear and logical, and goes down to the very foundation."—*Utica Herald.*

4. The Art of Securing Attention. By J. G. FITCH. Pp. 43.
"Perhaps I overestimate Fitch's works, but I fail to find in the statement of any other educational writer a juster comprehension of the needs and difficulties of both teacher and pupil, or more common sense put into neater, clearer style."—*The Student*, Philadelphia.

5. Learning and Health. By B. W. RICHARDSON. Pp. 39.
"A timely topic ably treated."—*N. E. Journal of Education.*
"Certainly worth many times its weight in gold."—*Eclectic Teacher.*

6. The New Education. By J. M. W. MEIKLEJOHN. Pp. 35.
"Absolutely the best summary we have seen of the doctrines of Frœbel in their present development."—*N. Y. School Journal.*

7. A Small Tractate of Education. By JOHN MILTON. Pp. 26.
"Far more important in the literature of the subject than the treatise of Locke."—*Encyclopædia Brittanica.*

8. The School Work-Shop. By Baroness VON MARENHOLZ-BUELOW. translated by Miss BLOW. Pp. 27.
"In this treatise the kindergarten view of Industrial Education receives its best exemplification."—*N. E. Journal of Education.*

9. Sex in Mind and in Education. By HENRY MAUDSLEY. Pp. 42.
"A masterly treatment of a delicate subject."—*N. E. Journal of Education.*

10. Education as Viewed by Thinkers. Pp. 47.
This contains 95 classified quotations from leading authorities of every time and country, and will be of use to every writer and speaker.

11. How to Teach Natural Science in Public Schools. By WM. T. HARRIS. Pp. 40.
Since this was first published in 1871 for the schools of St. Louis, it has been regarded as the standard authority upon the subject, and this edition, revised by the author, was prepared by the request of the Committee on Physics-Teaching in 1887 of the National Association.

C. W. BARDEEN, Publisher, Syracuse, N. Y.

Instruction in Citizenship.

1. Civil Government for Common Schools, prepared as a manual for public instruction in the State of New York. To which are appended the Constitution of the State of New York as amended at the election of 1882, the Constitution of the United States, and the Declaration of Independence, etc., etc. By HENRY C. NORTHAM. 16mo, cloth, pp. 185. 75 cts.

Is it that this book was made because the times demanded it, or that the publication of a book which made the teaching of Civil Government practicable led to a general desire that it should be taught? Certain it is that this subject, formerly regarded as a "finishing" branch in the high school, is now found on every teacher's examination-paper, and is commonly taught in district schools. Equally certain is it that in the State of New York this text-book is used more than all others combined.

2. A Chart of Civil Government. By CHARLES T. POOLER. Sheets 12x18, 5 cts. The same folded, in cloth covers, 25 cts.

Schools using Northam's Civil Government will find this chart of great use, and those not yet ready to introduce a text-book will be able to give no little valuable instruction by the charts alone. Some commissioners have purchased them by the hundred and presented one to every school house in the county.

3. Handbook for School Teachers and Trustees. A manual of School Law for School Officers, Teachers and Parents in the State of New York. By HERBERT BROWNELL. 16mo, leatherette, pp. 64. 35 cts.

This is a specification of the general subject, presenting clearly, definitely, *and with references*, important questions of School Law. Particular attention is called to the chapters treating of schools under visitation of the Regents—a topic upon which definite information is often sought for in vain.

4. Common School Law for Common School Teachers. A digest of the provisions of statute and common law as to the relations of the Teacher to the Pupil, the Parent, and the District. With 500 references to legal decisions in 28 different States. 14th edition, wholly re-written, with references to the new Code of 1888. By C. W. BARDEEN. 16mo, cloth, pp. 120. 75 cts.

This has been since 1875 the standard authority upon the teacher's relations, and is frequently quoted in legal decisions. The new edition is much more complete than its predecessors, containing Topical Table of Contents, and a minute Index.

5. Laws of New York relating to Common Schools, with comments and instructions, and a digest of decisions. 8vo, leather, pp. 867. $4.00.

This is what is known as "The New Code of 1888," and contains all revisions of the State school-law to date.

6. The Powers and Duties of Officers and Teachers. By ALBERT P. MARBLE. 16mo, paper, pp. 27. 15 cts.

A vigorous presentation in Sup't Marble's pungent style of tendencies as well as facts.

7. First Principles of Political Economy. By JOSEPH ALDEN. 16mo, cloth, pp. 153. 75 cts.

Ex-President Andrew D. White says of this book: "It is clear, well arranged, and the best treatise for the purpose I have ever seen."

C. W. BARDEEN, Publisher, Syracuse, N. Y.

————THE SCHOOL BULLETIN PUBLICATIONS.————

Teachers' Question Books.

1. The Regents' Questions in Arithmetic, Geography, Grammar and Spelling from the first examination in 1866 to June 1882. *(No questions of later date will be printed.)* Being the 11,000 Questions for the preliminary examinations for admission to the University of the State of New York, prepared by the Regents of the University, and participated in simultaneously by more than 250 academies, forming a basis for the distribution of more than a million of dollars. *Complete with Key.* Cloth, 16mo, pp. 478. $2.00.

2. Complete. The same as above but without answers. Pp. 340. $1.00.

In the subjects named, no other Question Book can compare with this either in completeness, in excellence, or in popularity. By Legislative Enactment no lawyer can be admitted to the bar in the State of New York without passing a Regents' Examination in these subjects.

3. The Dime Question Books, with full answers, notes, queries, etc. Paper, pp. about 40. By A. P. SOUTHWICK. Each 10 cts.

Elementary Series.

3. Physiology.
4. Theory and Practice.
6. U. S. History and Civil Gov't.
10. Algebra.
13. American Literature.
14. Grammar.
15. Orthography and Etymology.
18. Arithmetic.
19. Physical and Political Geog.
20. Reading and Punctuation.

These 10 in one book. Cloth, $1.00.

Advanced Series.

1. Physics.
2. General Literature,
5. General History.
7. Astronomy.
8. Mythology.
9. Rhetoric.
11. Botany.
12. Zoölogy.
16. Chemistry.
17. Geology.

These 10 in one book. Cloth, $1.00.

Extra Volume, 21. Temperance Physiology.

The immense sale of the Regents' Questions in Arithmetic, Geography, Grammar, and Spelling has led to frequent inquiry for the questions in the Advanced Examinations. *As it is not permitted to reprint these*, we have had prepared this series, by which the teacher need purchase books only on the subjects upon which special help is needed. Frequently a $1.50 book is bought for the sake of a few questions in a single study. Here, the studies may be taken up one at a time, *a special advantage in New York, since applicants for State Certificates may now present themselves for examination in only part of the subjects, and receive partial Certificates to be exchanged for full Certificates when all the branches have been passed.* The same plan is very generally pursued by county superintendents and commissioners who are encouraging their teachers to prepare themselves for higher certificates.

4. Quizzism. Quirks and Quibbles from Queer Quarters. Being a Mélange of questions in Literature, Science, History, Biography, Mythology, Philology, Geography, etc. By A. P. SOUTHWICK. 16mo, pp. 55. 25 cts. Key, $1.00.

A stimulus for home study, and invaluable for school or teachers' gatherings.

5. New York State Examination Questions. Cloth, 16mo, pp. 256. 50 cts.

This contains all the questions given at all the New York Examinations for State Certificates from the beginning. There are more questions and in greater variety than in any other collection. It does not give answers.

6. The Common School Question Book. By ASA L. CRAIG. Cloth, 12mo, pp. 340. $1.50. We can also furnish SHAW's *National Question Book*, pp. 351, $1.50; STILLWELL's *Practical Question Book*, pp. 400, $1.50; BROWN's *Common School Examiner*, pp. 371, $1.00; THOMPSON's *Teacher's Examiner*, pp. 378 $1.50; SHERRILL's *Normal Question Book*, pp. 460, $1.50.

C. W. BARDEEN, Publisher, Syracuse, N. Y.

―――*THE SCHOOL BULLETIN PUBLICATIONS.*―――

Helps toward Correct Speech.

1. Verbal Pitfalls: a manual of 1500 words commonly misused, including all those the use of which in any sense has been questioned by Dean Alvord, G. W. Moon, Fitzedward Hall, Archbishop Trench, Wm. C. Hodgson, W. L. Blackley, G. F. Graham, Richard Grant White, M. Schele de Vere, Wm. Mathews, "Alfred Ayres," and many others. Arranged alphabetically, with 3000 references and quotations, and the ruling of the dictionaries. By C. W. BARDEEN. 16mo, cloth, pp. 223. 75 cts.

Perhaps the happiest feature of the book is its interesting form. Some hundreds of anecdotes have been gathered to illustrate the various points made. These have the advantage not only of making the work entertaining, but of fixing the point in the mind as a mere precept could not do. The type indicates at a glance whether the use of a word is (1) indefensible, (2) defensible but objectionable, or (3) thoroughly authorized.

2. A System of Rhetoric. By C. W. BARDEEN. 12mo, half leather, pp. 813. $1.75.

3. A Shorter Course in Rhetoric. By C. W. BARDEEN. 12mo, half leather, pp. 311. $1.00.

4. Outlines of Sentence Making. By C. W. BARDEEN. 12mo, cloth, pp. 187. 75 cts.

5. Practical Phonics. A comprehensive study of Pronunciation, forming a complete guide to the study of elementary sounds of the English Language, and containing 3,000 words of difficult pronunciation, with diacritical marks according to Webster's Dictionary. By E. V. DE GRAFF. 16mo, cloth, pp. 108. 75 cts.

The book before us is the latest, and in many respects the best, of the manuals prepared for this purpose. The directions for teaching elementary sounds are remarkably explicit and simple, and the diacritical marks are fuller than in any other book we know of, the obscure vowels being marked, as well as the accented ones. This manual is not like others of the kind, a simple reference book. It is meant for careful study and drill, and is especially adapted to class use.—*New England Journal of Education.*

6. Pocket Pronunciation Book, containing the 3,000 words of difficult pronunciation, with diacritical marks according to Webster's Dictionary. By E. V. DE GRAFF. 16mo, manilla, pp. 47. 15 cts.

Every vowel that can possibly be mispronounced is guarded by danger signals which send one back to the phonic chart for instructions. We are glad to notice that the Professor is leading a campaign against the despoilers of the vowel *u;* he cannot hold communion with an educated man whose third day in the week is "Toosday."—*Northern Christian Advocate.*

7. Studies in Articulation: a study and drill-book in the Alphabetic Elements of the English language. *Fifth thousand.* By J. H. HOOSE. 16mo, cloth, pp. 70. 50 cts.

This work not only analyzes each sound in the language, but gives as illustrations hundreds of words commonly mispronounced.

Dr. Hoose's "Studies in Articulation" is the most useful manual of the kind that I know of. It should be a text-book in every Teachers' Institute. —*A. J. Rickoff, formerly Sup't of Schools at Cleveland and at Yonkers.*

8. Hints on Teaching Orthoëpy. By CHAS. T. POOLER. 16mo, paper, pp. 15. 10 cts.

9. Question Book of Orthography, Orthoëpy, and Etymology, with Notes, Queries, etc. By ALBERT P. SOUTHWICK. 16mo, paper, pp. 40, 10 cts.

10. Question Book of Reading and Punctuation, with Notes, Queries, etc. By ALBERT P. SOUTHWICK. 16mo, paper, pp. 38. 10 cts.

C. W. BARDEEN, Publisher, Syracuse, N. Y.

——THE SCHOOL BULLETIN PUBLICATIONS.——

Helps in Language Teaching.

1. Normal Language Lessons; being the instruction in Grammar given at the Cortland State Normal School. By Prof. S. J. SORNBERGER. 16mo, boards, pp. 81. 50 cts.

Whatever text-book the teacher uses, or if he uses no text-book at all, he will find this manual of great assistance. Its classification is simple, its definitions are careful, its tabular analyses are complete, and *its reference by page to all the best authors* makes it invaluable.

2. Exercises in English Syntax. By A. G. BUGBEE. 16mo, leatherette, pp. 87. 35 cts.

This differs from other handbooks of sentences for class-drill in that it does not print wrong sentences to be corrected,—a practice now generally condemned, because incorrect forms should never be put before the child's eye,—but leaves blanks in the sentence to be filled by the pupil from a choice of expressions given, thus calling in the most effective way to right usage and its reasons. It is of especial assistance in preparation for Regents' examinations, which always include much work of this kind. Send for special circular with specimen sentences, and recommendations.

3. The Regents' Questions in Grammar, from the beginning to June, 1882. By DANIEL J. PRATT, Assistant Secretary. 16mo, manilla, pp. 109. 25 cts.

This unequalled series of questions is recognized throughout the country as the best drill-book ever made, and the only satisfactory preparation for examination.

An edition of these Questions, *with complete answers, and references to the grammars of* Brown, Murray, Greene, Clark, Kerl, Quackenbos, Weld & Quackenbos, Hart, Fowler, Swinton, Reed & Kellogg, and Whitney, will be sent post-paid to any address on receipt of One Dollar. It contains 196 pages, and is handsomely bound in cloth.

4. Dime Question Book No. 14, Grammar. By ALBERT P. SOUTHWICK. 16mo, paper, pp. 85. 10 cts.

This is one of the best books in a deservedly popular series, giving full answers to every question, with notes, queries, etc. Conductor John Kennedy says: "The bad question book fosters cram; the good one suggests study. Mr. Southwick's system is good. It is happy and nourishing. I hope you may sell a million of them."

5. The Diacritical Speller. A practical course of exercises in Spelling and Pronunciation. By C. R. BALES. 8vo, boards, pp. 68. 50 cts.

This work is novel even in a field so thoroughly worked as spelling. Its striking features are conciseness and simplicity. The pupil is not drilled upon what all pupils know, but only upon what most pupils fall in. The collections of words are made with great skill, and the pupil who uses this book is not likely to say Toosday or Reuler. The selection of test-words is particularly happy, and the exercises in synonyms will afford material for many a spare ten minutes.—*California Teacher.*

6. An Aid to English Grammar; designed principally for Teachers. By ASHER P. STARKWEATHER. 16mo, boards, pp. 230. 75 cts.

This is a grammar aid book on a wholly original plan. It is simply a collection of words which are used as two or more parts of speech, with illustrative sentences to show their correct use.—*School Herald, Chicago.*

C. W. BARDEEN, Publisher, Syracuse, N. Y.

Helps in Teaching Literature.

1. A Series of Questions in English and American Literature, prepared for class drill and private study by MARY F. HENDRICK, teacher in the State Normal School, Cortland, N. Y. 16mo, boards, pages 100, interleaved. 35 cts.

This edition is especially prepared for taking notes in the literature class, and may be used in connection with any text-book or under any instruction.

2. Early English Literature, from the Lay of Beowulf to Edmund Spenser. By WM. B. HARLOW, instructor in the High School, Syracuse, N. Y. 16mo, cloth, pp. 138. 75 cts.

This handsome volume gives copious extracts from all leading authors, of sufficient length to afford a fair taste of their style, while its biographical and critical notes give it rare value.

3. Dime Question Book No. 2, General Literature, and *No. 13, American Literature.* By ALBERT P. SOUTHWICK. 16mo, paper, pp. 85, 89. 10 cts. each.

These are among the most interesting books in the series, abounding in allusion and suggestion, as well as giving full answers to every question. They afford a capital drill, and should be used in every class as a preparation for examination.

4. How to Obtain the Greatest Value from a Book. By the Rev. R. W. LOWRIE. 8vo, pp. 12. 25 cts.

No one can read this essay without pleasure and profit.

5. The Art of Questioning. By JOSHUA G. FITCH. 16mo, paper, pp. 36. 15 cts.

Mr. Fitch, one of Her Majesty's inspectors of schools, now recognized as the ablest of English writers on education, owed his early reputation to this address, the practical helpfulness of which is everywhere acknowledged.

6. The Art of Securing Attention. By JOSHUA G. FITCH. 16mo, paper, pp. 43. 15 cts.

The *Maryland School Journal* well says: "It is itself an exemplification of the problem discussed, for the first page fixes the attention so that the reader never wearies, till he comes to the last and then wishes that the end had not come so soon."

7. The Elocutionist's Annual, comprising new and popular Readings, Recitations, Declamations, Dialogues, Tableaux. etc., etc. Compiled by Mrs. J. W. SHOEMAKER. Paper, 16mo, pp. 200. *12 Numbers.* Price of each, 30 cts.

Though primarily designed for classes in elocution, the character of the selections is so high that any of these volumes may be used with profit in a literature class.

8. The Bible in the Public Schools. Paper, 24mo, 2 vols., pp. 214, 228. 50 cts.

These volumes contain the most important arguments, decisions, and addresses connected with the celebrated contest in Cincinnati, 1869.

C. W. BARDEEN, Publisher, Syracuse, N. Y.

———THE SCHOOL BULLETIN PUBLICATIONS.———

Helps in Teaching History.

1. A Thousand Questions in American History. 16mo, cloth, pp. 247. Price $1.00.

This work has been prepared by an eminent teacher for use in his own school—one of the largest in the State. It shows rare breadth of view and discrimination, dealing not merely with events but with causes, and with the side-issues that have so much to do with determining the destiny of a nation.

2. Helps in Fixing the Facts of American History. By HENRY C. NORTHAM. 16mo, cloth, pp. 298. Price $1.00.

Here all facts are presented in groups. The key-word to the Revolution, for instance, is LIBERTY, as shown in the accompanying table of *Key-Words;* and in like manner the events of the late civil war are kept chronologically distinct by the key-words SLAVES FREED. Chart No. 1 indicates by stars the years in each decade from 1492 to 1789, in which the most remarkable events occured, while the colored chart No. 2 arranges the events in twelve groups.

L—exington.
I—ndependence.
B—urgoyne's Surrender.
E—vacuation.
R—etribution.
T—reason.
Y—orktown.

3. Topics and References in American History, with numerous Search Questions. By GEO. A. WILLIAMS. 16mo, leatherette, pp. 50. 50 cts.

This is a book of immediate practical value to every teacher. The references are largely to the lighter and more interesting illustrations of history, of a kind to arouse the thought of pupils by giving vivid conceptions of the events narrated. By dividing these references among the members of a class, the history recitation may be made the most delightful of the day.

4. Dime Question Books, No. 5, General History, and No. 6, United States History and Civil Government. By ALBERT P. SOUTHWICK. 16mo, paper, pp. 37, 32. 10 cts. each.

5. Outlines and Questions in United States History. By C. B. Van WIE. 16mo, paper, pp. 40, and folding Map. 15 cts.

The outgrowth of four years' practical work in the school-room with map prepared by a pupil as a suggestive model.

6. Tablet of American History, with Map of the United States on the back. By RUFUS BLANCHARD. Heavy paper, mounted on rollers, 3½ by 5 feet. Price, *express paid*, $3.00.

The demand for a colored chart to hang upon the wall and thus catch the often-lifted eye of the pupil, has led to the preparation of this chart by an experienced author. The events of the four centuries are grouped in parallel belts of different colors, and upon the corners and sides are names of the States and Territories, with their etymology, etc., history of political parties, portraits of all the Presidents, Coats of Arms of all the States, etc. The map is engraved expressly for this chart by Rand & McNally, is *colored both by States and by counties*, and gives all the latest railroads, the new arrangement of time-lines, showing where the hour changes, etc.

C. W. BARDEEN, Publisher, Syracuse, N. Y.

Music in the School Room.

1. *The Song Budget.* A collections of Songs and Music for Educational Gatherings. By E. V. DE GRAFF. Small 4to, paper, pp. 76. 15 cts.

This book owes its popularity to two causes:

(1) It gives a great deal for the money.

(2) The songs are not only numerous (107), but *they are the standard favorites of the last fifty years.*

This is why the book contains more music *that will be used* than any other book published. For in all other books that we know of, two-thirds of the tunes are written by the compilers, who are of course partial to their own productions. Sup't De Graff wrote no songs of his own, but gathered those which his long experience as a conductor of teachers' institutes had shown him to be the most generally familiar and pleasing.

In fact, the success of this book has been due to the fact that only those songs were admitted that have proved to be universal favorites. This involved a large original outlay, as much as fifty dollars having been paid for the right to use a single song. But the best were taken, wherever they could be found and at whatever cost, and the result is a school singing-book of popularity unexampled. For instance, *a single firm* in Cleveland, Ohio, J. R. Holcomb & Co., had purchased of us up to Feb. 15, 1888, no less than 9730 copies, 4500 within the last six months, besides 2100 of the *School Room Chorus.*

2. *The School Room Chorus.* A collection of Two Hundred Songs for Public and Private Schools, compiled by E. V. DE GRAFF. Small, 4to, boards, pp. 148. 85 cts.

This is an enlarged edition of the *Song Budget*, with twice the number of songs. The plates of the last edition are so arranged that it is identical with the *Song Budget* as far as page 68, so that both books can be used together. The *Budget* and *Chorus* are particularly adapted for Teachers' Associations and Institutes. At these prices every meeting of teachers can be supplied with one or the other, while the fact that the tunes are standard favorites makes it easy for any audience to join in the singing at sight.

3. *The Diadem of School Songs;* containing Songs and Music for all grades of Schools, a new system of Instruction in the elements of Music, and a Manual of Directions for the use of Teachers. By WM. TILLINGHAST. Small, 4to, boards, pp. 160. 50 cts.

This book, of which Dr. French, the veteran institute-instructor was associate author, gives an exceedingly simple and practical system of instruction, as well as a valuable collection of songs.

4. *Half a Hundred Songs*, for the School-Room and Home. By HATTIE S. RUSSELL. 16mo, boards, pp. 103. 85 cts.

These songs are all original, but without music.

5. *The School Vocalist;* containing a thorough system of elementary instruction in Vocal Music, with Practical Exercises, Songs, Hymns, Chants, &c., adapted to the use of Schools and Academies. By E. LOCKE, and S. NOURSE. Oblong, boards, pp. 160. Price 50 cts.

6. *The School Melodist.* A Song Book for School and Home. By E. LOCKE and S. NOURSE. Oblong, boards, pp. 160. Price 50 cts.

7. *The Song Life,* for Sunday Schools, etc., illustrating in song the journey of Christiana and her children to the Celestial City. Small 4to boards, pp. 176. Price 50 cts.

Nos. 5, 6, and 7 are books that have had their day, but of which we have a few hundred copies of each on hand. These we will sell at 10 cts. each; if to go by mail, 6 cts. each extra. They contain much good music.

C. W. BARDEEN, Publisher, Syracuse, N. Y.

―――THE SCHOOL BULLETIN PUBLICATIONS.―――

Arithmetic by the Grubé Method.

1. *First Steps among Figures.* A drill book in the Fundamental Rules of Arithmetic. By LEVI N. BEEBE. Cloth, 16mo, 3 editions. *Pupils' Edition*, pp. 140, 45 cts. *Oral Edition*, pp. 139, 50 cts. *Teachers' Edition*, including all in both the others, with additional parallel matter, Index, and Key, pp. 326, $1.00.

These books give the only practical exposition of the *Grubé Method*, now generally admitted to produce the best results with beginners. It has been used ten years in the primary schools of such cities as Norwich, Conn., and Auburn, N. Y., and for many years *every student* in the Albany State Normal School has been directed to purchase a copy to take with him for his subsequent use in teaching.

From a multitude of testimonials we copy the following:

"We are still successfully using Beebe's *First Steps*. It has many admirable qualities."—*Sup't N. L. Bishop, Norwich, Conn.*

"I think it especially excellent for a system of graded schools, where uniformity of teaching is essential. It develops in practical shape an idea that I have long sustained as to the proper method of teaching arithmetic." *Sup't B. B. Snow, Auburn, N. Y.*

"I have recommended Beebe's *First Steps* as the best work in primary arithmetic. . . . The book is received with much favor, and is very helpful to me in my work."—*Prof. A. N. Husted, State Normal School, Albany, N. Y.*

"I am much pleased with the book, and wish every primary teacher to have a copy."—*Sup't J. M. Frost, Hudson, N. Y.*

"By vote of the Board of Education a copy of the Teachers' Edition was placed on the desk of every primary teacher in the city.—*Sup't Edward Smith, Syracuse, N. Y.*

"I consider Beebe's *First Steps* the best work of the kind that I have ever seen, and I take every opportunity to recommend it."—*Mary L. Sutliff, Haiku, Maui, Hawaian Islands, Feb. 9, 1888.*

2 *The Pestalozzian Series of Arithmetics.* Teachers' Manual and First-Year Text-Book for pupils in the first grade. Based upon Pestalozzi's method of teaching Elementary Number. By JAMES H. HOOSE. Boards, 16mo, 2 editions. *Pupils' Edition*, pp. 156, 35 cts. *Teacher's Edition*, containing the former, with additional matter, pp. 217, 50 cts.

This is a practical exposition of the *Pestalozzian Method*, and has met with great success not only in the Cortland Normal School, where it was first developed, but in many other leading schools, as at Gloversville, Babylon, etc. It is diametrically opposed to the Grubé Method, and good teachers should be familiar with both, that they may choose intelligently between them.

3. *Lessons in Number, as given in a Pestalozzian School, Cheam Surrey. The Master's Manual* By C. REINER. 16mo, pp. 224. $1.50.

This work was prepared in 1835 under the supervision of Dr. C Mayo in the first English Pestalozzian school, and has particular value as representing directly the educational methods of the great reformer.

C. W. BARDEEN, Publisher, Syracuse, N. Y.

———THE SCHOOL BULLETIN PUBLICATIONS.———
Useful Appliances in Arithmetic.

1. The Word Method in Number. A series of 45 Cards, on which are printed all the possible Combinations of Two Figures. In box. By H. R. SANFORD, Institute Conductor. Size 3¼ x 6 inches. Price 50 cts.

These cards need only to be seen, as the principle is familiar and accepted. The type, in *written* figures, is large enough to be seen across the room, and the combination on one side is given in reversed order on the other, so that as the teacher holds the card before him he knows the figures presented to the class. The pupil is taught to look upon the combination 4+9 as *itself* 13, not as "4 and 9 are 13," just as he looks upon DOG as an entire word, not as D-O-G. Success is certain if new combinations are introduced only after those already given are thoroughly learned. Reviews should be constant.

2. A Fractional Apparatus. By W. W. DAVIS. A box of eight wooden balls, three and one-half inches in diameter, seven of which are sawn into 2, 3, 4, 6, 8, 9, and 12 parts respectively, while the eighth is left a sphere. Price $4.00.

With this apparatus every principle and rule can be developed, and the pupils can be led to deduce rules for themselves.

Many other expedients are resorted to, but they are all objectionable. Suppose a teacher takes a stick and breaks it in the middle, will the pupil perceive two halves of a stick or two sticks? In teaching fractions objectively, that should be taken for unity from which if a part is taken unity is destroyed. This is not the case with a stick or cube. Apples are objectionable for three reasons; first because they cannot always be obtained; second because they are perishable; and third, because the attention of the pupils is diverted by a desire to know whether they are sweet or sour, etc. Nor can the teacher readily saw wooden balls into divisions even enough for the purpose designed, the charm of this method being the *exact* presentation to the pupil's eye of the fact illustrated.

3. A Manual of Suggestions for Teaching Fractions especially designed for accompanying the above apparatus. By W. W. DAVIS. Paper, 12mo, pp. 43. 25 cts.

This accompanying manual gives probably the best arrangement of the subject into sixty lessons ever made, with practical suggestions which all teachers will find valuable.

4. Cube Root Blocks, carried to Three Places. In box. $1.00.

Our blocks are unusually large, the inner cube being two inches, and the additions each one-half inch wide.

5. Numeral Frame, with 100 balls, $1.25; with 144 balls, $1.50.

"Initiate children to arithmetic by means of the *ball frame alone,* thereby making their elementary instruction a simple and natural extension of their own daily observation," says Laurie, in his standard book on *Primary Instruction* (p. 112), and as he leaves the subject of arithmetic, he adds this note (p. 117), as if in fear he had not been sufficiently emphatic:

"The teaching of arithmetic should be begun earlier than is customary, *and always with the ball-frame.*"

C. W. BARDEEN, Publisher, Syracuse, N. Y.

Maps, Charts and Globes.

1. Johnston's Wall Maps These are of three sizes, 27x33 inches, costing $2.50 each; 40x48, costing $5.00 each; and 63x72, costing $10.00 each.

The Common School Series includes (*a*) Hemispheres, (*b*) North America, (*c*) South America, (*d*) United States, (*e*) Europe, (*f*) Asia, (*g*) Africa. Others sometimes substituted or added are (*h*) World, Mercator's Projection, (*i*) Eastern Hemipphere, (*k*) Western Hemisphere.

We can furnish also in the 40x48 size: (*l*) England, (*m*) France, (*n*) Italy, (*o*) Spain, (*p*) Central America, (*q*) Orbis Veteribus Notus, (*r*) Italia Antiqua, (*s*) Græcia Antiqua, (*t*) Asia Minor, (*u*) Orbis Romanus, (*w*) De Bello Gallico, (*x*) Canaan and Palestine, (*y*) Bible Countries, (*z*) United States, historical, showing at a glance when and whence each portion of its territory was derived—a very valuable map in history classes.

All these maps are engraved on copper, and printed in permanent oil colors. All are cloth-mounted, on rollers. Spring rollers are added at an extra cost of $1.00, $1.50, and $2.50 respectively.

We offer a special consignment of T. Ruddiman Johnston's maps 40x48, *in sets only*, including Hemispheres, North America, South America, United States, political, United States, historical, Europe, Asia, and Africa, 8 maps, regular price $40.00, *at $15.00 per set.* They were prepared for a firm in the west who have been obliged to discontinue the business, and were sent to us by the Johnston Co. with instruction to close them out at once. Hence the unparalleled price, which applies only to this 100 sets.

3. Bulletin Map of the United States. Paper, on rollers, 3½x5 ft., with Blanchard's chart of the United States History upon the back. $3.00.

This is colored *both* by States and by Counties and gives correctly the new time lines.

4. Map of New York State, colored both by Counties and by Towns, 2½x3 ft. on rollers. Paper, $1.00; Cloth, $2.00.

5. Adams's Large Map of New York State, 61x66 inches. Cloth, on rollers, $10.00; on spring rollers, $12.00. We are now the sole proprietors of this latest and best map, and can hereafter fill all orders promptly.

6. Dissected Map of New York, sawn into Counties. 75 cts.

7. Dissected Map of the United States, sawn into States. 75 cts.

8. Chart of Life Series of Physiology Charts, 23x27 inches, four in number, including one to show the effects of alcohol on the system. These show every organ, *life-size* and *in place.* Per set, $10.00; on spring rollers, $12.50.

9. Eckhart's Anatomical Charts, consisting of 12 double plates, with more than 100 distinct and separate figures. Per set, $15.00.

10. Reading Charts of all kinds. Appleton's, $12.50; Monroe's Complete, $10.00. Monroe's Abridged, $6.00, etc.

The School Bulletin Globe. While we keep a dozen styles always in stock, we recommend this especially because: 1. It is 12 or 6 inches in diameter. 2. It has a low and heavy Bronzed Iron Frame. Its axis is adjustable. 4. It shows an entire Hemisphere. 5. Its Meridian is movable. 6. Its map is Johnston's. 7. It is shipped to any address at Fifteen Dollars for a 12-inch or Five Dollars for 6-inch size. 8. EVERY GLOBE IS GUARANTEED TO BE ABSOLUTELY PERFECT

C. W. BARDEEN, Publisher, Syracuse, N. Y.

——THE SCHOOL BULLETIN PUBLICATIONS.——

Blackboard Material.

No feature of the school-room is of more vital importance to the health of scholars and teachers than the Blackboard. If it be gray or greasy the amount of chalk used fills the air with dust, which produces catarrhal and bronchial difficulties, and yet makes so faint a mark that the children's eyes are permanently injured. Choice should be made among the following materials.

1. Solid Slate. This is durable, but costs from 30 to 50 cts. a square foot, is noisy, not black enough in color, and unhealthful because there is commonly used upon it the softest crayon. Where solid slate is already in, we recommend the Slate Pencil Crayon, as the only preventive of serious disease.

But it is better to put either upon the plastered wall, or upon the wall covered with manilla paper, or upon wooden boards, one of the following preparations.

2. Agalite Slating. This is the cheapest of all, may be sent by mail, and usually gives fair satisfaction. Price, *post-paid*, for box to cover 400 feet, one coat, $6.00; 200 feet, $3.25; 100 feet, $1.75; 50 feet, $1.00. We furnish the *Black Diamond* or *Silicate Slating* at the same price, but it can be sent only by express.

3. Slate Pencil Slating. This remarkable preparation does away altogether with chalk-dust, having sufficient grit to take a distinct mark from a slate-pencil. *Soft crayon should never be used upon it,* unless it is first rubbed down to smoother surface. It is a pure alcohol slating, and therefore durable. Price per gallon, covering 600 ft., one coat, $10.00; quarts, $2.75; pints $1.50.

In many schools using the Slate Pencil Slating, the State Normal at Potsdam, for instance, Faber's slate-pencils have taken the place of crayon. In other schools hard crayon, like Alpha H, is used.

4. Hornstone Slating. This is new, and altogether the best in the market, making a really stone surface which is yet absolutely black. There is no waste of chalk, even with soft crayon, while the Alpha H produces a beautifully clear mark. It contains no oil or grease, and grows harder with age. It is put on with a paint-brush, and adheres to *any* material, so that it may be put on walls, boards, paper, or any other smooth surface. Price $8.00 per gallon, covering 200 feet with *four* coats. It is somewhat expensive, and must be put on with care; but when properly finished it is a delight to the eye.

Sup't Smith, of Syracuse, says: "Your Hornstone Slating is now in use in four of our buildings, and I have no hesitation in saying that it is superior to solid slate or to any other blackboard surface I ever saw."—Principal Miner, of Skaneateles, says: "Its very smooth surface saves crayon and lessens the amount of chalk-dust in the room....I do not hesitate to say that it is the best board I ever used."

Cheney's Dustless Erasers work well on any of the boards named. Price 10 cts. each, $1.00 a dozen. The *School Bulletin Erasers* are made of the closest and best felt, and are very durable. Price 15 cts. each, $1.50 a dozen. Specimen of either by mail for 15 cts. *Alpha Crayon*, M or H, 75 cts. a box. *Ordinary White Crayon*, 15 cts. a box. *Colored Crayon*, 75 cts. a box. *Slate Pencil Crayon*, for solid slate, 50 cts. a box. (13)

C. W. BARDEEN, Publisher, Syracuse, N. Y.

School Records and Reports.

1. *The Bulletin Class Register.* Designed by EDWARD SMITH, Superintendent of Schools, Syracuse, N. Y. Press-board cover. *Three Sizes,* (*a*) 6x7, for terms of twenty weeks; (*b*) 5x7, for terms of fourteen weeks. When not otherwise specified this size is always sent. Pp. 48. Each 25 cts. (*c*), like (*b*) but with one half more (72) pages. Each 35 cts.

This register gives lines on each of 12 pages for 29 names, and *by a narrow leaf* puts opposite these names blanks for one entry each day for either 14 or 20 weeks, as desired, with additional lines for summary, examinations, and remarks. Nothing can be more simple, compact, and neat, where it is desired simply to keep a record of attendance, deportment, and classstanding. It is used in nearly two-thirds of the union schools of New York.

2. *The Peabody Class Record*, No. 1, with 3 blanks to each scholar each day for a year. Boards 4½x9½, pp. 100, $1.00. No. 2, with 5 blanks to each scholar, 8x11, $1.50. Like No. 1, but gives 3 or 5 blanks each day.

3. *Ryan's School Record*, 112 blanks to a sheet, per dozen sheets, 50 cts.

4. *Keller's Monthly Report Card*, to be returned with signature of parent or guardian, card-board 2¾x4, per hundred, $1.00.

5. *Babcock's Excelsior Grading Blanks*, manilla, 3x5, with blanks on both sides. Comprising (*a*) Report Cards; (*b*) Grade Certificates for each of 9 grades; (*c*) High School Certificate (double size). Price of (*a*) and (*b*) $1.00 a hundred; of (*c*) $1.50 a hundred.

6. *Shaw's Scholar's Register*, for each Week, with Abstract for the Term. Paper, 5x7, pp. 16. Per dozen, 50 cts. Each pupil keeps his own record.

7. *Jackson's Class Record Cards.* Per set of 90 white and 10 colored cards, with hints, 50 cts. Only *imperfect* recitations need be marked.

8. *Aids to School Discipline*, containing 80 Certificates, 120 Checks, 200 Cards, 100 Single and Half Merits. Per box, $1.25. Supplied separately per hundred: Half Merits, 15 cts., Cards, 15 cts., Checks, 50 cts., Certificates, 50 cts.

The use of millions of these Aids, with the unqualified approval of teachers, parents, and pupils, is assurance that they are doing great good.

They save time by avoiding the drudgery of Record keeping and Reports.

They abolish all notions of "partiality" by determining the pupil's standing with mathematical precision.

They naturally and invariably awaken a lively paternal interest, for the pupil takes home with him the witness of his daily conduct and progress.

They are neat in design, printed in bright colors. The Certificates are prizes which children will cherish. The Single Merits and Half Merits are printed on heavy card board, the Cards and Checks on heavy paper, and both may be used many times—hence the system is cheap, as well as more attractive than any other to young children.

9. *Mottoes for the School-Room.* By A. W. EDSON, State Agent of Massachusetts. Per set of 12 on heavy colored card-board 7x4 inches, printed on both sides, $1.00, post-paid, $1.10.

These mottoes are "Never too Late," "Above all, be Useful," "Dare to Say No," "God Bless our School," "Avoid Anger," "Be Good, Do Good," "Think, Speak, Act the Truth," "Fear to Do Wrong," "Misspent Time is Lost Forever," "Speak the Truth," "Act Well Your Part," "Strive to Excel," "Try, Try Again," "Be Diligent, Prompt, and Useful," "Think Good Thoughts," "Learn to Study," "Before Pleasure Comes Duty," "Think First of Others," "Dare to Do Right," "Order is Heaven's First Law," "A Will Makes a Way," "Study to Learn," "Hold Fast to Honor," "God Sees Me."

C. W. BARDEEN, Publisher, Syracuse, N. Y.

——— THE SCHOOL BULLETIN PUBLICATIONS. ———

Official Question Books.

1. The New York State Examination Questions from the beginning to the present date. Cloth, 16mo, pp. 274, 50 cts.

These annual examinations, only by which can State Certificates be obtained in New York, have a reputation all over the country for excellence and comprehensiveness. The subjects are as follows:

Arithmetic,	Grammar,	Physics,	Geography,
Book-Keeping,	Composition,	Chemistry,	Civil Government,
Algebra,	Rhetoric,	Geology,	Astronomy,
Geometry,	Literature,	Botany,	Methods,
Drawing,	History,	Zoölogy,	School Economy,
Penmanship,	Latin,	Physiology,	School Law.

No answers are published, except in the following special volume.

2. Dime Question Book on Book-Keeping, containing all the questions in that subject given at the first 15 New York Examinations for State Certificates, *with full Answers, Solutions, and Forms.* Paper, 16mo, pp. 31, 10 cts.

3. The Uniform Examination Questions. By voluntary adoption of the 113 School-Commissioners of the State of New York, certificates are now given only on examinations held under these questions, which are issued sealed from the State Department. They are published in the *School Bulletin* of the following dates, *with Complete Official Answers*; price of each, 10 cts.

June, 1888, *School Law*, 34 Questions and Answers.
July, 1888, *Arithmetic*, 167 " " "
Aug., 1888, *Geography*, 385 " " "
Oct., 1888, *Grammar*, 328 " " "
Nov., 1888, *Physiology*, 250 " " "
Dec., 1888, *Am. History*, 301 " " "

4. The Civil Service Question Book. Cloth, 16mo, pp. 282, $1.50.

42,000 places are now filled exclusively by appointments dependent on examinations. No favoritism is possible. You do not need the influence of Congressman or of politician. You have only to learn when the next examination is held, apply for the necessary papers, present yourself, and answer the questions asked. The appointments are made from those who stand highest, and are open to women as well as to men. All the particulars as to these examinations, the places and dates where held, and how to apply, are here given with 943 specimen questions in *Arithmetic*, 575 specimen questions in *Geography*, 400 specimen questions in *English Syntax*, 100 each in *American History* and *Civil Government*, with full treatises on *Book-Keeping* and on *Letter-Writing*. To prepare for competition for places at $1,000 and higher these subjects *and these only* are required. Any one who can answer the questions here given, *to all of which full and complete answers are added*, is ready to enter the next examination.

Hon JOHN B. RILEY, Chief Examiner, State of New York, July 10, 1888, says: "I am pleased with your Civil Service Question Book. It will not only be of service to those intending to try the Civil Service examinations, but teachers or others who are obliged to prepare questions for examinations in the common English branches will find it a great convenience."

The N. E. Journal of Education says, Aug. 23, 1888: "It is rarely that any book can be found with so many valuable and so few unimportant questions."

OTHER QUESTION BOOKS.

5. The Common School Question Book. By ASA L. CRAIG. Cloth, 12mo, pp. 340. $1.50. SHAW's *National Question Book*, pp. 351, $1.50: STILLWELL's *Practical Question Book*, pp. 400, $1.50; BROWN's *Common School Examiner*, pp. 371, $1.00; THOMPSON's *Teacher's Examiner*, pp. 378, $1.50; SHERRILL's *Normal Question Book*, pp. 400, $1.50.

C. W. BARDEEN, Publisher, Syracuse, N. Y.

www.ingramcontent.com/pod-product-compliance
Lightning Source LLC
Chambersburg PA
CBHW051733300426
44115CB00007B/548